Emerson's Angle of Vision

Through the individual fact there ever shone for him the effulgence of the Universal Reason. The great Cosmic Intellect terminates and houses itself in mortal men and passing hours. Each of us is an angle of its eternal vision. . .

WILLIAM JAMES, *Address at the Emerson Centenary in Concord,* 1903.

Emerson's Angle of Vision

MAN AND NATURE IN AMERICAN EXPERIENCE

Sherman Paul

HARVARD UNIVERSITY PRESS · CAMBRIDGE

Library of Congress Catalog Card Number *52–5039*
SBN *674-24925-9*
Printed in the United States of America

For My Mother and Father

Preface

This essay was first written under the direction of Professors Perry Miller and Kenneth B. Murdock; to them, I owe my greatest debt for guiding me with patience and kindness. Mr. Alec Lucas heard me out and helped me clarify the writing, and Professor Robert E. Spiller read the manuscript with great professional care, offering excellent criticism, by which I have tried to profit. Throughout, in the intellectual and mechanical crises, my wife responded and made the work her own.

I have a lasting debt to Mr. Edward W. Forbes and the Ralph Waldo Emerson Memorial Association for permitting me to use the Emerson manuscripts and for their material assistance in publication. Mr. William H. Jackson and Miss Caroline Jakeman of Houghton Library permitted me to use the Christopher Cranch drawings and William James's personally annotated copies of Emerson's *Works*. And Mr. Frederic W. Pratt generously gave permission to use the unpublished journals of Bronson Alcott, portions of which I was able to study because Mr. Murray Murphey offered me his transcriptions.

I owe permission to quote to the following authors and publishers: to the Houghton Mifflin Company for the Centenary Edition of Emerson's *Works, The Journals of Ralph Waldo Emerson, Young Emerson Speaks,* edited by Arthur C. McGiffert, and *The Writings of Henry David Thoreau;* to the Columbia University Press and the Ralph Waldo Emerson Memorial Association for Ralph Rusk's *The Letters of Ralph Waldo Emerson;* to Little, Brown and Company, Mr. Odell Shepard, and Mr. Frederic Wolsey Pratt for *The Jour-*

nals of Bronson Alcott; to Mr. Kenneth W. Cameron for his *Emerson the Essayist;* to the University of Pennsylvania Press for William Charvat's *The Origins of American Critical Thought;* to the Yale University Press for Perry Miller's edition of Jonathan Edwards' *Images or Shadows of Divine Things,* and Alice Snyder's *Coleridge on Logic and Learning;* to Longmans, Green and Company for William James's *The Pluralistic Universe,* copyright 1909; and to Mr. Ortega y Gasset and *The Partisan Review* for "On Point of View in the Arts." Chapter 6 appeared in a slightly different form in my Bowdoin Prize Essay, "Emerson's Literary Ethics." The frontispiece is by courtesy of The Houghton Library, Harvard University, Cambridge, Massachusetts.

For the convenience of the reader, I have used unpublished and inaccessible documents sparingly. Emerson's work, so much of which is available, grew by the accretion of stored thought, and what remains unpublished was taken up into his public expression. I have also incorporated in the text citations from the standard sources of Emerson's writing and refer to them by means of the following notations:

(*C,* I, 1): *The Complete Works of Ralph Waldo Emerson,* edited by Edward Waldo Emerson, 12 vols., Boston, 1903–1904. The Centenary Edition.

(*J,* I, 1): *The Journals of Ralph Waldo Emerson,* edited and annotated by Edward Waldo Emerson and Waldo Emerson Forbes, 10 vols., Boston, 1909–1914.

(*L,* I, 1): *The Letters of Ralph Waldo Emerson,* edited by Ralph L. Rusk, 6 vols., New York, 1939.

(*Y,* 1): *Young Emerson Speaks,* edited by Arthur C. McGiffert, Boston, 1938.

S. P.

July, 1951
Cambridge, Massachusetts

Contents

Emerson's Angle of Vision

All [philosophers] follow one analogy or another; and all the analogies are with some one or other of the universe's subdivisions. Every one is nevertheless prone to claim that his conclusions are the only logical ones, that they are necessities of universal reason, they being all the while, at bottom, accidents more or less of personal vision which had far better be avowed as such; for one man's vision may be much more valuable than another's, and our visions are usually not only our most interesting but our most respectable contributions to the world in which we play our part. . .

Let me repeat once more that a man's vision is the great fact about him. Who cares for Carlyle's reasons, or Schopenhauer's, or Spencer's? A philosophy is the expression of a man's intimate character, and all definitions of the universe are but the deliberately adopted reactions of human characters upon it. . . If we take the whole history of philosophy, the systems reduce themselves to a few main types which, under all the technical verbiage in which the ingenious intellect of man envelops them, are just so many visions, modes of feeling the whole push, and seeing the whole drift of life, forced on one by one's total character and experience, and on the whole preferred — *there is no other truthful word* — *as one's best working attitude.*

WILLIAM JAMES, *A Pluralistic Universe.*

Every man is uneasy until every power of his mind is in freedom and in action; whence arises a constant effort to take that attitude which will admit of this action.

EMERSON, "Find Your Calling,"
February 5, 1832.

Introduction

*Still am I a poet in the sense of a perceiver
& dear lover of the harmonies that are in the
soul & in matter, & specially of the correspondences between these & those.*

EMERSON, *Letters.*

This essay is a study of a way of thinking about the relatedness of man and the universe. The problem it examines, Emerson forewarns, "is the standing problem which has exercised the wonder and study of every fine genius since the world began" — the relation of spirit and matter, of man to nature. What moved Emerson to undertake its solution for his time — what compels me to return to Emerson — was the spiritual uneasiness he felt when he wrote: "We are as much strangers in nature, as we are aliens from God." The standing problem was, as Blake compacted it in a line, "Where man is not, nature is barren."

To bridge this gap between man and nature, Emerson created a structure of thought, of which "correspondence" was the most essential part. What he meant by "correspondence" and how it entered his thought and permeated his vision is the theme of this essay. For Emerson, who believed that men were disposed by temperament to take one or another philosophical stand, the human dimension of this idea is especially important. I have tried to give the idea the biographical perspective I felt it needed without ranging too far; but the thread of the essay is the enactment of the idea itself, not the biography, and, undoubtedly, a familiarity with the events of Emerson's life would give fullness to my presentation.

The idea of correspondence — I call it an "idea" for want of a better word — is not new, even though we are not inclined to entertain it today. Nor was it new for Emerson's generation. It was not a "metaphysical whim of modern times," he said, but a belief "as old as the human mind." Perhaps, then, we should call it a belief, for without the will to believe, correspondence loses its efficacy. In this sense it was not an idea to be taken up intellectually and applied to the estrangement of man and nature. Instead it was a faith which in turn became a way of seeing the universe in the light of human needs. "That only which we have within," Emerson wrote, "can we see without." A man sees what he is, becomes what he contemplates. The universe could be viewed correspondentially because correspondence itself was the prism through which one contemplated — a prism shaped by a temperamental need to see the universe that way.

The need to see the universe as friendly, beneficent, lawful, and related in every part is not new. It is a moral necessity. Men have always made this demand on the universe. And correspondence, therefore, has a long history. I have not attempted to trace that history, except in the most random way in Emerson's own appropriation of the past. For what prompted him, I think, to use the past (and the present) in the way he did was the very need correspondence was created to satisfy. This need was intensified by his religious heritage, and correspondence as he used it never surrendered its religious hold. What providence meant to his ancestors, correspondence meant to him; and if he had had available Edwards' treatise on *Images or Shadows of Divine Things,* he might not have had to turn from New England to Continental mystics like Swedenborg and Boehme. Even though his Calvinism was too severe for Emerson, Edwards was representative of the correspondential way of thinking Emerson appreciated in his forebears. Edwards gave two examples of the belief in correspondence that I think as serviceable as any as definitions:

8. Again it is apparent and allowed that there is a great and remarkable analogy in God's works. There is a wonderful resemblance in the effects which God produces, and consentaneity in His manner of working in one thing and another throughout all nature. It is very observable in the visible world; therefore it is allowed that God does purposely make and order one thing to be in agreeableness and harmony with another. And if so, why should not we suppose that He makes the inferiour in imitation of the superiour, the material of the spiritual, on purpose to have a resemblance and shadow of them? We see that even in the material world, God makes one part of it strangely to agree with another, and why is it not reasonable to suppose He makes the whole as a shadow of the spiritual world?

59. If there be such an admirable analogy observed by the Creatour in His works through the whole system of the natural world, so that one thing seems to be made in imitation of another, and especially the less perfect to be made in imitation of the more perfect, so that the less perfect is as it were a figure or image of the more perfect, so beasts are made in imitation of men, plants are [a] kind of types of animals, minerals are in many things in imitation of plants. Why is it not rational to suppose that the corporeal and visible world should be designedly made and constituted in analogy to the more spiritual, noble, and real world? It is certainly agreeable to what is apparently the method of God's working.

These passages give the fundamental meaning of correspondence: that the spiritual and natural universes share the same law, that although the natural is an imitation and therefore inferior world, its analogical identity with the Creator and the spiritual universe gives it (and the man who lives in it) a spiritual significance. For those who see the creation as broken in two, correspondence is a way of joining the spiritual and natural halves. It provides the assurance, as Emerson wrote, that "the laws above are sisters of the laws below."

This is the germ of the idea as one finds it in Plato. The actual universe of multiplicity, change, and imperfection is fashioned from and retains some impress of the real universe of universals, permanence, and perfection. For Emerson, however, correspondence meant all this and more. For him, it explained the epistemological problem. He transferred the dualism of the universe to the mind. "The fundamental fact in our metaphysic constitution is," he wrote, "the correspondence of man to the world, so that every change in that writes a record in the mind." For him, correspondence covered all the ways by which man came into relation with the world *outside* of himself, transformed the world *into* himself, and expressed the insight of the *experience* in words and character. To assert this correspondence he had to reconsider the nature of man, that is, how affection or sympathy provided ways into the universe that intellect alone did not. This meaning of correspondence I call the "sympathetic," following Cudworth, who in his analysis of the creative aspects of perception, wrote that sense alone would not admit one into the world of celestial harmonies, that one had to have an "active principle" to perceive it — to "correspond or vitally sympathise with it." I have been more concerned with *this* correspondence, because it is a dynamic, experiential correspondence, and because Emerson's affirmation of it is still needed.

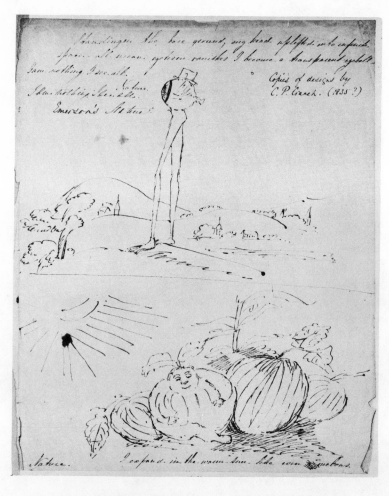

THE TRANSPARENT EYEBALL AND THE EXPANDING MELON

Drawings by Christopher Pearse Cranch

I

The Linear Logic

*The robust Aristotelian method, with its
breadth and adequateness, shaming our sterile
and linear logic by its genial radiation, conversant with series and degree, with effects and
ends, skilful to discriminate power from form,
essence from accident, and opening, by its
terminology and definition, high roads into
nature, had trained a race of athletic philosophers.*

EMERSON, "Swedenborg,"
Representative Men.

*It is not for time or space to set limits to the
effect of the life of a single man.*

SAMPSON REED, *Growth of
the Mind.*

In his quest for reality, and in his desire to stand at the
center of the universe, Emerson was an affirmer. The affirmative was his constant and characteristic mode of expression.
Familiar with the perils of doubt, he believed that "scepti-
cisms are not gratuitous or lawless, but are limitations of the
affirmative statement," and that "the new philosophy must
take them in, and make affirmations outside of them, just
as much as it must include the oldest beliefs" (C, III, 75).

More prudent perhaps than many of his transcendentalist contemporaries, and personally aware of the dissipation of his strength in denial (*C*, I, 356), Emerson practiced what he preached in "Prudence": "Neither should you put yourself in a false position with your contemporaries, by indulging a vein of hostility or bitterness. Though your views are in straight antagonism to theirs, assume an identity of statement, assume that you are saying precisely that which all think, and in the flow of wit and love roll out your paradoxes in solid column, with not the infirmity of a doubt" (*C*, II, 239). In doing this he was so successful that the literary stereotype of Emerson we have inherited presents a mild and cheerful, but denatured sage.

For Emerson was courageous enough to make affirmations outside of the intellectual framework that the generation from whose roots he sprang cherished as meaningful and necessary for acceptable life. "There are two ways of living in the world," he copied from his brother Charles's journal, "either to postpone your own ascetic entirely and live among people as among aliens; or, to lead a life of endless warfare by forcing your Ideal into act" (*J*, IV, 42). Of the two blameless courses open to the wise man, Emerson chose the more militant, to force his Ideal into act.

A halo of veneration settled over his later years. But before the Civil War and its aftermath swallowed up the transcendental awakening in its expansive materialism, leaving to the frenetic new generation an old gentlemanly Emerson as the representative of a passing order, he had been, in spite of his lineage and charm, a man suspect. For, first of all, his affirmations, especially when realized in the *Divinity School Address*, had been received only as rejection and antinomianism. This misinterpretation of his radicalism dismayed him, and the transcendental label galled him, before it amused him.[1] In the crucial years of his development — those unsettled and unsettling years of depression, the factory movement, Chardon Street conventions, Brook Farms, and abolition — he had turned from the society for which he had been traditionally prepared and which he had served with promise. But as the biographical early sermons make apparent, for Emerson this was never intended as overt rebellion from society; his withdrawal to Concord was necessary to his choice of calling.[2] As he told the young men at Dartmouth in 1838, "The hour of that choice is the crisis of your history" (*C*, I, 186). These sermons prepared his congregation for the precipitation of his character, and he departed in peace. And yet, by the very polarities of experience he came to champion, society recognized his radicalism. In time, after his retreat had served his purpose, he became acceptable enough: the generation he nourished saw to that, saw the old man tour Europe, the peer of nobility. But in the heyday of his revolt, when, for example, the English were warned that the radical Emerson was to lecture, he had to discipline his emotional forces, check them by the cheerful composure that remained his special outward claim.[3]

Seen in the historical perspective of a century, Emerson's life was a rejection of the past, and this, of course, was the strength of his affirmation. More and more, as one enters into and feels the anxiety of the first quarter of the nineteenth century, and realizes the currents and tributaries of that intellectual whirlpool, he appreciates the genius and sensitivity of the Emerson who mastered them in affirmative action and vision. Literary history, acknowledging, perhaps, the genuine function the people of Emerson's day felt he performed for them as no one else did, has given him his allotted space. But literary history has drained Emerson, if not of his reputed genius, of the courage his choice of calling — in an age much less individualistic and nonconformist than ours — demanded. To be a visionary with public commitments, a

visionary who acted on the belief that words are things —
that one's public statements are the expression of one's private
character and experience and that what one says is, therefore,
as forceful as action — required firm ground.[4] Some have said
with the assurance of Orestes Brownson that Emerson was
"one of the working men of this generation," that the self-
reliance and subjective center of his will to believe was a
"system of pure egotism." [5] And Stephen Whicher, in his
study of the development of Emerson's ideas in his formative
years, confirms Emerson's early identification of self-reliance
and greatness, and uncovers his almost overweening drive for
glory.[6] "You can never come to any peace or power," Emerson
omitted to say in his 1837 lectures on Human Culture, "until
you put your whole reliance in the moral constitution of
man" (*J*, IV, 406). He had made significant revisions after
the *Divinity School Address*, and self-reliance had become
reliance on God instead of the absorption of God by man.
Perhaps he had taken Sampson Reed's injunction to heart:
"Know, then, that genius is divine, not when man thinks
that he is God, but when he acknowledges that his powers are
from God." [7] But self-reliance was still associated with ego-
tistical individualism, with the Rev. Ezra Ripley's warning
against Egomites, and perhaps to some good purpose. Because,
if this watchword is driven to its biographical origins in
Emerson's needs, it intensifies our impression of the extent
to which Emerson had to go to find a place for his "genius"
and his energies in what he felt a paralyzing society. Men,
like the books they make, Emerson wrote, "should have a
commanding motive in the time and condition" of which
they are a part (*C*, X, 255). The freedom and action Emerson
desired, he achieved with youthful determination by withdrawal from society, and in solitude found the ecstasy of
self. This solitude, he later wrote, was essential to the great
leader (*C*, VI, 156). For "somewhere," he recorded in his

journal, "you must let out all the length of all the reins" (*J*, IV, 406). When he had done this, he ventured into the arena to proclaim the miracle of his experience — his possession of a living God. For "what were many thoughts," he wrote in contemplating Alcott's devotion to the Ideal, "if he had not this distinguishing Faith, which is a palpable proclamation out of the deeps of nature that God yet is?" (*J*, IV, 495). However much Emerson may have altered the idea of self-reliance to fit the drama of his life, the self and its experience of dependence on a higher source for spiritual power became the ground of his vision.[8]

Here was the experiential analogy [9] in terms of which he fashioned his "philosophy" and by example, without argument, condemned the past — more specifically, the English eighteenth century. He characterized this century by words, which for him were derogatory: "sterile," "linear," and, above all, "logic." And he condemned the slavish present by calling it "retrospective." When he appraised the England of the 1840's, he said, "It is wise and rich, but it lives on its capital. It is retrospective" (*C*, V, 246). And Emerson meant this, like so much of *English Traits*, for the New England as well as the old. The burden of those early liberating lectures to the young men — *The American Scholar*, "Literary Ethics," "The Young American," "Man, the Reformer," "The Conservative," "The Transcendentalist" — was heavy with patriotism, with the longing of youth to be needed and expended, in the course of empire, in the unfolding of their personal gifts. "Powerful and concentrated motive," Emerson wrote as early as 1823, "is necessary to a man, who would be great; and young men whose hearts burn with the desire of distinction may complain perhaps that the paths in which a man may be usefully illustrious are already taken up, and that they have fallen in too late an age to be benefactors of mankind" (*J*, I, 245–246). Like Emerson's, the frustration of Henry

Adams was the similar end of a youth who felt that the
control of his destiny was out of his hands. His was the frustration of the next generation, but its roots were also in the
eighteenth century.[10]

But unlike Adams, Emerson damned the eighteenth century and set out to transform it. He considered the reforming
mind a transforming mind, converting life into truth (*J*, IV,
232). His role, as he saw it, was not to reject totally, but, by
the alchemy of a fresh, energizing mind, secure in "principles," to adapt the usable content of his inheritance to the
living needs of the present. The scholar, he believed, by
pressing beyond the limitations of current abstraction, converted "the dishonored facts . . . into trees of life" (*J*, IV, 7).
It was in recognition of this that Brownson had called him a
working man. And sensitivity to these living needs made him
the "spokesman of our experience." [11] He refused the husk
of the past as unsustaining aliment for one intent on experiencing the living germ of the present. He felt the need to
harmonize his concrete experience of the universe — his ecstatic and limitless joy — with the intellectual formulas of the
day, and, if necessary, by shattering them. Like Thoreau (and
like the early expatriates, Margaret Fuller and Charles K.
Newcomb), like all who responded to transcendentalism, he
felt the desire to live totally, to taste life, to find ways to give
living, gone stale, its vital flavor. "Sad is this continual postponement of life," especially so when he knew that "every
soul has to learn the whole lesson for itself," that "what it
does not see, what it does not live, it will not know" (*J*, IV,
229, 306). He was the spokesman, then, as he said in the
opening pages of *The Dial*, for all those who felt the restrictions of a block universe, who felt in the verbal formulas of
the day barriers to fresh experience (*J*, V, 250–254). In that
mild manifesto, Emerson perhaps gave the most generally
acceptable statement of the transcendental demands: "to

reprobate that rigor of our conventions of religion and education which is turning us to stone, which renounces hope, which looks only backward, which asks only such a future as the past, which suspects improvement, and holds nothing so much in horror as new views and the dreams of youth." The spirit of the times, he pointed out, "is in every form a protest against usage, and a search for principles." [12]

After the fact, makers of "revolutions," especially intellectual and spiritual revolutions, usually appear from across the gap of history *naïf*, as Adams said. Their influence is hardly manifest in the bold outline of historical events. They work beneath its surface, rechanneling the streams of sensibility, altering perspectives and replacing attitudes;often, even when they are public men, they transmit the felt influence of their character to a small group. Fortunately, Emerson's family of influence was the Boston of the Saturday Club, of the *North American Review* and *The Atlantic*, the Boston that magnetized culture-hungry Midwesterners like Howells with a fascination as great as that of Europe for the Bostonian.[13] Emerson may have been, as many still say, only a spokesman for Emerson, a voice crying in the wilderness of materialism; but his wilderness was the capital of both American thought and American trade. Affirmer or rejector, usually misunderstood — as the newspaper accounts of his lectures constantly made him aware — his international acclaim, the glamor of his presence beyond the Mississippi, the intellects he germinated here and abroad for over fifty years, indicate that the sentiments he expressed were desired and shared by a wide community and that for them he had caught and voiced the tendency of the times. In an early sermon, before his language was molded to his vision, he expressed more simply the tendency of which transcendentalism was one eruption. "The governments, the laws, the customs into which we are born —

they are like the shell or outer skin of many animals. If it do not admit of growth the animal will cast it" (*Y*, 55).

If the method and expression of the mature Emerson were misunderstood, the tone of his literary and platform efforts found response.[14] Beneath the philosophic and poetic cloak of his vehicle, his audience recognized the authority of an individual vision that had cast the skin of the past.[15] When his eloquence raised them to a higher platform and charged them with emotion, they shared it. They were captivated by the tone — "No article so rare in New England as Tone," he said (*J*, V, 307). They were captivated by the character behind the words (*J*, IV, 364) and hung, as Emerson himself had in the power of speech, "on the lips of one man" (*J*, IV, 361). But Emerson's vision had a private center. It was never intended to be shared, that is, hypostatized for general use (see *J*, II, 282; V, 272). Instead, Emerson intended it as a representative expression of the tendency he proclaimed, intended to show by his example the sustaining power of vision and how its luminosity was generated — and especially, the value of its altitude in releasing the paralyzed will. His was an order of vision that each could adopt for himself, that each could find and affirm in the center of living personality. And the itinerant Emerson, the public Emerson, became the personification of what the rejection of the eighteenth century's linear logic meant to those who witnessed this spirit: a living distinction between the methods of the past and the present, of observation versus vision. "The great distinction," he wrote, "between teachers sacred or literary, — between poets like Herbert, and poets like Pope, — between philosophers like Locke, Paley, Mackintosh, and Stewart, — between men of the world . . . and here and there a fervent mystic . . . — is that one class speak *from within*, or from experience, as parties and possessors of the fact; and the other class, *from without*, as spectators merely" (*C*, II, 287). What Emerson meant by the affirmative principle was this vision or insight permitting men, like Jesus, to speak "from within the veil, where the word is one with that it tells of" (*C*, II, 287). Like Edwards nearly a century earlier, he asked men not only to entertain ideas intellectually but to realize them vitally with a sense of the heart. In this respect a later day Edwards come to announce that "where there is no vision, the people perish" (*C*, X, 252), Emerson represented the visionary to the country at large (just as Alcott did for him), and, in his crisp priestly black, was acceptable. And if, as he wrote, "The measure of a master is his success in bringing all men round to his opinion twenty years later," he found a large measure of acceptance (*C*, VI, 164).

II

The retrospective age was derivative and provincial, imitative in the sense of Emerson's distinction between imitation and originality. The original age made new use of what it borrowed. But the perversity of the New England of the early nineteenth century was annoying because, as the foundling of progress, America promised new glories, and in the boast appropriated eighteenth-century forms, and even worshipped them. The English eighteenth century, contrasted in Emerson's perspective with the glorious seventeenth, was a descent. "These heights," he wrote, "were followed by a meanness, and descent of the mind into lower levels; the loss of wings; no high speculation." The century of ideas was followed by "Locke, to whom the meaning of ideas was unknown;" and his "type of philosophy" and his " 'understanding' " became "the measure, in all nations, of the English intellect" (*C*, V, 243). Dedicated to the Lockean understanding, early nineteenth-century New England selected from the manifold riches of the eighteenth century those elements of method and philosophy which, in terms of their spiritual

needs, were showing most the effects of hardening and inutil-
ity. It had been slow to grasp the subterranean currents of
emotion already present in Edwards' use of Hutcheson, which
actually culminated in Wordsworth as a response to the irreconcilable beliefs in both physical mechanism and spiritual
free-will. In its intellectual determination to have both, New
England had lost the vitality and impetus to growth. James
Marsh pointed out the dilemma clearly: "According to the
systems of these authors [Locke and the Scottish Realists],
as nearly and distinctly as my limits will permit me to state
it, the same law of cause and effect is the law of the universe.
It extends to the moral and spiritual — if in courtesy these
terms may still be used — no less than to the properly natural
powers and agencies of our being. The acts of the free-will
are pre-determined by a cause out of the will, according to
the same law of cause and effect which controls the changes
in the physical world. We have no notion of power but uni-
formity of antecedent and consequent. The notion of a power
in the will to act freely is nothing more than an inherent
capacity of being acted upon, agreeably to its nature, and
according to a fixed law, by the motives which are present in
the understanding." [16]

Only after the *wanderjahre* of young New Englanders in
Germany in the first decades of the century did Wordsworth's
reputation increase and the heart and the will find new
worshippers among the Unitarians. The history of New England's allegiance to eighteenth-century rationalism need not
be retold here.[17] One must remember, however, that the in-
stitutionalization of the rational values in Unitarianism came
in the early nineteenth century, and that by this time the
limitations of the Lockean theory of knowledge had been
realized in Hume's *reductio ad absurdum*. On the Continent,
Kant had already printed his Copernican revolution, *The
Critique of Pure Reason* (1781), and Fichte and Schelling

had explored the dilemma of the Kantian self and its world. Except in "industrial activity and enterprise," [18] America was at least a quarter of a century behind the spirit of the times. And in the year of Emerson's *Nature* (1836), the year Perry Miller has called the *annus mirabilis*, many besides Emerson recognized it.[19]

Emerson got to the heart of the eighteenth century in New England, and for that matter in Western intellectual history, when he described the atmosphere of ideas into which Swedenborg was born. Here was the background to the appreciation of the current sterility in method (*C*, V, 238 ff.; IV, 103 ff.). The age of hypotheses and ideas, of the wide generalization, of the dramatic intuitive discovery; the age of Harvey, Gilbert, and Newton; the age Whitehead called the "century of genius," when science was gloriously opening a wider universe,[20] he contrasted with the analytical, cumulative, inductive science of his day — with the linear logic. The science of the seventeenth century was still moral, ethical, imaginative — in an Emersonian word, poetic; that of the eighteenth searched piecemeal into a nature no longer spiritually intimate with man. "The eye of the naturalist must have a scope like nature itself," Emerson wrote, " a susceptibility to all impressions, alive to the heart as well as the logic of creation. But English science puts humanity to the door. . . It isolates the reptile or mollusk it assumes to explain; whilst reptile or mollusk only exist in system, in relation. The poet only sees it as an inevitable step in the path of the creator. But, in England, one hermit finds this fact, and another finds that, and lives and dies ignorant of its value . . . the natural science in England is out of its loyal alliance with morals, and is as void of imagination and free play of thought, as conveyancing" (*C*, V, 253).[21] By balancing poetry and science, the two forms of intellectual activity by which he characterized the seventeenth and eighteenth centuries, Emerson revealed the need for reconciliation, the need in a mechanistic present for a more organic or spiritual philosophy of nature. Like Whitehead, he knew that "the only way of mitigating mechanism is by the discovery that it is not mechanism." [22] And like Christopher Cranch, in his poem, "A Word to Philosophers," he had found that "the Tree of Life / Flaunts your narrow classifying." [23] Without the imaginative union of man and nature, which gave him a morally animating sense of life, and without man's controlling idea as the thread of universality and significance, the eighteenth-century science offered man "No hope, no sublime augury . . . no secure striding from experience onward to a foreseen law. . . A horizon of brass of the diameter of his umbrella shuts down around his senses. Squalid contentment with conventions, satire at the names of philosophy and religion, parochial and shop-till politics, and idolatry of usage, betray the ebb of life and spirit. . . In the absence of the highest aims, of the pure love of knowledge, and the surrender to nature, there is the suppression of the imagination, the priapism of the senses and the understanding; we have the factitious instead of the natural; tasteless expense, arts of comfort, and the rewarding as an illustrious inventor whosoever will contrive one impediment more to interpose between man and his objects" (*C*, V, 254). If, for Emerson, life and action were perfected science (*J*, IV, 32), then the sterility of rationalism informed the conduct of life with its lifelessness. Wanting a concept of "series and degree," and the penetration of insight and vision, it limited those who lived in its climate to the brass ring of materialism and sensualism. It shut out faith and hope and the dreams of youth. "The mind of the race," Emerson wrote as the reason for the lack of genius in America, "has taken another direction, — Property. Patriotism, none. Religion has no enthusiasm. It is external, prudential" (*J*, IV, 109). The genius, he wrote, became a drudge, died of disgust or suicide because of the discord between the claims of a higher morality and the imperatives of actual conduct. "Young men of fairest promise," Emerson observed in *The American Scholar*, "inflated by the mountain winds, shined upon by all the stars of God, find the earth below not in unison with these, — but are hindered from action by the disgust which the principles on which business is managed inspire" (*C*, I, 114).

For Emerson, this was the dead end of the science founded on Lockean sensationalism. This mechanical science collected facts and failed to find them, as he did, raw and insignificant without the teleological immediacy of God — the qualitative presence of the whole. Like the contemporary idolators of progress, he was not going to discard science; but unlike them, he wanted to humanize and vivify the facts by restoring the dynamic vitalization of imaginative perception. What they had left atomized and isolated, he wanted to unify at the life-giving source. This, he wrote to Lidian, was his choice of calling: "a poet in the sense of a perceiver & dear lover of the harmonies that are in the soul & in matter, & especially of the correspondences between these & those" (*L*, I, 435). For what they saw with the outer eye capable only of receiving atomic sensation, he saw with the inner eye, the "fluid consciousness" of form-giving perception (*C*, II, 138), and the new perspective was revolutionary for early nineteenth-century America.

For although that America gloried in the "intellectual consolation" of rational optimism — certain that the Lockean mind was adequate to the Newtonian universe — that optimism, as James Marsh pointed out to them, was reared on cosmic determinism.[24] The Unitarian and Calvinist universes were equally cast in granite, and the evidences of beneficence and evil-turned-to-good the Unitarian polished into its surface were not enough. Without the immediate presence of

God, its determinism was intellectually and emotionally un-
relieved. Somewhere, Emerson hoped to find instead "that
fragrant piety," the "beautiful mean, equi-distant from the
hard, sour, iron Puritan on the one side, and the empty nega-
tion of the Unitarian on the other" (*J*, IV, 31). This, the
rational theodicy did not permit.

Speaking of its intellectual consolation, Lovejoy said that
"it was usually designed to produce . . . a mood [of] rea-
soned acquiescence in the inevitable, based upon the conviction that its inevitableness was absolute and due to no
arbitrary caprice." [25] Such an optimism unrolled a future as
irremediable as the past. The cosmic certainty that whatever
is, or has been, is right and good, left change to the uninter-
rupted Newtonian mechanism. Change was linear, merely the
reorientation in time and space of bodies smoothly operating
to the divine purpose, but in themselves, will-less and isolated.
Nowhere did the system admit of growth in an organic sense.
Nowhere did it admit the perception that anticipated the
future (*C*, VIII, 141). For Emerson it admitted only an optimism of submission.

Even the last stay of those who clung to "faith," the possibility (unlikely in *their* present) of the miracle of divine
intervention, was shaken by a faith, rooted in rationalism,
that the universe was already so perfectly designed that secondary causes could do the work of the deity. Hume contributed to their dilemma the reasonableness of unreason
and unsettled their optimism. Skepticism was, a writer in
The Dial remarked in an article on the significance of Kant,
the natural consequence of Lockean sensationalism. For "even
if we were willing to receive phenomena as facts [as the
Scottish Realists were], still this would not bring us much
farther; for they would still be mere detached existences,
unrelated except by accidental position, and consequently we
could not reason from one to the other, nor even classify

them, without at the same time acknowledging the accidental nature of our classification." The author, characteristically branding Hume as the arch-representative of the immediate past, continued: "The general dismay and resistance with which Hume's doctrine was received . . . is attributable to its peculiar excellence as an expression of the thought of his age. So keen was the unconscious feeling of the correctness of the result at which he had arrived . . . and so violent the resistance against these results of the inmost nature of man, that a convulsion was produced which opened new depths in the human consciousness." [26] The method that Hume carried to its logical conclusion, the transcendentalist regarded with reverent horror, because he had been nourished in reason as a child and because his realization of the sterility of the linear logic was often traumatic.[27] If cause and effect were, as Brownson discovered, truly "invariable antecedence and consequence," the universe was literally linear. And the more one glorified the perfect machinery of the universe, the more difficult it became to avoid its relentless determinism by a faith in one's own agency or the promise of miracles.

For Emerson, the linear logic conveyed this sense of the despair of the times. One sign, on the prudential level, was the depression of 1837. "Young men," he wrote, "have no hope. Adults stand like day-laborers idle in the streets. None calleth us to labor. The old wear no crown of warm life on their gray hairs. The present generation is bankrupt of principles and hope, as of property. I see man is not what man should be. He is the treadle of a wheel. He is a tassel at the apron-string of society. He is a money-chest. He is the servant of the belly. This is the causal bankruptcy, this the cruel oppression, that the ideal should serve the actual, that the head should serve the feet" (*J*, IV, 242). Another sign, on the spiritual level, was the paralysis of the will: "A new disease has fallen on the life of man . . . our torment is Unbelief, the Uncertainty as to what we ought to do; the distrust of the value of what we do, and the distrust that the Necessity (which we all at last believe in) is fair and beneficent. Our Religion assumes the negative form of rejection." [28]

The linear logic, then, marked the failure of a method. Its Necessity was cruel (linear), not benevolent and progressive. It could not affirm. But nowhere, unless in the large of his life, did Emerson analyze that method with the rigor of Brownson or Parker. Like them, however, Emerson meant it to unfold all the discontent following from an epistemology limited to the passive reception of sensations. For, unless the mind contributed something to perception beyond its machinelike manipulations — and the mind, Hume had shown, had no necessary assurance that the sensations it put together revealed the actual but unknowable relations of the universe — the mind received only an impression of surface: the self found itself outside the universe. If one sought the common-sense solution, believing that in perception he actually seized a real objective world, he was still limited to surface. For Scottish Realism only partially "solved" the epistemological problem: it naïvely supposed that the perception of a real universe eliminated the problem of the moral significance of a related universe. For one could no more explain connectedness by the distinction between fact, as the really known objective world, and phenomena, as all that the mind beholds of a universe *out there*. The consequences for action in both the Scottish and Lockean epistemologies remained the same; one still perceived only the material world of secondary causes, and the problem of the meaning the self gives to its experience of the world was left unanswered. With this question, Emerson wrote, science was not concerned (*C*, I, 66–67). To follow Lockean sensationalism was to reduce the universe to one dimension — that, as Whitehead said, of "one-eyed reason, deficient in its vision of depth." [29] Without the dimension of

the human and/or divine minds, human significance, meaning and value (all that the youth of Emerson's day demanded)
were similarly reduced to the space of a point, and progress
to its extension as a line.

Furthermore, the method of ordering the chaos of sensation
was that of reason considered as discursive logic. For Locke,
knowledge resided only in the comparison of ideas with their
objects, and the spontaneous play of intuition was lawless and
irresponsible. Significance was not to be found in the illu-
mination of insight, but was a matter guaranteed by the rules
of association. These rules, however, applied only to the
analyzable workings of the intellect, not to the unanalyzable
feelings.[30] The human personality or self was merely the addi-
tive product of circumstance (the Emersonian word for environment), was educated by "nature," by the rational laws
that reasoning man had observed in what amounted to a
stimulus-response universe. Such a self developed "logically,"
traversing the line of its sensations, but it could neither extri-
cate itself from the pressures of the external nor command
them. Caught in this "trap of so-called sciences," Emerson
saw no escape for man, "from the links of the chain of physical
necessity." "Given such an embryo," he wrote, "such a history
must follow. On this platform, one lives in a sty of sensualism"
(C, III, 54). Lacking the creative spontaneity of the will, the
direction of the line toward what Emerson called self-culture
or growth was uncertain. "Linear," to Emerson, was "horizontal." And the course of spiritual ascent was withheld from
those who relied wholly on the outer world for the spur to
action. Reliance on the outward victimized those who, like
Emerson, needed a central reality as the basis of faith and
action. What did it matter, if the approved mold had already
been formed?

The problem, then, that Emerson faced and stated meta-
phorically as the linear logic, was that of erecting the vertical

standard of value perpendicular to the horizontal enslaving his day. His purpose can be represented graphically by a diagram proposed by Philip Wheelwright, who says in response to our philosophical malaise, "If we see the world only as patterns of phenomena, our wisdom will be confined to such truths as phenomena can furnish." [31] The horizontal line represents for him these patterns of phenomena, the descriptive achievements of empiricism — Emerson's linear logic. The horizontal line represents "the ground line of familiar facts" (*C*, I, 30), the one dimensional world of fact, of space, time, and history, a world limited to the experience of sense impression. It gives us — to use the transcendental label distinguishing the superficially outward and the meaningful inner [32] — only the world's *surface*. "We dwell amidst surfaces;" Emerson wrote, "and surface laps so closely on surface, that we cannot easily pierce to see the interior organism." [33] Again: "It is the depth at which we live, and not at all the surface extension, that imports. We piece to the eternity, of which time is the flitting surface" (*C*, VII, 183). Looking out of the inner eye, he said: "How does everybody live on the outside of the world!" (*J*, III, 159). And regarding America he said: "Our culture or art of life is sadly external" (*J*, VIII, 253).

Emerson felt called on to raise the vertical axis, to give the universe its spiritual dimension, to reinstate its mystery and wonder by giving scope to the mythic, symbolic, and religious components of human experience: the vertical was the inner and spiritual and "put nature underfoot" by making nature serve the moral needs of man (*C*, I, 58). The linear logic was sterile, to use the words of Wheelwright that Emerson might have copied, because "it ignores or deprecates that haunting awareness of transcendental forces peering through the cracks of the visible universe." [34] Not attuned to the emotional resonance of transcendental experience, literalists or sensualists —

all those who take the horizontal and outward experience merely for what it gives them — never respond to the spiritual vibrations of which it is possible.[35] For the vertical is, in a sense, an optical or experiential illusion; it arises only when we experience the horizontal in a "genial" manner, when we live in the recognition that "everything in the universe goes by indirection" and that "there are not straight lines."[36]

As a dimension of the human consciousness, the vertical represents the fact of consciousness known as projection. Experiencing horizontally, one recognizes the separation of the self and nature, and also one's dependence on the senses for any communion with it: one is limited to what nature provides, and from this base in nature all men begin. But the nature they know is transformed by their own imaginative perception, by their desires, feelings, fears, and so forth. As I. A. Richards extends this idea of psychologically different natures, the nature of science is a selection of the universal perceptions that make for the control of nature in everyday life. Science necessarily selects what its further progress requires, but it also eliminates those projections of aspiration and belief, that is, one's total response to nature, that myth and art try to incorporate more fully. From this essential difference develops the often irreconcilable tensions that the more sensitive feel in their own conflicting apprehensions of nature: the feeling of dependence on and limitation to the external, and the feeling that projections are somehow justified by something corresponding to them in and/or behind nature, and that this correspondence promises an infinite scope for activity.[37]

This distinction in the *meaning* of nature — between the partial materialist and the total moral and spiritual response — was fundamental in the transcendentalists' attempt to extend the meaning of nature. An explicit example, in the language of transcendentalism, is Fordyce Mitchel Hubbard's "Study of the Works of Nature" (1835). "The various meanings of Nature," Hubbard wrote, "may be mainly reduced to two classes — the logical, addressing itself to the understanding, and comprehended by the reason, — and the tasteful or moral, addressed to the sentiments, and apprehended and perhaps shaped by the imagination — the first, that which she presents to the eye of a philosopher; the second, that which she conveys to the mind of a poet. The logical includes those laws and forms of matter and motion, which can be precisely measured, and enunciated by the formulae of mathematics; comprising also those principles of moving force, and the great living energy, of which these laws and forms are but the formulae and manifestations. The distinction between these two orders of meaning, may be compared to that between a finely chiseled statue in the perfect form and exact dimensions of a man, and the form and dimensions only, and the same marble wrought into the Laocoon, writhing and crushed in the serpent's folds, expressing his sacred horror, and parental anguish. Or it may perhaps be better illustrated by the different feelings which would arise in the mind of an anatomist and of a child, in looking on the pleasant countenance of a mother. The anatomist sees a combination of bones and processes, and articulations, the circulation of the blood, the insertion and movements of muscles. The child rests his head upon his mother's bosom, and with his eye upturned in quiet confidence to the face which has been wont to repay his every look with a smile, sees, and thus first learns, the calmness of contentment, or the joy of a satisfied affection, the intenseness of a mother's love, the chastened pensiveness of resignation, or the subdued glow of a fervent devotion.

"Diverse as are the ideas imparted to these two minds, so unlike are the impressions produced in the two classes of those who, each in his own way study Nature; and in the elements of character generated by them; or rather by one of them, since the mechanical philosophy has no direct moral *sense* and of course has no *direct* effect on moral character." [38]

For Emerson, at least, the transcendentalism of the vertical axis was not a mysticism of irresponsible flight from the mundane horizontal.[39] By raising the vertical he intended to assert a multi-dimensional universe of spiritual possibilities rather than to overcome the restraints and trivialities of everyday prudential life. For him, the new standard incorporated the world of common sense; in fact, relying as he did on his sensuous experience and on the direct confrontation of nature, all of his transcendental energy was earth-derived. His daily problem was to maintain a living connection between the horizontal-worldly and the vertical-otherworldly, to live on as many of the platforms of experience that intervened as he could (*C*, IV, 55). The paradoxes and polarity of his thought reflect this struggle to inform the life of the horizontal with the quality of the vertical, and by means of the horizontal to raise himself into the erect position. He did not want to sacrifice his sense of individuality and free will for a formulated, dependent mysticism: he wanted both freedom and merger, just as he sought for some way to express inclusively what he had experienced of the infinite and the finite, of the ideal-abstract and the actual-concrete, of the supernatural and the natural, of insight and action, contemplation and conduct, solitude and society. Like William James after him, he found the multiplicity of life too rich to be impoverished by the metaphysician's sentiment of rationality. That multiplicity, he believed, could not be simplified, but it could be used in all its potentialities as the stuff of analogy by which to achieve the unity of vision. He preferred, then, to mediate in poetic vision the higher and lower universes of his experience. And the difficulties of maintaining both transcendental ascent and earthy base formed for him the provoking tensions shared as well by Thoreau and Alcott.[40] For he knew that his highest realizations could only be mirrored in the concrete, that whatever value merger promised was not to be dissipated in the rare atmosphere of Reality, but transformed for the grosser world of the Actual. He knew that this knowledge was inseparable from its expression, that his vision was seeing by means of, as well as through, the objects he contemplated. Affirmation may have been, as he believed, the socially useful concomitant of such vision (*J*, VII, 245), but it could only be displayed (was only morally justifiable) in an act. It was in this sense that his affirmation was an attempt to force the ideal into act, to make visioning a conduct of life. And for this reason he needed a technique of vision, needed to discover the prism, which was in itself the product of vision, its promise, and its fulfillment.

2

The Staircase of Unity

Their minds loved analogy, were cognizant of resemblances, and climbers on the staircase of unity.

EMERSON, *English Traits.*

To seek unity is a necessity of the mind.

EMERSON, *Journals.*

The fact is that the human mind is impatient of things finite . . . and loves to lose itself in the contemplation of the vast and unbounded.

EMERSON, "The Choice of Theisms," 1831.

Emerson turned to vision because, for him, it was the only way to "lop off all superficiality and tradition, and fall back on the nature of things" (*J*, IV, 90–91). He wanted to find "the adamant under all the upholstery," and thereby preach, as he felt Coleridge, Southey, and Wordsworth did, "the nullity of circumstances" and the centrality of man (*J*, IV, 92–93). The unity he proclaimed, he asserted in the assumption of the identity or correspondence of the natural and spiritual worlds; but this correspondence, if it were to fulfill its promise of moral certainty in the conduct of life, had to be renewed daily in man's dynamic experience of self-consciousness. To affirm it forced man to take a central position in nature, where in the presence of the overwhelming flux of his sensations, vision was stimulated and he realized the informing unity that for the moment of inspiration played *through him.* The guarantee of the connection of the moral and physical worlds was, then, the experience of one's perception of the spirit in the mind and in and behind nature. As the possessor of the intuitive faculty, man was necessarily, in Emerson's view, the center of unity, the psychological apex of the angle of vision, and correspondence, therefore, was a self-evident truth of his first philosophy.

The coherence of this vision,[1] however, needed, as Emerson's extensive reading shows, the support of a considerable philosophical scaffolding.[2] Unconcerned with the subtle distinctions of philosophical thought, Emerson seized from the past speculation about the nature of man and the universe any idea that pointed in the direction of their correspondence. From his reading in the history of philosophy he found, up until Descartes at least, a tendency — the general acceptance of this assumption cosmologically stated — which supported his own more psychological view. In this respect, Western thought was to Emerson, what Whitehead said of it, merely the footnoting of Plato's philosophy. And in the vast store of Platonic writing — which he read first in de Gérando's detailed survey and in Cudworth's collection of ancient lore, and later in the Neo-Plotinian tainted translations of Thomas Taylor — he found the distinctions necessary for the restoration of vision as a source of higher knowledge in a universe divided into visible and intelligible realms. What he needed from philosophy in order to provide the support of the vertical axis, in order to put his mind in its best working attitude, he was fortunate to have available; for he was temperamentally unfit for this painstaking metaphysical work. He needed those elements which the eighteenth century had discarded and which current academic training in Lockean and Scottish common-sense philosophy minimized: a universe of levels, rising to the summit of the spiritual and Real; an account of perception, restoring an intuitive, imaginative faculty of Reason; and a theory of the relation of language to nature, making possible, as the role of the poet, the expression of the Real in the concrete objects of everyday experience.

Fortunately, again, in the general reaction to the eighteenth century which had been provoked by Hume, he discovered several thinkers who brought out those elements he needed in relation to the more pressing epistemological solution of the dualism of subject and object, the self and the world. In Kant, Fichte, Schelling, and especially Coleridge, who transmitted their distinctions along with high praise for the unitary function of Platonic ideas, he recognized the builders of the defense against Locke: and on Locke's home ground, the psychological process.[3] But it was chiefly Carlyle who startled Emerson to emulation by his forthright personal expression of the new ideas in the Everlasting Yea. Here, as we shall see again and again in considering Emerson's sources, what stimulated Emerson was the biographical *use* of ideas, the vindication of ideas by living them, the idea personified in the act. This, he admired in Alcott and Thoreau, and he entertained many ideas with a personal loyalty to those whom he believed represented them. In fact, his desire for an intellectual community of friends was shaped considerably by his need for seeing ideas enacted, and much of his thought was prompted by personal influence.

At any rate, by Emerson's time the ideas he needed were already being swept into the American stream of thought and were beginning to find expression if not wholehearted enactment. Channing, for example, was sensitive to them. Emerson wrote Aunt Mary Moody that Channing seemed "sometimes as the sublime of calculation, as the nearest that mechanism could get to flowing genius" (*J*, VI, 285). But in his calculation, Channing voiced many of the ideas that Emerson afterward domesticated, by living them. For what was "new" in Emerson's work was the thorough application or enactment of these ideas in character and vision. And this enactment was made less difficult when the ideas were taken seriously in the market place. By 1831, when James Marsh introduced the first American edition of Coleridge's *The Friend*, it was becoming apparent that the battle for their recognition, at least, was over. Marsh wrote that "it is now no longer hazardous to one's reputation to call in question the authority of those philosophers who have been most popular among us; and the article on Brown's theory of perception in a late number of the Edinburgh Review shows, that language and thoughts derived from German metaphysics may now be used to a much greater extent, than they have been done by Coleridge — in a work, where formerly they would have been rejected with contumely . . . one who would be thought not ignorant of philosophy hereafter, must acquaint himself with something beyond empiricism, which has so long assumed its name among us." [4]

When Emerson asked those leading questions in *Nature* — "Why should not we also enjoy an original relation to the universe? Why should not we have a poetry and philosophy of insight and not of tradition?" — he was preparing for the subsequent unfolding of his method. *Nature*, as the massive scholarship of Kenneth Cameron shows, was his distillation of all his previous reading, culled for an answer to these questions. The chief idea it developed, the idea which made correspondence as the symbolic expression of the Real one of its central proofs as well as ends, was that of *nature as use* as the mediating agency between man and God. For it was by means of nature that man attained insight and moral growth, and had ready the language of its expression. The meaning of nature, then, was its use.

The rehabilitation of nature, therefore, as more than a field for scientific investigation, terminated in nature's ultimate discipline — Idealism. "Idealism," Emerson wrote, "is a hypothesis to account for nature by other principles than those of carpentry and chemistry" (*C*, I, 62–63). Its advantages over other theories, he wrote, in what we have since come to acknowledge as the pragmatic attitude, "is this, that it presents the world in precisely that view which is most desirable to the mind" (*C*, I, 59). "Grant us the Ideal theory," he wrote, "and the universe is solved. Otherwise, the moment a man discovers that he has aims which his faculties cannot answer, the world becomes a riddle" (*J*, IV, 14; see also *L*, II, 384–385). And even though its solipsistic dead end, the denial of the existence of matter, haunted him, Emerson found Idealism useful because it indicated the dualism of the soul and the world (*C*, I, 59, 63). This dualism was necessary even for a seeker after unity, if God as the unconditioned and absolute ground were to be reinstated as the unifying source who made the laws of nature answer to the self-evident ideas He planted in the mind of man. Nature, now, could serve man in his quest for the moral certainty of a living God, could stand between him and God, not as a barrier, but as a promise that its exploration would be spiritually rewarded. This was "the true position of nature in regard to man," Emerson wished to affirm in *Nature*, "wherein to establish man, all right education tends; as the ground which to attain is the object of human life, that is, of man's connexion with nature" (*C*, I, 59). Confronting nature in this religious perspective, man would no longer be content to ferret out the facts, but instead would go into its presence feeling it "the expositor of the divine mind," searching for the analogies between its phenomena and his thoughts, assured that they were manifestations of the divine unity.

Emerson's poetry and philosophy of insight affirmed that this insight was possible and shared in the experience of every man; and that, although private and perhaps incommunicable, such vision was not wayward, but on the contrary the only possible revelation (*Y*, 203 ff.). The structural and functional premises of this vision, which made it the only possible revelation and guide, he found in an essentially Platonic or idealist cosmology, and in a complementary epistemology which restored the faculty of Reason and accorded to its trans-empirical perceptions the truth of being. In language he found the penetrating and conceptualizing instrumentality of vision. As the gift of God most closely connected with the mind, language could be made responsive to the burdens of expressing a universe emotionally felt and experienced beyond the object in and by which it was first superficially "known." The cosmological-epistemological framework of correspondence permitted language this symbolic function. For if, Emerson wrote, "the Greek was the age of observation; the Middle Age, that of fact and thought; ours, that of reflection and ideas," then, the Reflective Age needed a theory of symbol-using in which "the near explains the far; a drop of water tells all that is true of the ocean; a family will reveal the State, and one man the All." If he were to be the center of unity, man needed to believe "that all Nature is only the foliage, the flowering and the fruit of the soul, and that every part therefore exists as an emblem and sign of some fact in the soul" (*J*, IV, 110, 282). And when Emerson wrote in 1859, "The fundamental fact in our metaphysic constitution is the correspondence of man to the world, so that every change in that writes a record in the mind," he used "correspondence" as the all-enclosing word to describe this cosmology, the symbolic use of language, and the dynamic process of inspiration and insight by which the spiritual mediation of nature was realized (*C*, VII, 300–301).

It is understandable, then, that the word itself and its many derivative forms and synonyms — analogy, analogon, connexion, identity, resemblance, sign, symbol, signature, type, emblem, hieroglyph, and so forth — had a considerable popularity. In the transcendentalist writing of this period, "correspondence" was the catch-all word for much of the work of the shift from the conception of the universe as a mechanism from which God was estranged to that of the universe as organism in which the mind was a unifying necessity. For example, in William Kirby and William Spence's *An Introduction to Entomology* (1815–1816), a book noted by Coleridge in his *Aids to Reflection,* and perhaps brought to Emerson's attention in Sampson Reed's extended review in the *New Jerusalem Magazine* (1828–1831), nature was viewed organically as a chain of affinities. "When," Kirby and Spence wrote, "the Almighty Creator willed to bring into existence this mundane system, he formed it according to a preconcerted plan, with all its parts beautifully linked together and mutually corresponding." [5] In their system of *Correlation* nature became a book of symbols "in which one thing represents another in endless alteration," from which, by drawing analogies in the situation, structure, and use of animals, one could symbolize the gradual ascent of animal life to man. But having achieved his position "in the centre of all," God also provided that his book of nature read symbolically "might *instruct* his creature man in such civil, physical, moral and spiritual truths, as were calculated to fit him for his station in the visible world, and gradually prepare him to become an inhabitant of that invisible one for which he was destined." [6]

As it is used here, the word served a life-giving function, signifying connections in the organic world beyond the scope of antecedence and contingency, beyond mere linear cause and effect. The correlation of the parts of nature existed not only to supply the physical wants of all creatures, but to make nature a process of ascent and a book of symbolic verities. All of the many uses of "correspondence" depended on a similar assumption of the relatedness of man and the universe (*J*, IV, 67); and all of its uses domesticated man in nature, destroying the homelessness he had felt in the cold and "dead" physical mechanism. Then, again, as Kirby and Spence, among others, illustrate, it provided a way of reviving the sense of a purposive, growing natural universe in which man's development was the highest end, and whose spiritual preparation was therefore a concomitant and significant necessity. Formerly on the rim of the world of sensation, the mind now took a central position, connected in its new spiritual capacities with the heart and cause of the spiritual organism. The ways of its relatedness, for which "correspondence" spoke, were, therefore, many.

But in considering the world as organism as we know it, man could be implicated in its natural processes in the way the evolutionary naturalism of the post-Civil War period described. In the Darwinian view, unable to transcend the nature of which he was admittedly the highest product, confined to remorseless processes that degraded him as much as Hume's description of the self as a bundle of perceptions, man was denied the religious perspective that one finds in the poetic science of Kirby and Spence. Without a higher universe there could be no drama of spiritual and moral ascent, no transcendence of evil, no sense of beneficent purpose. And the shudder that swept the post-Darwinian religious mind was no less than that awakened in Emerson's time by the similar materialism of sensationalism. The unity that Emerson demanded was not to be achieved by restricting man to one level, either that of material or spiritual monism. Such a reduction would have been one of those "metaphysical terrors" that he prayed he would have strength enough to endure (*J*, IV, 494).

Instead, Emerson retained the cosmological dualism of the Platonic tradition.[7] His universe was a universe of levels and platforms, a progressive staircase leading to unity. Worldliness and other-worldliness, lower and higher, material and spiritual — he needed these polarities; they described the tensions he experienced and that as facts of consciousness his vision reconciled. Of course, they had been a part of his religious and intellectual inheritance. The Puritans, whose stern moral fervor he admired, had distinguished between nature and revelation; and Edwards had fractured the universe with the humanly unbridgeable chasm of common and supernatural grace. But content with neither the unknowableness of the supernatural — Emerson gave the religious experience a natural base — nor with the awful sovereignty of a God who forbade human agency in the religious ascent, Emerson still needed to maintain the dualism of prudence and spiritual laws. Without this conception of a polar universe, correspondence-as-connection or as the axis would have been unnecessary. And only when this structural dualism was represented psychologically — "Blessed is the day when the youth discovers that Within and Above are synonyms" (*J*, III, 399) — was correspondence, as the act of intuitive perception that spanned the gap of finite (outer) and infinite (inner) and unified them in the experience of the self, a necessary assumption of this thought.

For perception bridged this epistemological gap opened in modern thought by Descartes. If the world was to be put together again, what happened in the act of perception had to be reëxamined and the convenient, intellectual split in the universe challenged by the intimate experience of its unity and wholeness. Thus the apprehension of unity, represented by the moral sentiment in Emerson's thought, fused subject and object with a religious warmth, and by uniting man with God, sanctified perception as a moral duty. By showing the limits of the understanding, Kant, too, had dichotomized the universe into the realms of noumena and phenomena, and the impossibility of knowing the things-in-themselves had disturbed Emerson. He followed in the writings of Coleridge the line of Kant in the thought of Fichte and Schelling that developed from Kant's own discontent with the empirical analysis of knowledge. For Kant had opened the way out of his own epistemological dilemma by asserting that the moral self in its acts of will transcended the limits of the knowing self and took its imperatives from noumenal sources. Rising above the phenomenal world, the self that willed and acted was morally at home. Later Fichte and Schelling made action and knowing inseparable; for in the activity of knowing, in perception as the expressive unfolding of the self, the two worlds melted into unity. The self that made the world of its experience, fashioned it after the higher instincts that beckoned it to a transempirical world.[8]

It is in this sense that we can understand how necessary the assumption of correspondence was to the relief of Emerson's "metaphysical pathos." The world was indeed split, but between its terminals, man generated in every perceptive act the spark that momentarily united them. This bipolar unity was an article of Emerson's faith. In his journal he wrote, in reply to Hedge's doubts: "If, as Hedge thinks, I overlook great facts in stating the absolute laws of the soul; if, as he seems to represent it, the world is not a dualism, is not a bipolar unity, but is *two*, is Me and It, then is there the alien, the unknown, and all we have believed and chanted out of our deep instinctive hope is a pretty dream" (*J*, V, 206). But nevertheless, that the universe was two was a fact in his experience: "A believer in Unity, a seer of Unity, I yet behold two." This was the reason for the inescapable ebb and flow of life, of merger and individuality, that he experienced. "Whilst I feel myself in sympathy with nature," Emerson wrote, "and rejoice with greatly beating heart in the course of Justice and Benevolence overpowering me, I yet find little access to this me of me. I fear what shall befal: I am not enough a party to the great order to be tranquil. I hope and I fear. I do not see. At one time I am a Doer. A divine life, I create scenes and persons around and for me, and unfold my thought by a perpetual, successive projection. At least I so say, I so feel, — but presently I return to the habitual attitude of suffering.

"I behold; I bask in beauty; I await; I wonder; where's my godhead now? This is the Male and Female principle in nature. One man, Male and Female, created he him. Hard as it is to describe God, it is harder to describe the individual.

"A certain wandering light comes to me which I instantly perceive to be the cause of causes. It transcends all proving. It is itself the ground of being; and I see that it is not one, and I another, but this is the life of my life. This is one fact then; that in certain moments I have known that I existed directly from God, and am, as it were his organ, and in my ultimate consciousness am He. Then, secondly, the contradictory fact is familiar, that I am a surprised spectator and learner of all my life. This is the habitual posture of the mind — beholding. But whenever the day dawns, the great day of truth on the soul, it comes with an awful invitation to me to accept it, to blend with its aurora.

"Cannot I conceive the Universe without a contradiction?" (*J*, IV, 248–249).

The contradiction was experiential, just as for Emerson the Platonic dualism was always psychologically undeniable: it was health and decay, genius and talent, imagination and fancy, reason and understanding. Its mediation was inspiration. Doing and beholding, Male and Female [9] — here was the mystery of the self, as Schelling taught, the ideal self as knower and the real self as known, the unconscious self that produced from itself the stuff of consciousness.[10] As Emerson wrote of the soul, "It is a watcher more than a doer, and it is a doer, only that it may the better watch" (*C*, I, 60). So in projecting a natural history of the Reason, Emerson advised himself: "Recognize the inextinguishable dualism." But he added, "Also show that to seek Unity is a necessity of the mind. . ." (*J*, IV, 435–436).[11]

II

"The best read naturalist," Emerson wrote, "will see that
there remains much to learn of his relation to the world, and
that it is not to be learned by any addition or subtraction or
other comparison of known quantities," but "by untaught sal-
lies of the spirit, by a continual self-recovery" (*C*, I, 66). The
relatedness and unity the Emersonian naturalist demanded
was not to be had in the manipulations of logic, but instead in
the act of perception which expressed the whole man. The
higher knowledge of value would come, Emerson believed,
when seeing became a unitary act involving both the emotional and intellectual responses of man. Perception, then,
could not be too narrowly accounted for as the passive reception of sense-impressions, and their consequent accumulation
as knowledge. A fuller description was needed, emphasizing
the active contribution of man's total nature, his *desire* for
unity, and the ways and means by which this desire was
fulfilled.

Following Coleridge, Emerson distinguished this total perception from Locke's contriving faculty. "Reason," he wrote
in 1834, "is the highest faculty of the soul, what we mean often
by the soul itself: it never *reasons*, never proves; it simply perceives; it is vision. The Understanding toils all the time, compares, contrives, adds, argues; near-sighted but strong-sighted,
dwelling in the present, the expedient, the customary." [12] But
to call the Reason a faculty is misleading. For Emerson, like
Coleridge, never intended to separate man's consciousness
into faculties. What was intended in the distinction was a
reëmphasis of the dynamic and imaginative aspects of the
mind in its totality as compared with its tool-like capacities for
"reasoning." Coleridge, Alice Snyder points out, "tried method after method of bringing the distinction home, contrasting
now *thought* with mere *attention*, now the *imagination* with

the *fancy*, and again, and more frequently, the *reason* with the *understanding*." "For," she continues, "the experience of knowing involved, Coleridge insisted, the 'total man,' not merely the 'understanding.' He found that ordinary thinking fell far short of adequacy because it was based on uncriticized premises and assumptions, and determined by often unrecognized bias. The processes with which ordinary formal logic dealt were futile unless supplemented by what he called 'mental initiative' when he thought the word 'Idea' would be misunderstood, and so the enlightenment that came through true experience in the world of nature. The thinking that counted involved the will to postulate premises instead of merely taking them for granted; it involved the power to perceive afresh the materials of thought, instead of accepting them passively as ready-made materials for intellectual manipulation. It was a physical experience, conditioned largely by 'feeling' and attitude." [13] Because of the physical experience of imaginative apprehension which he himself knew as the miracle of his being, Emerson felt the Coleridgean distinction "a philosophy itself" and "very practical";[14] and he welcomed in the writings of Coleridge, the "thorough examination of thought as an 'instrument of real life.'"[15]

In Coleridge's essays on method in *The Friend*, Emerson found joined with Kantian Reason a Platonic emphasis on ideas, and in the distinction between science and scheme, he found science transformed. Just as Reason, another key word of the eighteenth century, had been filled with the new content of intuition and imagination, that is, brought more into accord with the facts of mind, so science, as the architecture of ideas and laws became the highest expression of the desire for unity in the mind. Requiring mental initiative, science was no longer "false by being unpoetical" (*C*, VIII, 10); it was, indeed, a form of the highest poetry (of the imaginative faculty) and its revelation of the grandeur of Law, a support of religion. This was the sense Emerson meant "intellectual" to convey when he wrote: "The religion which is to guide and fulfil the present and coming ages . . . must be intellectual. The scientific mind must have a faith which is science" (*C*, VI, 240).

Emerson read *The Friend* carefully as early as 1829 (*J*, II, 277–279). Here was one of the few "self-imprinting" books, he wrote to his aunt, Mary Moody Emerson. "I like to encounter these citizens of the universe, that believe the mind was made to be spectator of all, inquisitor of all, and whose philosophy compares with others much as astronomy with the other sciences, taking post at the centre and, as from a specular mount, sending sovereign glances to the circumference of things." That Emerson compared Coleridge's work with astronomy, one of the imaginative constituents of Emerson's vision,[16] was the highest praise. For Emerson believed that the religious revolution was the result of modern science, of the Copernican system. "The irresistible effect of the Copernican Astronomy has been," he also wrote in "Historic Notes of Life and Letters in New England," "to make the great scheme for the Salvation of man absolutely incredible." Taking salvation out of the hands of "dogmatic theology," proving theism, the new astronomy operated "steadily to establish the moral laws, to disconcert and evaporate temporary systems" (*J*, II, 490–491). Emerson felt that Coleridge's method promised as much; for wasn't astronomy an example of its application?

Coleridge's "Science of Method" proposed as the way out of the Humean wilderness of association what Emerson called the tyrannization of the universe by ideas (*C*, XII, 21). Science and scheme described the method or manner of operation of the faculties of the Reason and the Understanding treated in *Biographia Literaria* psychologically as fundamental differences in the mind's approach to reality. The Imaginative Reason was a means of apprehending Reality, and by its imaginative apprehension, the mind created its universe, that is, created and so coalesced with the objects it perceived (see *J*, IV, 99–100, 380 ff.). In these moments of vision, one felt or was conscious of the growth of the mind, of its development from within outward. And in his account of ideas (Reason, of course, was their seed-bed),[17] Coleridge was describing from a logical rather than a psychological viewpoint the grounds of this progressive dialectic. Understanding, on the other hand, was characterized by being manipulative: it could not create nor fuse the objects with which it worked. It could only obey the laws of association, and reassemble what the mind, in its imaginative aspect, had already created.[18] Scheme was, therefore, as the logic of the Understanding, a secondary method, by which one arranged what was previously perceived; and Science, as the logic of the Reason on which the Understanding depended, was a method of unity and progression, of the self's development in its interaction with nature.

As long as the understanding, Coleridge wrote in *The Friend*, submitted "to mere events and images as such . . . independent of any power in the mind to classify or appropriate them," unity and progression remained impossible. Instead of passively observing things, one had, if he were to think methodically, to contemplate the relations of things. And of the two kinds of relation that Coleridge distinguished, Law fitted the needs of Science, and Theory those of Scheme. Law as the highest order of relation was the result of the creative *idea* of God, who "not only appoints each thing to its *position*, gives it its qualities . . . [but also] its very existence as *that particular* thing." Similarly, whenever the human mind apprehended Reality by its Reason and originated a truth "not abstracted or generalized from the observation of parts," and, as in geometry, by that truth or idea predetermined the order of things, the second order of the relation of law prevailed. But to apprehend the first order of the relation of law, that is, the ideas in the mind of God from which all the "grounds and principles necessary to Method" were derived, one had to avail himself of insight — Coleridge queried, "Intuition shall we call it, or stedfast faith?" For only in God was the absolute law and the "sufficient cause of the reality correspondent thereto." Thus, for Coleridge, the only guarantee of Law was its contemplation "as exclusively an attribute of the Supreme Being, inseparable from the idea of God." [19]

In contradistinction to Law and its intuitive perception — its realization only by the penetration to Reality — Coleridge placed Theory. Coleridge's account of Theory was close to the eighteenth-century notion of law or the usual inductive proceedings of scientific method. Theory, he wrote, was discovered by observation or experiment, was a "given arrangement" for purposes of control and utility, and was founded on the "general idea of cause and effect." In Theory, one did not originate ideas, but applied them, arranging facts from their point of view. These arrangements were, Coleridge commented, "at best but approximations to the first [the Science of Law], or tentative exercise in the hope of discovering it." [20] Its failure was in its arbitrary imposition of "unity" and its lack of organic fusion or interrelatedness.

Both Emerson and Coleridge criticized eighteenth-century science because they had an intimate knowledge of the intellectual-spiritual paralysis created by the limitation of the concept of law to the level of Theory. Restricted to the mechanical superimposition of concepts (which, freshly perceived in the seventeenth century, had extended the frontiers of the universe), the scope of law had now to be extended beyond its mere manipular function and made the guarantee of purposeful organic order. Stemming originally from the belief in God's providence, but now excluding God in its "scientific" application to nature, the concept of law had to be given a metaphysical status as the absolute ground from which to derive its moral and teleological emphasis. Again another level had to be added to the reduced scope of human activity: the limited abstractions of science — the "counters" — had to be reconciled with man's direct and total apprehension of nature, with the self-evident truths of his consciousness. Aware of this, and yet unwilling to sacrifice the cardinal virtue the eighteenth century found in science, its verification of law in the universe (*Y*, 220–225), Emerson felt with Coleridge that science had to be reoriented in the larger framework of a purposive, evolutionary nature. The perception of the quality of the whole and the sense of its flowing relatedness from which in turn its chief value to the spirit of man derived shattered narrow abstractions and manipulated theories. These theories any new fact might upset, and one was therefore at the mercy of events. But in a purposiveness and relatedness grounded in Law, Coleridge taught that man might share by contemplating its corresponding ideas, and that this constituted his freedom.[21] The concept of absolute law, then, was another way of asserting that there was both more depth and direction in the universe (and in man's consciousness) than rational science admitted, and that what it omitted was necessary to man's freedom and spiritual growth. By adding the spiritual dimension to the universe of science, they were not rejecting it, but, on the contrary, making possible its reconciliation by means of the experience of correspondence. For representing an ever-present fact of consciousness, science could not be eliminated: instead, it had to be controlled, and control was provided for in the mediation of Ideas as the central fact of correspondence.

But what eighteenth-century Theory chiefly omitted was the possibility of Ideas, in the self-originating, trans-empirical sense Coleridge intended. When plagued by the disciples of Locke, Hume, and Reid for an Idea of an Idea, Coleridge wrote in his *Autograph Notebook*: "What meaning I attached to the *word*, Idea, I had already declared. The *term*, Idea, I had already defined, in the only way, in which the name of *anywhat*, that really or actually is, can be defined — viz, first, negatively . . . positively, by some character common to all Ideas — ex gr. that in all we contemplate the Particular in the Universal, or the Universal in the Particular, the Qualified (or determinate) in the Absolute, and the Absolute in the Qualified. This, however, is not *the* Idea — which is *the* Form, in which the Absolute distinctly yet entirely and indivisibly is realized and revealed. This is that which cannot be *generalized*, on which the mind can exercise no modifying functions — that which is deeper than all intelligence, inasmuch as it represents the element of the Will, and it's [sic] essential inderivability." [22] Perhaps what is most significant for Emerson here is the statement that an Idea "is *the* Form, in which the Absolute *distinctly yet entirely and indivisibly* [italics supplied] is realized and revealed." The idea is a *way* of contemplating, that is, a form of intuition or direct perception through which what is revealed is always the Absolute Reality. An Idea, for Coleridge, was, therefore, the Law realized. "The words Idea and Law are correlative terms," he wrote, "differing only as object and subject, as Being and Truth." "Thus an IDEA conceived as subsisting in an object becomes a LAW; and a Law contemplated subjectively (in a mind) is an Idea." [23]

And Emerson immediately following the passage he took from Coleridge (" 'The problem of philosophy . . . is, for all that exists conditionally, to find a ground unconditioned and absolute.' ") wrote: "It proceeds on the faith that a law determines all phenomena, which being known, the phenomena can be predicted. That law, when in the mind, is an idea" (*C*, I, 55). More concretely, what Emerson meant by an idea, he recorded in his Journal: "The Idea according to which the Universe is made is wholly wanting to us; is it not? Yet it may or will be found to be constructed on as harmonious and perfect a thought, self-explaining, as a problem in geometry. The classification of all natural science is arbitrary, I believe; no method philosophical in any one. And yet in all the permutations and combinations supposable, might not a cabinet of shells [see his own experience at the Jardin des Plantes] or a Flora be thrown into one which would flash on us the very thought? We take them out of composition, and so lose their greatest beauty. The moon is an unsatisfactory sight if the eye be exclusively directed to it, and a shell retains but a small part of its beauty when examined separately. All our classifications are introductory and very convenient, but must be looked on as temporary, and the eye always watching for the glimmering of that pure, plastic Idea. If Swammerdam forgets that he is a man, and when you make any speculative suggestion as to the habits or origin or relation of insects, rebukes you . . . he is only concerned for the facts, — he loses all that for which his science is of any worth.

"This [the pure, plastic Idea] was what Goethe sought in his Metamorphosis of plants. The Pythagorean doctrine of transmigration is an Idea; the Swedenborgian of Affections Clothed, is one also" (*J*, III, 292–293). The prospective affirmative aspect of his vision needed the idea which could dissolve "the solid-seeming block of matter" (*C*, I, 55) and reshape it. Coleridge best expressed this futuristic and controlling role of ideas when he contrasted Theory and Law once again in those terms: "The Conception or synopsis of a plurality of phaenomena so schematized as to show the compatibility of their coexistence, is THEORY — a product of the Understanding in the absence or eclipse of IDEAS, or Contemplations of the Law, and *hence necessarily conditioned by the Appearances*, and changing with every new or newly-discovered Phaenomenon, which Theory always follows never leads — while the Law being constitutive of the phaenomena and in order of Thought necessarily antecedent, the Idea as the Correlative and mental Counterpart of the Law, is necessarily prophetic

and constructive." [24] As an example of this difference in
method, Coleridge contrasted the Ptolemaic and Newtonian
astronomies: "The dependence of the understanding on the
representations of the senses, and its consequent posteriority
thereto, as contrasted with the independence and antecedency
of reason, are strikingly exemplified in the Ptolemaic System
(that truly wonderful product and highest boast of the faculty
judging according to the senses!) compared with the Newtonian, as the offspring of a yet higher power, arranging, correct-
ing, and annulling the representations of the senses according
to its own inherent laws and constitutive ideas." [25] Emerson,
then, had good reason for hanging a picture of Newton in his
study and for saying in an early sermon on "Astronomy" that
"the discoveries of astronomy have reconciled the greatness of
nature to the greatness of mind" (*Y*, 176).

But Coleridge also knew that this power in the idea depended on "proving" its correlative relation to law, and that
the only proof was in the fact of its experience. This only "the
conscience . . . can at once authorize and substantiate." For,
he added, "From whichever point the reason may start, from
the things which are seen to the one invisible, or from the idea
of the absolute one to the things that are seen, it will find a
chasm, which moral being only, which the spirit and religion
of man alone, can fill up." [26] When faced with this problem,
Coleridge wrote, Plato also believed that the only solution lay
in a Reason which could "pass out of itself and seek the
ground of agreement in a supersensual essence, which being at
once the *ideal* of the reason and the cause of the material
world, is the pre-establisher of the harmony in and between
both." [27] The basis of correspondence, upon which the method of science rested was, therefore, "a principle deeper than
science, more certain than demonstration." [28] It was to be
verified in the self-conscious life of the Reason itself, in its
awareness of the "sense of a principle of connection given by

the mind." [29] Correspondence was, as Emerson said of Swedenborg, this genuine vision upon which man's intimate relation
depended. The spirit of man could fill up the chasm because,
for Coleridge, the essence of this spirit in man was self-repre-
sentativeness.[30] Spirit saw only itself in the object it viewed:
was the original identity of subject and object.[31] If the organs
of sense found a corresponding world of sense, and the organs
of spirit a corresponding world of spirit,[32] this was so because
*the senses were living growths and developments of the mind
and spirit.*" [33] The faculties fitted the world, as Emerson also
believed, as channels for the anticipations of spirit. They
helped one realize the potential working in man [34] by provoking the instinct for unity which Reason fulfilled in the progressive unfolding of ideas. "It is essential to a true theory of
nature and of man," Emerson began his chapter on "Spirit" in
Nature, "that it should contain somewhat progressive. Uses
that are exhausted or that may be, and facts that end in the
statement, cannot be all that is true of this brave lodging
wherein man is harbored, and wherein all his faculties find
appropriate and endless exercise" (*C*, I, 61). For the realization
of spirit, nature had to be its symbolic mirror, providing (via
the faculties of sense) the objects in which the spirit somehow
resided and in which, at the same time, it saw itself projected.

Reason, as the faculty in which spirit had its life, that is, as
the faculty capable of self-intuition or philosophic imagination, of reading the symbol,[35] expressed its penetration into
the spirit behind objects and events by means of ideas. When
reason had grasped the idea — in terms of which for Emerson
it perceived "the analogy that marries Matter and Mind" (*C*,
I, 35) — it acquired a universal truth; and, again thinking in
terms of astronomy, a Universal truth, Emerson wrote, "is like
a great circle on a sphere, comprising all possible circles;
which, however, may be drawn, and comprise it, in like manner. Every such truth is the Absolute Ens seen from one side"

(*C*, I, 44). The vindication of these universal truths was, for Emerson, one of the most rewarding results of Coleridge's methodization of the life of Reason. For what Emerson wanted from the reassertion of ideas in science and poetry was an assurance that he could live by his own moral ideas without wasting himself in mysticism. Without this dedication to a lawful universe in which, regardless of individual perspective, man might share, correspondence would be mere whim, moral readings of natural tendencies merely relative, and the control of circumstance illusory. The anchor of individual perception, therefore, was the *law* which informed the totality of which man was a part, and whose only connection was the faculty of Reason. In the equation: Law is to Necessity as Perception (Reason and Ideas) is to Freedom, Emerson found his solution to the problem of determinism and free will. If ideas were truly the correlatives of law, the life of Reason promised release from prudential interference. It meant, as Emerson wrote at the conclusion of "Idealism," a revitalization of religion by "the practice of ideas, or the introduction of ideas into life" (*C*, I, 57).

The introduction of ideas into life, like the mental initiative of Bacon, who was "capable of ideas, yet devoted to Ends" appealed especially to Emerson. He was, of course, indebted to Coleridge for reinstating Bacon, the traditional father of British empiricism, in the Platonic camp. Bacon represented modern Platonism or the "poetic tendency" in science, for according to Coleridge, Bacon had said that "one fact is often worth a thousand" and that "an idea is an experiment proposed, an experiment is an idea realized." [36] Even more for Emerson, Bacon represented the "mental materialism" he desired for himself and admired in Montaigne. Coleridge's comparison of Plato and Bacon made this clear. The distinction was "simply this: that philosophy being necessarily bi-polar,

Plato treats principally of the truth, as it manifests itself at the *ideal* pole, as the science of intellect . . . while Bacon confines himself . . . to the same truth, as it is manifested at the other, or material pole, as the science of nature . . . [Plato directed] his inquiries chiefly to those objective truths that exist in and for the intellect alone, the images and representatives of which we construct for ourselves by figure, number, and word . . . [while Bacon attached] his main concern to the truths which have their signatures in nature, and which . . . may be revealed to us *through* and *with*, but never *by* the senses.[37] Although his attachment to the material pole was so tenacious, Bacon was not to be mistaken for an empiricist. For first of all, Emerson wrote, "he required in his map of the mind . . . universality, or *prima philosophia*, the receptacle for all such profitable observations and axioms as fall not within the compass of any of the special parts of philosophy, but are more common, and of a higher stage" (*C*, V, 240). For his first introduction to *prima philosophia*, Emerson was probably more indebted to Baron de Gérando than Coleridge, for Gérando prefaced his *Histoire comparée des systèmes de philosophie* (1822) with a study of Baconian method as a model for his own treatment of diverse systems under general ideas.[38] But Emerson merged what he learned of method from Gérando with Coleridge's *Science*; and this can be seen in his journal record: "I endeavor to announce the laws of the First Philosophy. It is the mark of these that their enunciation awakens the feeling of the moral sublime, and great men are those who believe in them. Every one of these propositions resembles a great circle in astronomy. No matter in what direction it be drawn, it contains the whole sphere. So each of these seems to imply all truth. Compare a page of Bacon with Swift, Chesterfield, *Lacon* [by Charles C. Colton], and see the difference of great and less circles. These are gleams of a world in which we do not live: they astonish the understanding"

(*J*, III, 489–490).[39] And it can be seen more dramatically in his persistent concern with first principles in the long preparation for the writing of *Nature*.[40]

Once he had made the method of ideas his own, Emerson applied it sweepingly to discomfort the materialists. All those who believed in the correspondence of the worlds of matter and spirit and in the mediation of ideas, he broadly identified as Platonists. And the test that distinguished materialists from spiritualists, men of the world from poets, Lockists from Platonists was "how far the sense of unity, or the instinct of seeking resemblances predominated" (*C*, V, 239). He characterized the Platonic mind by its love of analogy; idealists were analogists. But so were all men, Emerson believed, in the constitution of their minds. "Man is an analogist," he wrote. "He cannot help seeing everything under its relations to all other things and to himself" (*J*, IV, 33). In this way "the humanity of science or the naturalness of knowing" was possible. And so, he wrote, in denouncing the Lockists, "Whoever discredits analogy and requires heaps of facts, before any theories can be attempted, has no poetic power and nothing original or beautiful will be produced by him." Only the poetic power of the Reason, through the prism of an idea, could build a *uni*-verse out of the chaotic multitude of facts. Locke, therefore, stood for prose and the "influx of decomposition . . . as Bacon and the Platonists, of growth." Assured that "the Platonic was the poetic tendency," Emerson was certain that "Spenser, Burns, Byron and Wordsworth will be Platonists; and that dull men will be Lockists" (*C*, V, 239). He believed, as he remarked of Bacon (who "held of the analogists, of the idealists"), "that no perfect discovery can be made in a flat or level, but you must ascend to a higher science" (*C*, V, 240). To live possessed of God, to put nature under your feet, that was the spiritual mission of the idea and of the poet who converted man's "daily routine into a garden of God, by suggesting the principle which classifies the facts" (*J*, IV, 7–8). In terms of inner and outer, of vertical and horizontal, "the Idea is spiritual sight"; Emerson wrote, "the idealess research of facts is natural sight." And Emerson asked, "Cannot the natural see better when assisted by the spiritual?" (*J*. IV, 147).

III

The emphasis on the need for double vision, for spiritual as well as natural sight, slowly strengthened during Emerson's formative years. Long before he read Coleridge and Swedenborg, he recorded personal spiritual observations for which his later appropriation of the word "correspondence" was well suited. At the age of seventeen, he described the fact of consciousness that constituted the Reason: "When those magnificent masses of vapour which load our horizon are breaking away, disclosing fields of blue atmosphere, there is an exhilaration awakened in the system of a susceptible man which so invigorates the energies of mind, and displays to himself such manifold power and joy superiour to other existences, that he will triumph and exult that he is a man. . . We feel at these times that external analogy which subsists between the external changes of nature, and scenes of good and ill that chequer human life" (*J*, I, 26). At twenty, he found the Rev. Joseph Stevens Buckminster "remarkable for a 'philosophic imagination.'" "It is the most popular and useful quality which a modern scholar can possess to become a favourite in society," because, Emerson explained, "It imparts a spirit of liberal philosophy which can impress itself by the applying of beautiful images" (*J*, I, 323).

Writing at the same time to Aunt Mary Moody Emerson of the metaphysical difficulties of holding fast to intellectual and moral truth in the face of skepticism, he said, "It was one of my youngest thoughts that God would not confound the weak-

eyed understandings of his children whilst they read on earth
the alphabet of morals." If moral truths are difficult to grasp,
he wrote, "an acquaintance with mind, indefatigable pursuit
and accumulation of all demonstrable truths; science, deep
and high and broad as Newton's may ally consciousness to so
many certain truths; may extend our vantage ground of existence so widely and tie it with so many fast knots to such a
various multitude of thoughts as to confirm our hold. A man
with one proposition can hardly go far in its illustration or
defence, and his knowledge increases in a far faster proportion
than the number of single propositions he amasses, because
he continually discerns new connexions and inferences growing out of and between them. And Newton's bright eye, which
glanced in every direction into the vast Universe, and saw
each fact corroborated by correspondencies springing up on
every side, was perhaps [too] wholly absorbed in the extent,
the consistency and beauty of the show . . . to doubt" (*J*, I,
325–326). And before he accepted the call to the Second
Church in 1829, he had asked himself "whether the business
of the preacher is not simply to hunt out and to exhibit the
analogies between moral and material nature in such a manner as to have a bearing upon practice" (*J*, II, 241–242). He
was already reaching out for a means of expression that could
accommodate his spiritual experience, that could, as he said of
spiritual sight, help the natural sight to see better.

Emerson's "bishop," William Ellery Channing, a student of
the Platonist Richard Price, had indicated the way to him as
early as 1824. In an ordination sermon, "The Demands of the
Age on the Ministry," Channing summarized the shift in sensibility by remarking on the change in poetry (which for him
and Emerson was an index of man's spiritual depth): "It has a
deeper and more impressive tone than comes to us from what
has been called the Augustan age of English literature. The
regular, elaborate, harmonious strains, which delighted a for-

mer generation, are now accused, I say not how justly, of playing too much on the surface of nature and of the heart. Men want and demand a more thrilling note, a poetry which pierces beneath the exterior of life to the depths of the soul, and which lays open its mysterious workings, borrowing from the whole outward creation fresh images and correspondences with which to illuminate the secrets of the world within us." [41] In the seminal "Remarks on National Literature," delivered in 1830, Channing voiced so many ideas that Emerson was to make a part of his own thought that his influence often seems more plausibly direct than that of others. Literature, the vehicle Emerson chose for himself, Channing linked with morality, religion, and politics as the expression of the nation's mind and as "the mightiest instrument on earth." He claimed for it "the first rank among the means of improvement." [42] Its offices were not limited to the mind alone, because "the worlds of matter and mind are too intimately connected" and "all the objects of human thought flow into one another." The "moral and physical truths" that constitute literature "have many bonds and analogies"; and the mind, which is the creative center of the literary structure, "was made to act on matter," to grow "by expressing itself in material forms." [43] The call to literature (and from Father William Emerson on, all the Emersons had responded) opened the way to the highest utility; for if "life is the means; action and improvement the end . . . who will deny that the noblest utility belongs to that knowledge by which the chief purpose of our creation is accomplished? According to these views," Channing wrote, "a people should honor and cultivate, as unspeakably useful, that literature, which corresponds to, and calls forth, the highest faculties; which expresses and communicates energy of thought, a thirst for the true, and a delight in the beautiful. . . Poetry, is useful, by touching deep springs in the human soul; by giving voice to its more delicate feelings; by breathing out, and making more intelligible, the sympathy which subsists between the mind and the outward universe; by creating beautiful forms of manifestations for great moral truths." [44] And the writer who would make literature the means of achieving fame, "who would make it [moral truth] visible and powerful, must strive to join an austere logic to a fervent eloquence; must place it in various lights; must create for it interesting forms; must wed it to beauty; must illuminate it by similitudes and contrasts; must show its correspondence with the outward world." [45]

These prospects suggest something of the emotional intensity, the hope and fervor of the atmosphere in which the young Emerson made his choice of calling. In its demands for symbolic depth, Channing had related the new poetry with "correspondence" as the visible embodiment of moral truths. But in relating correspondence to poetry, Channing was not limiting it. For poetry was the exalted yearning of man's deepest instinctive nature, and as the means of expressing man's relation to the ideal — to the "true end of life" — poetry warranted his praise. Poetry was the corresponding (the fitting, the natural) vehicle for man's highest faculty: the imagination. This faculty, Channing said, was able to conceive "a more perfect beauty than exists within the limits of actual experience." Instead of distorting reality, it "ever . . . sees in the visible the type of the invisible, and in the outward world an image of the inward, thus bringing them into harmony, and throwing added brightness over both." [46] The vision by which this was accomplished, and the "proof that we are created to look above everything outward to a spiritual end," Channing also meant by correspondence. For to find harmony and to feel at home in the universe, one had to see the universe *that way*. To the young Emerson, then, seeing the inseparableness of correspondence and poetic insight, Channing's apostrophe to poetry was irresistible.

"It is the glorious prerogative of this art," Channing wrote in *On the Character and Writings of Milton*, a paper Emerson singled out for praise in his "Historic Notes," [47] "that it 'makes all things new' for the gratification of a divine instinct. It indeed finds its elements in what it actually sees and experiences, the world of matter and mind; but it combines and blends these into new forms and according to new affinities; breaks down, if we may so say, the distinctions and bounds of nature; imparts to material objects life, and sentiment, and emotion, and invests the mind with the powers and splendors of the outward creation; describes the surrounding universe in the colors which the passions throw over it, and depicts the soul in those modes of repose and agitation, of tenderness or sublime emotion, which manifests its thirst for a more powerful and joyful existence. To a man of a literal and prosaic character, the mind may seem lawless in these workings; but it observes higher laws than it transgresses — the laws of the immortal intellect; it is trying and developing its best faculties; and in the objects which it describes, or in the emotions which it awakens, anticipates those states of progressive power, splendor, beauty, and happiness, for which it was created. . . Its great tendency and purpose is, to carry the mind beyond and above the beaten, dusty, weary walks of ordinary life; to lift it into a purer element; and to breathe into it more profound and generous emotion. It reveals to us the loveliness of nature, brings back the freshness of early feeling, revives the relish of simple pleasures, keeps unquenched the enthusiasm which warmed the spring-time of our being, refines youthful love, strengthens our interest in human nature by vivid delineations of its tenderest and loftiest feelings, spreads our sympathies over all classes of society, knits us by new ties with universal being, and, through the brightness of its prophetic visions helps faith to lay hold on the future life." [48] Channing's claims were not extravagant, for the poetry of which he speaks was the end of the new assessment of the projective powers of the mind. It embodied the new vision: what he claimed for poetry was claimed for the vision through or by which it was created; and what gave that vision its moral value was its power to tax man's highest faculties — those which yearned for and felt the unity of the universe and found the correspondences in which this unity was accomplished. A literature formed for such a moral purpose vindicated the utility of poets.[49]

Channing, a champion of the "utility" of Wordsworth, was representative of the changing theories of aesthetics that prepared the way for the full flowering of correspondence in Emerson's works. Without the questioning of neoclassical theory and without the growing familiarity with Wordsworth, Emerson's achievement would have been made more difficult. Emerson's originality, where ideas were concerned, was chiefly that of recognition and transformation. The representative man, as Emerson conceived him in his own image, incorporated the ideas of his time. His solitude was not intellectual, but rather a condition for work. And the amazing thing about the solitary Emerson was his openness and responsiveness to the flow of ideas and how much he was in the rapids of the intellectual current.

As a student at Harvard College, Emerson had no doubt met with the Scottish common-sense critics in his training and reading.[50] These "psychological aestheticians" — Lord Kames, Hugh Blair, Archibald Alison — and the American adapter of Blair, Edward Tyrell Channing, brother of William Ellery Channing and Boylston Professor of Rhetoric at Harvard from 1819 until 1851, had initiated the process of change in literary taste.[51] By applying David Hartley's and Francis Hutcheson's theories of the association of ideas to the problem of taste, "the old, necessarily conservative, idea of the intrinsic beauty of objects was undermined, and the conception of subjectivity

. . . took its place." The mind no longer passively perceived, but in its projection created the beauty it apprehended.[52]

But the idea of subjectivity, which Alison buttressed with the authority of Plato,[53] was only a step in the freedom of perception that Emerson needed. Afraid of individual associations that tended to irresponsible "expression," the Scottish philosophers tried to restrict them to the universal. To maintain their theory of knowledge, that the senses seized an objective reality, they had to maintain also that the faculties of all men operated in the same manner — that their processes of association (their subjectivities) were uniform and therefore universal. This was unfortunate for the nineteenth century, Charvat shows, because to catalog associations "as static and unchanging — as universal rather than individual — was to keep poetry in its old channels and to discourage new and original reactions." [54] This, incidentally, was the fault Emerson was, in time, to find with Swedenborg.

The recognition in America of Wordsworth's poetry was, perhaps, the sign that these limitations of Scottish aesthetics had been overcome and that new and original reactions — morally edifying, to be sure — were now acceptable. Charvat has traced the course of the critical acceptance of Wordsworth in America, showing that by 1830, even the orthodox trinitarian *Christian Spectator* had regretted its early neglect and now approved "his idea of the moral beneficence of nature" and "his simple style." [55] Wordsworth, whose "influence on American thought was penetrating," was the major figure of the 1820's. "It was his work," Charvat says, "that vitalized American moralism into a dynamic and creative force. It was he who gave American idealism a philosophy to work with. Without him, American transcendentalism might have reached only a few minds capable of philosophic subtlety, for he prepared a common-sense and practical nation for the visions of Coleridge and Emerson. . . American criticism seemed to sigh that here at last was what it had been looking for: spirituality without unintelligibility, vitality without sensuality, edification without didacticism." [56] Wordsworth, then, was as important to the preparation of the transcendental soil as Coleridge was in planting the seeds of the necessary philosophic distinctions. For it was chiefly in Wordsworth that "by 1833 the battle against neo-classical diction was won." By then the critics had discovered "that the universal moral conceptions were best described in terms of the concrete." [57]

Emerson, whose own literary progress in the years leading up to *Nature* parallels this pattern of changing taste, and whose changing style reveals it, at first found nothing appealing in Wordsworth beyond an occasional "flash of divine light." "The genuine bard," he wrote to Aunt Mary when he was twenty-three — and the definition remained serviceable for him for the rest of his life — "must be one in whom the extremes of human genius meet . . . [whose] judgment must be as exact and level with life as his imagination is discursive and incalculable." Wordsworth he felt, when judged by this, was "too much a *poet*." His sins were egotism and imagination, he wrote "mystic and unmeaning verses," and what proved his aberration, he wrote "verses on a theory" and "agreed with two or three antics more to bring the public over to a new taste in poetry." His confidence was so overweening that he tried "to break the marble silence of Nature and open some intercourse between man and that divinity with which it seems instinct." And in doing this he "discarded that modesty under whose influence all his great precursors . . . resorted to external nature sparingly for illustration and ornament, and have forborne to tamper with the secret and metaphysical nature of what they borrowed." Because he was "foolishly inquisitive," he would not "let what Heaven made small and casual remain the objects of a notice small and casual" (*J*, II, 105–110).[58]

Emerson, here, was practicing the neoclassical critical attitude. He was perceptive enough to find the faults in Wordsworth that he realized later were his virtues; and his definitions — poetry, for example, was the "relation of thoughts to
things, or of language to thought" — were sound enough to
stand the shift. But it took the long struggle with the expressions of his own perceptions to help him see Wordsworth's
courage in vision. Recollecting in *English Traits*, his visit to
Wordsworth in 1833 — and he thought him important enough
to seek out — he told how hard it was for him to suppress his
laughter (and for Emerson laughter was a forbidding, self-
devastating eruption) when the seer declaimed a poem (*C*, V,
23). But by 1836, he altered his former criticism of Wordsworth's failure to eliminate the poet from the poem and found
"nothing vulgar in Wordsworth's idea of Man." Now, "to believe your own thought . . . is genius," and "to believe that
a man intended to produce the emotion we feel before his
work is the highest praise" (*J*, IV, 55). This was the gauge of
sincerity: that the private association rested on the sure
ground of self, was the legitimate expression of its realization
of correspondence.

Emerson recognized this when he wrote in 1832 that he
found in Swedenborgianism a system of associations congruent
enough, but hardly true. How could Swedenborgianism be
true when other systems of associations endeavored to "shadow forth" the same truth? What he found, instead, was the
element of poetry which for him became one manifestation of
correspondence. Acknowledging his reading in Scottish aesthetics, he wrote that one "sees in this [Swedenborgianism],
and in them all, the element of poetry according to Jeffrey's
true theory, the effect produced by making every thing outward only the sign of something inward: Plato's *forms or
ideas*" (*J*, II, 473–474). Poetry, Emerson had written in 1822,
fulfilled the "tendency in the passions to clothe fanciful views

of objects in beautiful language. It seems to consist in the pleasure of finding out a connection between a material image and a moral sentiment" (*J*, I, 105). Jeffrey had said as much in his article on beauty.[59] The germ of correspondence — what Emerson found true in his theory of poetry, Jeffrey discovered in the "relation which external objects bear to our internal feelings . . . the power they may acquire of suggesting them in consequence of a sort of resemblance or analogy which they seem to have to their natural and appropriate objects." The language of poetry, he said, was "founded to a great degree on this analogy," and the poet, therefore, was a maker of "original similes and metaphors."[60] But for an explanation of the mystery of original similes and metaphors — Jeffrey had confused the poet as maker and the poet as seer — Emerson had to go beyond the Scottish aestheticians. They had, however, indicated the point at which Scottish philosophy had to expand beyond its own explanation of mind.

From whatever side it was viewed, considering the various channels through which it came to Emerson, correspondence focused the age's discontent. Sterile language or hardened forms of sensibility, which no longer intimated man's awareness of his immediate relation to nature, merely presented the problem in another light. And inevitably, Coleridge again helped Emerson understand the philosophic and psychological complexities. For the problem of a language of correspondences connecting the material image and the moral sentiment returned once more to the mystery of the Reason and the Imagination: One had "to perceive afresh the materials of thought" and reflect on the projective and unifying powers of the mind.[61] Metaphors, similes, allegory might be "original" in Jeffrey's sense and still remain the products of fancy. But true symbolic correspondences originated in and were constitutive of the life of the Reason. As Emerson wrote of his own experience in *Nature*, "The moment our discourse rises above the ground line of familiar facts, and is inflamed with passion or exalted by thought, it clothes itself in images. A man conversing in earnest, if he watch his intellectual processes, will find that always a material image, more or less luminous, arises in the mind with every thought, which furnishes the vestment of the thought. . . This imagery is spontaneous. It is the blending of experience with the present action of the mind. It is proper creation" (*C*, I, 30–31).

Coleridge used "symbol" in a similar sense. Looking for living or organic expression to stand between the literal or "dead letter" and the metaphorical or "counterfeit product of the mechanical understanding," he had only abuse for the achievements of the fancy. He wrote, for example, "Allegory is but a translation of abstract notions into a picture-language, which is itself nothing but an abstraction from objects of the senses." A symbol, however, "is characterized by a translucence of the special in the individual, or of the general in the special, or of the universal in the general; above all by the translucence of the eternal through and in the temporal. It always partakes of the reality which it renders intelligible; and while it enunciates the whole, abides itself as a living part in that unity of which it is the representative." [62] As an expression of correspondence, similar to the idea in its relation to law, a symbol fixed a moment of insight, but to communicate this insight (which was Emerson's standing problem with expression), the reader, in order to recreate it, had to be brought to a similar intensity of imagination. For this reason, whenever he was able to penetrate a writer's thought, Emerson felt the promise of his own creative imagination.

The maker of original similes and metaphors had, therefore, to be a seer. For the metaphor, as the product of vision, became the apparatus of vision in others, and so a way of extending consciousness. Among Emerson's representative men,

Swedenborg was the seer (and mystic) who gave the name "correspondence" to this metaphorical or symbolical extension of consciousness. He was the convenient historical personage whom Emerson could use to represent the fulfillment of vision.

The convenience of the word "correspondences" in Swedenborg's theological writings to cover the idealization or spiritualization of the sensual and material probably brought it to Emerson's already prepared and predisposed attention. Although Emerson had been working simultaneously toward and anticipating this doctrine in the wider frames of cosmology and method and had found it emerging in the changing aesthetic theories, in Swedenborg he found it explicitly expressed and applied; and more important for him, he found a man with whom he could identify it. What he made of the Swedenborgian idea was perhaps typical of Emerson's transformation of ideas; for although, undoubtedly, the word always carried a Swedenborgian association for him — specifically with the doctrine of "Affections Clothed" (*J*, III, 293) — the range and application of the idea in Emerson's work was significantly different.

The fundamental difference, of course, lay in Swedenborg's theological and static conception of its use. Emerson's universe was organic and dynamic; its fluidity demanded a flexible and secular adaptation of the idea. Not content to limit correspondence to a mechanical doctrine of symbol-making, Emerson appropriated the word and adjusted it to cover the metaphysical and psychological needs of relatedness in a universe of evolutionary flux. For him it was an instrument of spiritual exploration, not of dogma. Emerson, in a way, viewed spiritual truth pragmatically, as something discovered in an activity, in process. His theory of the moment and therefore of symbolism recognized the fragmentary, perspective grasp of truth and the necessity of continually taking new positions and sights. For this reason he repudiated Swedenborg's application of correspondence as a static one-to-one relationship.

What Emerson knew of the doctrine of correspondence he got at second-hand from J. J. Garth Wilkinson's English translation of *The Economy of the Animal Kingdom*. In his essay on Swedenborg, he quoted — with several mistakes in copying[63] — an important footnote from this source. The passage was significant, because by giving the explicit Swedenborgian idea, it showed the limits to which it was confined by the Swedish theologian. " 'In our doctrine of Representations and Correspondences, we shall treat these symbolical and typical resemblances [an Emersonian substitution for 'representations'], and of the astonishing things which occur, I will not say, in the living body only, but throughout nature, and which correspond so entirely to the supreme and spiritual things, that one would swear that the physical world was purely symbolical of the spiritual world; insomuch, that if we choose to express any natural truth in physical and definite vocal terms, and to convert these terms only into the corresponding and spiritual terms, we shall by this means elicit a spiritual truth, or theological dogma, in place of the physical truth or precept: although no mortal would have predicted that anything of the kind could possibly arise by bare literal transposition; inasmuch as the one precept, considered separately from the other, appears to have absolutely no relation to it. I intend, hereafter, to communicate a number of examples of such correspondences, together with a vocabulary containing the terms of spiritual things, as well as the physical things for which they are to be substituted. This symbolism pervades the living body' " (*C*, IV, 115–116).[64] The doctrine was obviously a theory of symbol-using that helped to make the external inner. Emerson needed such a theory because it corroborated his own poetic experience of the transformation of natural facts into spiritual facts. But it could only suggest a general method which he himself had to fashion in his particular way. For the conversion of terms, "bare literal transposition," "substitutions" were mechanical and contrary to Emerson's experience of the alchemization of nature. He made fun of the rigid and dogmatic dictionary of spiritual symbols: "a horse signifies carnal understanding; a tree, perception; the moon, faith; a cat means this; an ostrich that; an artichoke this other" (*C*, IV, 121). "The slippery Proteus," he knew from *his* experience, "is not so easily caught." For Swedenborg, Emerson willingly admitted, the original perception of the possibility of symbolic correspondences had been the genuine vision of an idea or law of the first philosophy. Lifted in this experience, Swedenborg had been a true poet; his vision had been "true in transition." But congealed into a system — and system horrified Emerson as much as it did William James — it had a "theological cramp," was no longer "vital," had no individual in it to humanize it. Like any other system, it became "false if fixed" (*C*, IV, 121 ff., 133 ff., 108, 109, 112).

Emerson's theory and use of symbols indicates the essential difference between Swedenborgian correspondence and his own. "In nature," he wrote, "each individual symbol plays innumerable parts, as each particle of matter circulates in turn through every system. The central identity enables any one symbol to express successively all the qualities and shades of real being. In the transmission of the heavenly waters, every hose fits every hydrant" (*C*, IV. 121).[65] If symbolization was to give each mind its individual freedom to create the universe over and over again in the moments of its perception, the symbol, like the universe it pierced, had to be fluid. The mind had to be free to grow, to seize and unify the moving universe anew in each experience, and by the progressive deepening of its insight into the central identity, reflect its moods in wider ranges of natural facts. The truly religious experience, the life of insight, lay in the act of perception, in the self's confrontation of the universe by which it realized itself. And in his attempts at friendship with other transcendentalists, Emerson found little life-giving light in the Swedenborgian hypostatization of insight. His theory of the image, which was the basic fact of the mind making possible an organic language, was closer to Coleridge. His theory of unfolding the idea was, as we shall see, closer to Plato's dialectic.

In spite of this difference in symbol-use, Swedenborg remained one of Emerson's great men because his doctrine of correspondences introduced a new era. Emerson gave this doctrine as much importance in the history of the world's thought as Newton's law of gravitation and Dalton's atomic theory (*J*, IX, 295). The importance, however, did not lie in the novelty of the idea, but in its propitious enunciation in the spiritually blind eighteenth century. The doctrine, Emerson knew, was "implied in all poetry, in allegory, in fable, in the use of emblems, and in the structure of language." And as Emerson reviewed the place of this idea in the history of philosophy, Swedenborg followed in the course of Plato and Bacon. Plato had revealed it in "his twice bisected line, in the sixth book of the Republic"; and Bacon had found "that truth and nature differed only as seal and print." But after the long estrangement of the soul and nature (as a result of eighteenth-century science), Swedenborg "first put the fact into a detached and scientific statement" (*C*, IV, 117). Nevertheless, Swedenborg had no proprietary claim on the "fruitful idea" that furnished "a key to every secret" (*C*, IV, 114): he was only one of the great number of idealists or spiritual thinkers whom Emerson had rediscovered in his reading, who had proclaimed the identity of inner and outer, of the microcosm and the macrocosm, of the spiritual and material worlds.

Certainly, Swedenborg had a tremendous influence in the early nineteenth century in rehabilitating the idealist perspective and the symbolic method. In England and in France, Blake and Baudelaire,[66] for example, accepted his doctrine of correspondence. And in America, that unregenerate Swedenborgian, Henry James, Sr., discovered a similar need for the theory of symbolism by way of the problems of Biblical interpretation.[67] Emerson could hardly have overlooked so quickening an idea, and the numerous references to, besides the ambivalent essay on Swedenborg show his indebtedness.[68] But it can scarcely be claimed that Swedenborg was the single or even catalytic influence in Emerson's use of correspondence.[69]

Emerson found Swedenborg difficult to read. Even by the time he finished *Nature,* in which correspondence was a central idea, he had not read an English translation of the seer. His earliest knowledge of, as well as enthusiasm for, Swedenborg he got from Sampson Reed's *Growth of the Mind.* Although the book does not mention Swedenborg, coming as early as 1826, with its lyrically spiritual portrayal of the mind and its revelation of the powers of analogy, it captivated Emerson and drove him to reading *The New Jerusalem Magazine.* That Emerson was enthusiastic — and this would be a way of evaluating his sources — can be seen in the eagerness with which he dispatched the book to numerous friends. He sent a copy to Carlyle in 1834, and the clothes-philosopher, perhaps like the young Emerson, at first picturing Swedenborg "as an amiable but inane visionary," altered his views.[70] What Emerson did read in the theologian (whom he preferred to receive as a poet because then his correspondences were more acceptable), he found in J. J. Garth Wilkinson's English translations. Wilkinson and Reed, then, were Emerson's living representatives of Swedenborgian thought, and with them, for many years, he maintained a cordial friendship.

An early reader of Coleridge, Reed was the more formative influence, whose thought often found reëxpression in Emerson's writing. But more important than the tags that appear in his work is the conception of mind that Emerson, in many respects, found awaiting his adoption in the *Growth of the Mind*. "The mind," Reed wrote, "must grow, not from external accretion, but from an internal principle." But it was in the natural world that the mind found the soil for its labors. With its earthbound spirituality, mind terminated in deed; once again man could look upward and remain a unitary creature.[71] And this especially attracted the Emerson who worked to force the ideal into act. "It is remarkable," he wrote in 1826, "for the unity into which it has resolved the various powers, feelings, and vocations of men, suggesting to the mind that harmony, which it has always a propensity to seek, of action and design in the order of Providence in the world" (*J*, II, 117). As the seat of man's desires, as well as intellect, the mind grew by concentrating on "those objects which correspond to the peculiar organization of our minds" and so had a "foretaste of that which is coming, in those internal tendencies of which we are conscious." [72] Correspondence was here a principle of mind, a law of attraction holding together the world of the heart's desire and the world of action; it was a principle of self-realization.

Unlike Reed, whom Emerson ranked among the men of genius, Wilkinson was an editor and annotator, but still one of the few men who saved England from complete spiritual decline. Known too late to be as liberating as Reed in Emerson's development, Wilkinson confirmed Emerson's tendency. Emerson said that he lacked centrality, but that he had the saving grace of "a catholic perception of relations" [73] (*C*, V, 250). And no one, it is true, tried so extravagantly to extend the idea of correspondence as Wilkinson did.

In his article on "Correspondence," included in Elizabeth

Peabody's *Aesthetic Papers* (in itself an attempt to secularize the idea), Wilkinson proposed correspondence as the science of sciences. Although he was Swedenborgian enough to insist on a universe in which there were enough particulars in heaven to correspond to those on earth, the relations he enumerated as correspondences were significant as a classification of its uses in Emerson's thinking. Wilkinson's aim was to show that the doctrine had lapsed because of the linear logic, but that there was "a theology in existence which not only admits the notion of correspondence, but fills it with details." [74]

Wilkinson built the foundation of his science of correspondence on the literal one-to-one symbolic transposition of Swedenborg, and this Emerson rejected. "There must be at least as much detail," Wilkinson wrote, "in the higher sphere, as the mind or the senses discern in the lower, with which the higher is to correspond." For without "apposite particular equivalents" comparison was impossible. If, for example, light was equated with truth, truth was not an acceptable correspondence (but was "occult") because "light" was also a general word standing for "reflection," "refraction," "polarization," and so forth. To assure this detail, as well as the unity of all the particulars, Wilkinson made the belief in God as a divine Idea and Unity essential. For if reasoning were analogizing, then the universe had to stop being a "vast charnel-house" and become an orderly whole.

Emerson, as we have seen, subscribed to the latter, and he subscribed to Wilkinson's activist and pragmatic conception of correspondence. First of all, man-as-microcosm was the image of the world and also the image of God. This permitted what Emerson called "the angle of vision": possessed of a "Divine Humanity" (as Wilkinson called the possession of God), "our finite nature is the delegated centre of the correspondential world." Then, just as man was the image of God, so man's body was the "microcosm of the microcosm." And just as man — fitting his desire to modify the world to the creative needs of God — was the agency of creation and modification in the world, so the body was also the connective link of service, love and use by which the soul established the universal principle of connection between spirit and nature.

For the body corresponded to the soul in the sense of doing the soul's service in the natural world. The soul created the body for use just as man builds him a house.[75] Man's faculties were also provided for use and had their corresponding objects. Or, as Wilkinson said: "For the uses of things are the reasons why they are used." The notion of fitness as use — the way an axe fits the hand and augments its powers (the essential idea of functionality) — contained the correspondences of ends and means and of cause and effect. And therefore, the perception of the connections of nature and spirit were, for Wilkinson, "the exact measure of the perception of the uses of nature." Anything to which man found himself related and could use in Wilkinson's science was said to correspond. And so nature was discipline and language in Emerson's *Nature* because it was to be used to *unfold* the soul or self. Similarly in Emerson's idea of power, one finds expressed Wilkinson's belief that progress is the transformation of chaos into a world that corresponds to man's needs. Man overcame circumstances as much by adapting them by transformation (one variety of correspondence seen in Emerson's approval of inventions) as by transcending them (another, and higher, order of correspondence). And such was the correspondence its ardent users desired of it: "the relation and friendliness of truth subsisting between all things." Toward this end, perception had its uses too, for by revealing correspondences it fitted man into the seamless fabric of the universe. These expansions of the idea show that both Reed and Wilkinson made more of the doctrine of correspondence than Emerson acknowledged in their master. Swedenborgians, they nevertheless placed the idea in the broader current of early nineteenth-century thought. But even more than they, Emerson took the static idea and fitted it to the demands of spirit-piercing perception. It was the prism (idea or law of first philosophy) through which he saw the universe. It was the perception of correspondence itself that for him made perception "the armed eye." In the post-Kantian universe of the self and the not-self, he made the electric perception of correspondence the "miracle of experience," and demanded for all who would *live* that they take "such rightness of position, that the poles of the eye should coincide with the axis of the world" (*C*, IV, 117). For once the framework of vision had been erected, the chief problem became the renewal of vision, and the renewal depended upon avoiding parallax. Inspiration was achieved by getting into position, and in that moment when the poles of the eye coincided with the axis of the world, the spiritual circuit was completed.

3
The Angle of Vision

What is life but the angle of vision? A man is measured by the angle at which he looks at objects.

EMERSON, "Natural History of Intellect."

For the whole world converts itself into that man and through him as through a lens, the rays of the universe shall converge, withersoever he turns, on a point.

EMERSON, *Journals.*

For the Emerson who defined the problem of insight in terms of the alignment of the axis of vision and the axis of things — "The ruin or the blank, that we see when we look at nature, is in our own eye. The axis of vision is not coincident with the axis of things, and so they appear not transparent, but opaque" (*C*, I, 73) — the passage on the transparent eyeball is justly the representative anecdote of his experience of inspiration. "In the woods," he wrote, "we return to reason and faith. There I feel that nothing can befall me in life — no disgrace, no calamity (leaving me my eyes), which nature cannot repair. Standing on the bare ground — my head bathed by the blithe air, and uplifted into infinite space — all mean egotism vanishes. I become a transparent eyeball; I am nothing; I see all; the currents of the Universal Being circulate through me; I am part or particle of God" (*C*, I, 10). The original *Journal* record (*J*, III, 452–453) is less compact, and except for an afterthought, less significant. The transparent eyeball is omitted, but its characteristic power is added: "There the mind integrates itself again. The attention, which had been distracted into parts, is reunited, reinsphered. The whole of nature addresses itself to the whole man. . . It is more than a medicine. It is health" (*J*, III, 453). In terms of Emerson's visual experience, the transparent eyeball was more than a lucky image. Twenty-five years later he noted that Plotinus had said of the heavens, "There . . . every body is pure (transparent), and each inhabitant is as it were an eye" (*J*, IX, 285). And throughout his many observations of the inspirational process, Emerson often converted thought into its visual counterpart, light: "Thought is nothing but the circulations made luminous" (*J*, VIII, 397). As a representative experience of inspiration, then, the famous passage in *Nature* indicates that for Emerson the primary agency of insight was seeing.

The eye was Emerson's most precious endowment. Everywhere in his writing it was a symbol of all the stages of inspiration, and still he could not resist the extended tribute he gave it in "Behavior." [1] He confessed his own poor ear, knowing that he had compensation in his eye: "My lack of musical ear is made good to me through my eyes. That which others hear, I *see*" (*J*, V, 138). What his ear brought him, he often described visually; he compared the "thread of sound" in a singer's voice to "a ray of light" (*J*, V, 255–256), and the rippling pond struck his eye with a delight as great as that of an aeolian harp to the ear (*J*, IX, 179–180). Light and music were analogous in their law, and he felt that in "the splendid function of seeing" he had the power of "recurring to the Sublime at pleasure" (*J*, IV, 173, 440).

The eye, then, was his prominent faculty. (Christopher Cranch, perhaps unwittingly, caricatured Emerson as an eye mounted on two spindly legs.) Seeing, for him, was constitutional: by bringing his total sensual response to nature, it was tantamount to spiritual health. He was aware of this in his youth because his eyesight wavered with his indecisions. The Emerson heritage (more dramatically revealed in the mental collapse of Edward) was transmitted, perhaps, in his weak eyes (see *L*, I, 208). When his eyesight failed him early in his striving for greatness,[2] he wrote of his convalescence, "I rejoice in the prospect of better sight and better health. . . Loss of eyes is not exactly one of Socrates's superfluities" (*J*, II, 99). How intimately his sight and health were connected, he was far from realizing here; but by the time of *Nature*, he could think of no greater calamity than the loss of his eyes.

For Emerson, the eye, in its own functions, focused the problem of his double consciousness of nature-as-sensation and nature-as-projection. Without the awakening stimulus of light, he was spiritually blind: "The light of the body is the eye." He would have agreed with Sampson Reed's attribution of the powers of Reason and Understanding to the eye, and especially with its unifying role in bringing the two awarenesses of nature into controlled equilibrium. "The eye," Reed wrote, "appears to be the point at which the united rays of the sun within and the sun without, converge to an expression of unity."[3]

Emerson found this true of his own experience. The eye brought him two perceptions of nature — nature ensphered and nature atomized — which corresponded to the distant and proximate visual powers of the eye. These powers, in turn, he could have called the reasoning and understanding modes of the eye. And to each he could have assigned its appropriate field of performance: the country and the city. The sympathy with nature he hoped to attain by seeing, he found in cultivating the distant powers of vision of the eye; for in distant vision he discovered a state of perception in which he felt a heightened intimacy with the natural process itself. Dorothy Emmet has called this *feeling* of organic intimacy "the adverbial mode of perception." [4] As a qualitative feeling of the total presence of nature, it might be compared to William James's pure experience or stream of consciousness. For from this undifferentiated total awareness, by focusing the attention, one selected or differentiated objects. Emerson, especially after he wrote "Experience," was aware of the selecting or accusative mode of perception (*J*, VI, 242, 253). But before he saw nature as *flux*, he found one of the difficulties of attaining insight by seeing, in the almost inescapable accusative perception of the natural eye. As Dorothy Emmet has pointed out, of the senses sight is the most highly developed, seldom perceiving in the "primitive" adverbial mode. In seeing, one is usually aware of specific objects, unless one rises to the higher level of "aesthetic seeing" in which one again consciously attempts to enjoy the whole as well as to differentiate its parts.[5]

As the agency of correspondence with nature and of inspiration, sight demanded a consciousness of its behavior that in itself might prohibit influx. It demanded, as well, scope of activity — the wide panorama — or the widening of Emerson's literal angle of vision, that is to say, the diffusion of his focus into a blur of relatedness. Before "strained vision" reconstructed his experience in nature, he had to achieve the "indolent vision" of reception (*C*, VI, 178). In this way, Emerson's sensory equipment provided initial difficulties that Thoreau, for example, did not have. Thoreau was fortunate in his exceptional hearing — the sense that discriminates least — and held easier converse (sympathetic correspondence) with nature.[6] But in other ways, Emerson found sight rewarding: chiefly, by converting his inspirational experiences with the stars and heavens into an astronomy of the imagination, he had the formal means for intellectualizing his experience that Thoreau never acquired.

The blur of relatedness of adverbial perception was achieved by Emerson in distant vision. When he began his essay, "Circles," he diagramed the need for this mode of vision: "The eye is the first circle," he wrote, "the horizon which it forms is the second" (*C*, II, 301). The distance between the eye and its horizon, however, could be progressively extended, and for Emerson, had to be extended. For one could view trifles as well as the stars: "Our little circles absorb us and occupy us as fully as the heavens; we can minimize as infinitely as maximize, and the only way out of it is (to use a country phrase) to kick the pail over, and accept the horizon instead of the pail, with celestial attractions and influences, instead of worms and mud pies" (*J*, X, 238). And what (or how much) one viewed made the difference between Reason and Understanding. With this in mind, he would have welcomed Ortega y Gasset's comment that " 'Near' and 'far' are relative, metrically . . . to the eye they have a kind of absolute value. Indeed, the *proximate vision* and the *distant vision* of which physiology speaks are not notions that depend chiefly on measurable factors, but are rather two distinct ways of seeing." [7] Bearing out Emerson's own experience (*J*, V, 21), Ortega explains that in proximate vision the eye converges on a central object, thereby limiting its horizon or field of vision. The object closely seen *is taken possession* of by the eye: it takes on "corporeality and solidity." In this respect, proximate vision is atomic — dissociating, analyzing, distinguishing — and, for Ortega, a feudal mode of seeing.[8] To the political implications of proximate vision, especially in the identification of a similar atomism in Lockean perception with the commercial but spiritually sterile England of the 1840's, Emerson might have assented.[9] He knew that "there is nothing of the true democratic element in what is called Democracy." True democracy had to transcend a commercialism that possessed trifles (*J*, IV, 95).

Democratic vision, for him as well as for Ortega (and Whitman should be recalled throughout), was the distant vision in which synthesis and relatedness were achieved. It was the wider look in which all things were alike or equalized (*C*, II, 136). In distant vision, as in Emerson's angle of vision, "the point of view becomes the synopsis." [10] In the "optical democracy" of distant vision, if "nothing possesses a sharp profile; [if] everything is background, confused, almost formless," still "the duality of proximate vision is succeeded by a perfect unity of the whole visual field." [11] Democratic vision was a mode of sympathy, the result of the love that blends and fuses (*L*, II, 377).[12] Describing this change from proximate to distant vision, from feudal to democratic vistas, in respect to the almost tactile sense of objects or "trifles" that one has in the former, Ortega corroborates Emerson's own experience of the dislimning of objects: "As the object is withdrawn, sight loses its tactile power and gradually becomes pure vision. In the same way, things, as they recede, cease to be filled volumes, hard and compact, and become mere chromatic entities, without resistance, mass or convexity. An age-old habit, founded in vital necessity, causes men to consider as 'things,' in the strict sense, only such objects solid enough to offer resistance to their hands. The rest is more or less illusion. So in passing from proximate to distant vision an object becomes illusory. When the distance is great, there on the confines of a remote horizon — a tree, a castle, a mountain range — all acquire the half-unreal aspect of ghostly apparitions." [13] Emerson made the same distinction in the reality of objects by distinguishing the masculine and feminine traits of the eye. "Women," he wrote, "see quite without any wish to act." And so with men of genius: "They have this feminine eye, a function so rich that it contents itself without asking any aid of the hand. Trifles may well be studied by him; for he sees nothing insulated" (*J*, V, 335–336). When he wrote that he was easily untuned by necessary domestic concerns and needed "solitude of habit" for inspiration, he confessed his "more womanly eyes" (*C*, VIII, 289). For the same reason he had to distance an object to see it: "If you go near to the White Mountains, you cannot see them; you must go off thirty or forty miles to get a good view" (*J*, VI, 156). Freed from the object, "the eye," he discovered, "possesses the faculty of rounding and integrating the most disagreeable parts into a pleasing whole" (*J*, III, 556).

This power to dislimn and integrate objects, an original endowment of the youthful eye, Emerson found hampered by culture or education: Even the first shock of Reason, by destroying one's faith or instinctive belief in the indissoluble union of man and nature, interrupted its functioning. After this momentary skepticism, however, the eye of Reason helped the natural eye renew its distant powers. "Until this higher agency intervened," he wrote, "the animal eye sees with wonderful accuracy, sharp outlines and colored surfaces. When the eye of Reason opens, to outline and surface are at once added grace and expression. These proceed from imagination and affection, and abate somewhat of the angular distinctness of objects. If the Reason be stimulated to more earnest vision, the outlines and surfaces become transparent, and are no longer seen; causes and spirits are seen through them" (*C*, I, 49–50).

And just as Emerson restores the distant powers with the eye of Reason, so Ortega connects the need for the integration of distant vision with the post-Renaissance trend toward subjectivism in epistemology. For when one tries to diffuse the focus of the eye and thereby "to embrace the whole field," objects lose their solid-convexity and the whole field becomes concave: the horizon literally becomes circular, as Emerson felt when he viewed "the bended horizon" (*J*, V, 46). The "limit," Ortega says, "is a surface that tends to take the form of a hemisphere viewed from within." [14] And this concavity begins, as Emerson also noted, at the eye. The result was the exhilaration of feeling one's centrality and penetration of space, and Emerson felt this in viewing the landscape and the heavens. He noted Aristotle's notion of space as container (*J*, VI, 6) and pictured the world as "a hollow temple," the beauty and symmetry of which depended on the eye (*J*, VIII, 52). Ortega confirms this sense of space in distant vision: "What we see at a distance is hollow space as such. The content of perception is not strictly the surface in which the hollow space terminates, but rather the whole hollow space itself, from the eyeball to the . . . horizon." [15] In this way the eye can be said to form the first circle, because, paradoxically, in distant vision the object "begins at our cornea." "In pure distant vision," Ortega explains, "our attention, instead of being directed farther away, has drawn back to the absolutely proximate, and the eye-beam, instead of striking the convexity of a solid body and staying fixed on it, penetrates a concave object, glides into a hollow." [16] Emerson recognized this *nearness*: "Really the soul is *near* things, because it is the centre of the universe, so that astronomy and Nature and theology date from where the observer stands" (*J*, VIII, 22). The eye (or soul), then, becomes the center of the angle of vision. Or, as Ortega says, "in fixing upon the object nearest the cornea, the point of view is as close as possible to the subject and as far as possible from things." [17] The eye no longer revolves "ptolemaically" about each object, "following a servile orbit." In the Copernican change to distant-subjective vision — in the visual revolution of the epistemologies of Descartes, Hume, and Kant — "the eye . . . is established as the center of the plastic Cosmos, around which revolve the forms of objects." [18] Emerson realized this change as early as 1831, when he wrote, "The point of view is of more importance than the sharpness of sight" (*J*, II, 399).

The requirements of distant vision compelled Emerson to arm the natural eye. Extremely "sensible . . . to circumstances" — he felt mean in the city streets (*J*, V, 146) — he needed as a condition of inspiration the wide, panoramic view. When only seventeen years old, he remarked on the scope of vision: "It is a singular fact that we cannot present to the imagination a longer space than just so much of the world as is bounded by the visible horizon" (*J*, I, 13). For the higher seeing he needed to go beyond this horizon (*C*, IV, 82); but, at least for the dislimning of objects by which inspiration was achieved, he needed to see *to* the horizon. The horizon, he would have admitted, was essential to his best working attitude: it was what the German Romanticists called the *Idealeferne*. He complained to his brother Edward, "I am trying to learn to find my own latitude but there is no horizon in C[hardon] St." (*L*, I, 330). And after he left the church, free to follow a literary life, he wrote to Lydia Jackson that in Concord he could possess his soul but that to go to Plymouth "would be to cripple me of some important resources" (*L*, I, 437–438). He felt that he must have "a scope like nature itself, a susceptibility to all impressions . . . the heart as well as . . . the logic of creation" (*C*, V, 253). For this, Concord was preferable.

One important resource was nature: in the rural landscape he found an attractive release from the visual confines of city life. "We need nature," he wrote, "and cities give the human senses not room enough. I go out daily and nightly to feed my eyes on the horizon and the sky, and come to feel the want of this scope as I do of water for my washing" (*J*, IV, 34). But even in the woods, unless he could fuse the detail by walking rapidly, he felt annoyed (*J*, IV, 439). Of what use was his genius, he wrote, "if the organ . . . cannot find a focal distance?" (*J*, VI, 519).

His best focal distance was the unlimited extent: the heavens, the sea, the fields, and preferably the line of the horizon in which heavens and earth, sea and sky met. "The imaginative faculty of the soul," he wrote, "must be fed with objects immense and eternal" (*C*, I, 216). In the horizon he felt "the true outline of the world" (*J*, III, 264), and the "astonishment" of landscape was "the meeting of the sky and the earth" (*J*, VI, 76). Here was the mystic line, the visible symbol in nature itself of the dualism of the universe. And if the finite limit of the horizon suggested the illimitable, its hazy fading in the distance promised the bipolar unity of the moment of inspiration. For Emerson, the far was "holy," especially when the world itself began to dislimn (*J*, IV, 13); and haze, by doubling the distance (*J*, IV, 489), seemed to double the quantity of nature one grasped in his angle of vision. "From your centre," Emerson recorded, "Nature carries every integral part out to the horizon, and mirrors yourself to you in the universe" (*J*, VIII, 525). In this way the hazy distance tempted his eye and compensated for "the cramp and pettiness of human performances" (*C*, VII, 298). By providing intimations of spiritual release, a landscape — "a long vista in woods, trees on the shore of a lake coming quite down to the water, a long reach in a river, a double or triple row of uplands or mountains seen one over the other" (*J*, V, 470) [19] — rewarded Emerson not only with first sight, but with second sight and insight (*J*, V, 422). With only the horizon before him, he could launch himself into the sea of being, certain that he was able "to possess entire nature, to fill the horizon, to fill the infinite amplitude of being with great life, to be in sympathy and relation with all creatures, to lose all privateness by sharing all natural action, shining with the Day, undulating with the sea, growing with the tree, instinctive with the animals, entranced in beatific vision with the human reason" (*J*, V, 272).

This sympathetic correspondence with nature, the harmony of man and the vegetable, followed from breaking the artificial bonds of city life and expanding with the horizon of the "medicinal" fields. Coming into nature, Emerson wrote, "We come into our own and make friends with matter" (*C*, III, 171). This sympathy with matter, in a sense opening up the circulations of being, was the ground of the moment of ecstasy. Following the rapture of the transparent eyeball, Emerson immediately and significantly added: "I am the lover of uncontained and immortal beauty. In the wilderness, I find something more dear and connate than in streets or villages. In the tranquil landscape, and especially in the distant line of the horizon, man beholds somewhat as beautiful as his own nature.

"The greatest delight which the fields and woods minister, is the suggestion of an occult relation between man and the vegetable . . . [and] the power to produce this delight does not reside in nature, but in man, or in a harmony of both" (*C*, I, 10).

Emerson's retreat to nature, then, having the precipitancy of constitutional need, was an advance on Reason. In the city he found more to be discontented with than the communion service. And, as we will see, he was much too gregarious (and ambitious) to seek forgetful solitudes for "romantic" reasons or for the picturesque alone.[20] In an early sermon on "Trifles" (1829), he illustrated the wide range of the mind by comparing it with the distant and proximate powers of the eye: "It is like the range of vision of the eye that explores the atmosphere and catches the dim outline of a mountain a hundred miles distant and examines the anatomy of the smallest insect" (*Y*, 47). But then he pointed out the dangers of close vision

with which he himself was familiar. "If you bury the natural
eye too exclusively on minute objects," he said, "it gradually
loses its powers of distant vision" (*Y*, 48). And this tendency
to magnify things, to lose the sense of relationship in an ob-
session with trifles, distinguished society (*C*, VI, 153). In the
perspectives of nature he tried to escape this tyranny of things.

For the city (and society) dissipated his energy and concentration, and waylaid his senses. He said the age was ocular
(*J*, IV, 236), but he diagnosed its difficulties as ophthalmia
(*L*, III, 400). The city was shortsighted business. In America,
he wrote Margaret Fuller, "We cannot see where we are going,
preternaturally sharp as our eyes are at short distances . . .
strange malady, is it not?" (*L*, III, 400). And the reason for
the disease was that "the City delights the Understanding. It
is made up of finites; short, sharp, mathematical lines, all
calculable. It is full of varieties, of successions, of contrivances.
The Country, on the contrary, offers an *unbroken horizon*,
the monotony of an *endless* road, or *vast* uniform plains, of
distant mountains, the melancholy of uniform and infinite
vegetation; the objects on the road are few and worthless, the
eye is invited ever to the horizon and the clouds. It is the
school of Reason" (*J*, V, 310–311; italics supplied). One of the
serious needs of America, he noted, was a " 'general education
of the eye' " (*J*, VIII, 550).

For the same reason, he would have put telescopes on every
street corner! There they could remind the shortsighted —
men with "microscopic optics" (*J*, III, 308–309) — that "they
were born heirs of the dome of God" (*J*, IV, 281) and that the
stars were the last outpost of God's providence. "God be
thanked," Emerson wrote of his own need for the heavens,
"who set stars in the sky! planted their bright watch along the
infinite deep and ordained such fine intelligence betwixt us
and them" (*J*, IV, 47). The stars seemed to him to take him
beyond the horizon: "The blue zenith," he wrote, "is the

point in which romance and reality meet" [21] (*C*, III, 172). And in astronomy he felt the visual promise of "everything"; the lawful heavens promised him successful moral navigation, and he took nightly walks under the stars to take his spiritual bearings (*J*, VI, 187). Obsessed with astronomy throughout his life, he even symbolized the mind as a quadrant. By sighting the sun and stars, he hoped to find his latitude (*J*, IV, 107). In the contemplation of the stars he participated in their animating law: "I please myself rather with contemplating the penumbra of the thing than the thing itself." And he found that this referred him "to a higher state than I now occupy" (*J*, III, 197–198).

When Emerson suggested that the American scholar — "the world's eye" — become an astronomer, he was speaking from this experience, and he was contrasting observation and vision (*C*, I, 101). He wanted the scholar to feel "the grandeur of the impression the stars and heavenly bodies make on us." Then they would value their gleams more than an "exact perception of a tub or a table on the ground" (*J*, VII, 93). They would literally have a wide horizon for every fact (*J*, X, 331) and discover "the inextinguishableness of the imagination" (*J*, X, 330). In their penetration of space they would realize the "immense elasticity" of the mind (*J*, X, 330), and would be startled into wonder — and wonder reborn was the first affirmation of transcendental experience.

Even more than the distant vision it satisfied, astronomy gave Emerson a chance to speak for "the sovereignty of Ideas" (*J*, IV, 32). As a student of thirteen, he chose astronomy for the subject of a free theme (*L*, I, 29), and astronomy — imaginatively interpreted — excited him during the long remainder of his life.[22] Herschel's great astronomy was his source book, and his "The General Nature and Advantages of the Study of the Physical Sciences," [23] as much as Emerson's own delight in the Jardin des Plantes, directed him to the natural sciences (*L*, I, 343; *J*, III, 197). In them, he was searching for the moral law, and astronomy — "thought and harmony in masses of matter" (*C*, I, 219) — seemed to Emerson its most grandiloquent expression. Calvinism and Ptolemaic astronomy lacked this moral grandeur for Emerson: they had yet to grasp the moral beauty of the Newtonian universe. They did not know "the extent or the harmony or the depth of their moral nature." Like the Unitarians, "they are clinging to little, positive, verbal versions of the moral law, and very imperfect versions too, while the infinite laws, the laws of the Law, the great circling truths whose only adequate symbol is the material laws, the astronomy, etc., are all unobserved" (*J*, III, 199). For to observe the stars was, for Emerson, to "come back to our real, initial state and see and own that we have yet beheld but the first ray of Being" (*J*, IV, 417). It was in the search for this experience that he began *Nature* (*C*, I, 7), and it was the end of all he said in *Nature* to bring men "to look at the world with new eyes" (*C*, I, 85). In viewing the stars he escaped into loneliness and health (*J*, III, 263, 390), because alone in an atmosphere "transparent with this design" he felt "a perpetual admonition of God and superior destiny" (*J*, III, 264). Again he undulated with the sea of being (*J*, IV, 417), rested his immortality in the immortal stars, and found in their great circles the laws that merger transformed into ideas. Properly *distant*, the natural unarmed eye achieved an angle of vision in which perception had a destiny (*J*, VIII, 321). Properly distant, restored to its natural scope, the eye was no longer retrospective, but prospective (*J*, VI, 190).

II

Emerson's critics, understandably, seized the central and striking image of the eyeball. Cranch has left us nothing that will give him as much fame, perhaps, as his good-natured sketch of this passage (*L*, II, 190). But the Very Rev. Henry

A. Braun, reviewing *Nature* in *The Catholic World*, cited the passage as evidence of insanity: "We wonder, when he wrote that, whether he was not bilious and his 'eyeball' bloodshot as he looked at it in the glass?" [24] He was using this "critical" bludgeon to prove that "Nature is not the correlative of the mind." *The Westminster Review* of London also singled it out as full of familiar truths, but here too much relied on and simplified: "They are propounded as if they lay on the surface of truth and within the grasp of all men, and contained not problems . . . in the solution of which the lives of thoughtful men have gone by, leaving the giant contradictions of our moral being just as they were, standing face to face, irreconcilable." [25]

What these and other critics have often failed to see is that the transparent eyeball is only representative for Emerson of one aspect of the mind, and that the angle of vision as a metaphor of inspiration has its origins in Emerson's thought in the religious affirmation of compensation. For the problem of the mind, as it presented itself to Emerson, was that of a twofold process. Structurally, this process was represented by the two poles or termini of the mind: Intellect Receptive and Intellect Constructive (*C*, II, 334). They recreated in man-the-microcosm the cosmological dualism of the universe. Functionally, they presented the problems of inspiration and its control, of passivity or "pious reception" and concentration or form. Between these poles the life of the mind played like a sputtering spark,[26] and Emerson's creative task was to prohibit a surplus of energy to store itself at either pole and thus intermit the circuit. "Human life," he wrote, "is made up of two elements, power and form, and the proportions must be invariably kept, if we would have it sweet and sound" (*C*, III, 65). Seen in another way, this mental equilibrium required innocence and sophistication, that is, the openness of response and mature judgment that modern critics of the arts often remark on as impossible: "The lover of nature is he whose inward and outward senses are still truly adjusted to each other; who has retained the spirit of infancy even into the era of manhood" (*C*, I, 9). Although the receptive aspect of this process — certainly the more primary in Emerson's experience — was mystical merger, Emerson was not a mystic in the usual "visionary" sense of the word.[27] He was not seeking in the angle of vision an escape from the world; as it formed, the angle of vision was to make *use* of the world. But mystical union, for him, was an epistemological necessity. Vision, he said of the inner seeing of the mind, "is not like the vision of the eye, but is union with the things known" (*C*, II, 325). The knowledge of merger, however, had its use only in the prudential world; if knowledge *began* in reception, it ended in action. Mysticism ended in rest. And "Man," he wrote, "was made for conflict, not for rest. In action is his power; not in his goals but in his transitions man is great" (*C*, XII, 60).

The transitions, or better, the transmutation of mystical power into form was his best description of the life of the mind. In this process the mind was a transmitter, a conduit through which the infinite was funneled from the spiritual reservoir to the prudential tap. Or again, to switch the metaphor, mind was the lens converging the rays of spirit on the daily affairs of man. Standing between the worlds of spiritual laws and prudential affairs, man's "health and erectness," Emerson wrote, "consist in the fidelity with which he transmits influences from the vast and universal to the point on which his genius can act" (*C*, I, 208–209). The point of action was found in everyday life, just as the only way of making the mystical power of insight available was by conveying it to men in the "language of facts." The ray of spiritual light, he pointed out in illustration, "passes invisible through space, and only when it falls on an object is it seen." Similarly, "when the spiritual energy is directed on something outward, then it is a thought" (*C*, II, 335). Speaking of his own experience of transition as ebb and flow, Emerson described the same process more "psychologically": "The daily history of the Intellect is this alternating of expansions and concentrations. The expansions are the invitations from heaven to try a larger sweep, a higher pitch than we have yet climbed, and to leave all our past for this enlarged scope. Present power, on the other hand, requires concentration on the moment and the thing to be done" (*C*, XII, 58).

In this twofold process of expansion and concentration, nature was instrumental both as the activator of insight and as the object of focus. Correspondence, therefore, as an inspirational means, was sympathy with nature, as well as the doctrine of its expression. And Emerson had in mind the natural history of its agency in inspiration when he gave his course in philosophy at Harvard in 1870–1871. He proposed early in "Natural History of Intellect" an aim that had absorbed the full span of his life. "My belief in the use of a course on philosophy," he explained, "is that the student shall learn to appreciate *the miracle of the mind*; shall learn its subtle but immense power, or shall begin to learn it; shall come to know that in *seeing* and in no tradition he must find what truth is; that he shall see in it the source of all traditions, and shall see each one of them as better or worse statement of its revelations; shall come to trust it entirely, as the only true; to cleave to God against the name of God. When he has once known the oracle he will need no priest. And if he finds at first with some alarm how impossible it is to accept many things which the hot or the mild sectarian may insist on his believing, he will be armed by his insight and brave to meet all inconvenience and all resistance it may cost him. He from whose hand it came will guide and direct it" (*C*, XII, 6–7; italics supplied). How biographical this passage was, only those students knew whose fathers or grandfathers had wit-

nessed and told them of the storm following *The Divinity
School Address* (1838). To appreciate the miracle of the mind
then had been to challenge the reigning miracle of tradition.
Emerson had taken the word "miracle" in its traditional,
linear sense and had reinterpreted it in terms of the vertical
dimension of human consciousness. He said that "the word
Miracle as pronounced by Christian churches gives a false
impression. . . It is not one with the blowing clover and the
falling rain" (*C*, I, 129). By divorcing the miracle from an
immediate sense of the presence of God in the process of
nature, only known by man by sharing that process, the
miracle that remained applied only to past events credited by
historical testimony. "By withdrawing it [the preaching of
the miracle] from the exploration of the moral nature of man,
where the sublime is, where are the resources of astonishment
and power . . ." the miracle as a support of faith became a
dead word, not a living thing (*C*, I, 141). In its sterility was
the history of fifty years of America's waning spiritual life.
And because of this, for Emerson, redemption was no longer
to be sought in the Church but in the soul — in man's own
experience of self-reflection. To his generation, long given to
thinking of miracles as events of the past, his reaffirmation of
their immediacy in consciousness was revolutionary. But as
a result of this tremendous semantic shift, a generation later
he could quietly say that truth was more likely to be revealed
in psychology than in history.

In the early sermons one can trace Emerson's growing
awareness of the fact that the revitalization of faith had to
come not from "Miracles" (1831) but from "The Miracle of
Our Being" (1834). Miracles were important to faith, because,
as Emerson said, "a miracle is the only means by which God
can make a communication to men, that shall be known to
be from God" (*Y*, 120). For this reason Emerson retained it
as historical fact (although he modified the usual interpreta-

tion by making the miracle accord with the moral expectations of man). To deny the miracle would have been to deny
that God can communicate with man, and this was sufficient
reason for him to keep it, in the face of a mechanistic universe
that seemed to dull men's senses to the need for miracles.
"There are thousands of men who, if there were no histories
and if the order of natural events had never been broken,
would," he explained the miracle as a departure from the
order of nature, "never ask in the course of their lives for
anything beyond a secondary cause and never ask for the first"
(*Y*, 121). Never shocked into wonder, unless by a breach in
nature itself, these "secondary" men (*Y*, 108) [28] found sufficient the explanation afforded by secondary causes. But for
Emerson, primary man himself must startle nature with "an
instructed eye." He must discover the genuine miracle in his
own life, that is, in his relation to the laws of nature — in the
fact, for example, that he can will the raising of his arm, communicate his thoughts, and conduct his life, certain that the
law of compensation will not fail him. Then he will realize
that he can believe in miracles because he is "such a manifestation," because "all our life is a miracle. Ourselves are the
greatest wonder of all" (*Y*, 122). Once he has recognized the
informing law of his life and of nature, he will no longer find
the miracle in departures from natural order, but in the moral
bond uniting his constitution and that of the universe. Miracle at this stage in Emerson's sermon has been transformed
into the awareness of a higher source of law operating in both
nature and man: in the fact that man's sympathy with nature
is the basic correspondence revealing God. What he omitted
here, but emphasized in the later sermon, was the fact that
only in self-reflection (as opposed to the observation of nature)
man became aware of the need for a higher law as explanation
of his sympathy with nature. For to reflect, he wrote, "is to
receive truth immediately from God without any medium"

(*J*, II, 409). And the noblest fact was that of "being addressed on moral grounds": "This fact is so close to the first fact of our *being*, that, like the circulation of the blood, or the gravity of bodies, it passes long unnoticed from the circumstance of its omnipresence" (*J*, II, 327).

When Emerson asked men to reflect on the miracle of their being he first pointed out the wonderful sympathy between nature and man, the way the universe was made to serve man and unfold his faculties. He distinguished, however, between superficial wonder in the external fitness of things and ecstatic wonder of man in the "bare fact" of his existence as a man. He significantly added, "This external fitness is wonderful, but I doubt if to those who saw this only, it would ever have occurred to remark upon the marvel . . . [because] it may be said of the things apprehended by the senses, that they are so nicely grooved into one another that the sight of one suggests the next preceding, and this the next before, so that the understanding in the study of the things themselves would run forever in the round of second causes, did not the soul at its own instance sometimes demand tidings of the First Cause" (*Y*, 203–204). The recognition of the *moral* fitness of the universe to man's needs, therefore, required one to get above the round of secondary causes, to get free from the enslavement to trifles, and to view the spectacle from the soul's vantage in the wonder of direct union with the First Cause. This was the supreme moment in the spiritual life of man, and it was toward this moment that Emerson had been groping in his need to destroy "the Chaos of Thought" of a morally unredeemed universe. "Rend away the darkness," he journalized when he was twenty, "and restore to man the knowledge of this principle [a moral universe], and you have lit the sun over the world and solved the riddle of life" (*J*, I, 257 ff.). And it was in "the exercise of reason, the act of reflexion" that man lit the sun: "the chief distinctions of his condition begin with that act." Echoing Coleridge, he glorified man's release from "brutishness": "Awakened to truth and virtue — which is the twofold office of Reason, he passes out of the local and finite, he inspires and expires immortal breath" (*Y*, 206–207).

When the inspired primary man now *contemplates* [29] the world about him, he discovers in himself "a point or focus upon which all objects, all ages concentrate their influence." He is now at "the heart of the world," at "the centre of the Creation." From this angle of vision the universe seems to exist only for his benefit. Life is no longer "an insupportable curse." Now "man lives for a purpose. Hitherto was no object upon which to concentrate his various powers. Now happiness is his being's end and aim" (*J*, I, 257). Now, like the "lowest natures" — a leaf, a grain of sand — he is intimately allied to the organic process. Emerson best described this intimacy — and he was a naturalist only to reveal it — when he wrote: "Look at the summer blackberry lifting its polished surface a few inches from the ground. How did that little chemist extract from the sandbank the spices and sweetness it has concocted in its cells? By any cheap or accidental means? Not so; but the whole creation has been at the cost of its birth and nurture. A globe of fire near a hundred millions of miles distant in the great space, has been flooding it with light and heat as if it shone for no other. It is six or seven months that the sun has made the tour of the heavens every day over this tiny sprout, before it could bear its fruit. The sea has evaporated its countless tons of water that the rain of heaven might wet the roots of this little vine. The elastic air exhaled from all live creatures and all minerals, yield this small pensioner the gaseous aliment it required. The earth by the attraction of its mass determined its form and size; and when we consider how the earth's attraction is fixed at this moment on equilibrium by innumerable attractions, on every side, of distant bodies, — we shall see that the berry's form and history is determined by causes and agents the most prodigious and remote" (*Y*, 207–208). By recognizing in the humble blackberry one instance of the focusing of the beneficence of the universe, man himself could see that he, too, was a "center round which all things roll, and upon which all things scatter gifts" (*Y*, 208). Knowing the benefits of his implication in nature, he no longer felt caught in the web of circumstances; instead, in his new freedom, "he stands upon the top of the world; he is the centre of the horizon" (*Y*, 208). Emerson found this a favorite way of expressing the new release from events man discovered in viewing the activity of his mind as an angle of vision. When he looked at the rainbow, he believed himself "the center of its arch," and this feeling of centrality he found in viewing a landscape between his legs or in the rapid movement of a train (*C*, I, 50–51). But he realized that these experiences were true of all men, that the angle of vision equalized, by making available to any man as much of the universe as his vision could contain. In this way, although dependent on nature, man was "absolutely, imperially free" (*J*, II, 272).

But the freedom of perception went beyond this awareness of the benefit of nature. Man, Emerson added, "is not designed to be an idle eye before which nature passes in review, but by his action is enabled to learn the irresistible properties of moral nature, perceived dimly by the mind as laws difficult to be grasped or defined, yet everywhere working out their inevitable results in human affairs" (*Y*, 209). Freedom was only to be found in the perception of the correspondence of the physical and moral laws. The whole message of compensation — the animating force in Emerson's vision — depended on perceiving this, that "the Creation is so magically woven that nothing can do him [man] any mischief but himself" (*Y*, 209). The secondary man (the unregenerate), with his idle eye, will be ground to powder by the laws, will find in nature as much obstacle as benefit. But the primary man, armed by his perception of the moral necessity of law, will be defended "from all harm he wills to resist; the whole creation cannot bend him whilst he stands upright" (*Y*, 209). The only freedom, like perception, was of this moral order.

The awakening of Reason was, for Emerson, this moral awakening: inspiration *was* moral regeneration. The moral sentiment (or Reason) was the "tie of faith" made alive by the human mind. The law it revealed as the basis of the human mind was the content of inspiration; when seen in nature it was "fatal strength" (*C*, VI, 221). And, as he repeated in his Harvard lectures, what was of greater worth than the dangerous knowledge of this power of the mind? "To open to ourselves — to open to others these laws — is it not worth living for? to make the soul, aforetime the servant of the senses, acquainted with the secret of its own power; to teach man that by self-renouncement a heaven of which he had no conception, begins at once in his heart; — by the high act of yielding his will, that little individual heart becomes dilated as with the presence and inhabitation of the Spirit of God" (*Y*, 210). Not only is this the religious burden of this sermon (as of the more secular essays on "Worship," "Inspiration," and "Spiritual Laws"), it is the religious context in which Emerson always thought of the experience of inspiration. When he enjoins men to see in the exaltation of Reason the transcendence of evil and the hidden spiritual good of their worldly failings, he is not mistaking the sense of power in inspiration for an irresponsible release of energies. "What is it," he says of the insight of inspiration, "but a perception of man's true position in the universe and his consequent obligations. This is the whole moral and end of such views as I present" (*Y*, 211). The power to overcome trifles resided in *this insight* and in no other, because, for Emerson, inspiration had no other "meaning" than that of compensation. If vision was to release him from the bondage of the senses, its message had to be a response to his most deeply felt need, had to answer his "metaphysical pathos." And in his moments of vision he found this assurance, "that the Father who thus vouchsafes to reveal himself . . . will not forsake the child for whom he provideth such costly instruction — whom every hour and every event of memory and hope educate. What does it intimate but presages of an infinite and perfect life? What but an assured trust through all evil and danger and death?" (*Y*, 212).

Inspiration experienced only as the ecstatic moment of heightened power was irresponsible, as one suspects from the passage on the transparent eyeball. But bringing with it the obligation (as well as the power) to communicate this insight to others, it made expression, either in act or word, its moral end. Men might feel at the receptive pole the spontaneous, instinctive flood of inspiration; they might balance it by reflecting on it, that is, by standing above it watch its operation and grasp its law. But at the constructive pole, this thought — "always a miracle" — demanded for its publication the control of the spontaneous flow (*C*, II, 335). For in the very way he described the mind, for Emerson inspiration was always saddled with a moral rider; intuition was always coupled with duty (*C*, VI, 224). "The poet," he instructed, "who shall use nature as his hieroglyph must have an adequate message to convey thereby" (*C*, VIII, 65). And because insight had to end in a message, the freedom of intuition demanded the necessity of precise form; and once Emerson became aware of this condition, he found, as all conscious artists have, that the reception of inspiration became even more difficult (*L*, II, 342–343). He found that he needed *two* inspirations, one by which to see, the other by which to write (*J*, VII, 113); and by intellectualizing his vision of the laws, he saved himself from the decay of the first, and had more and more only to consider the ebb and flow of the second.

III

Emerson intellectualized his vision by constructing an astronomy of the imagination. His constitutional need for *seeing* determined the spatial character of his thought; and his devotion to astronomy, especially the Newtonian revelation of gravitational attraction beyond the surface of the earth, provided him his symbols for expressing the fundamental correspondence of physical and moral laws. In the circle he not only found an equivalent for the Coleridgean Idea, but in its compensatory action he saw the moral law of compensation (*C*, VI, 218–219). The daily life of the mind, its ebbing and flowing, he found he could express in the solar cycle of day and night; and this almost "primitive" dependence on the sun and stars, he made the visual metaphor of the process of inspiration.[30] He believed that the most ordinary symbols were adequate to the fullest expression, and day and night were, indeed, the common pulse of the universe (*C*, III, 17–18).

Men were literally born in darkness, he wrote: "Out of darkness and out of the awful Cause they come to be caught up in this vision of a seeing, partaking, acting and suffering life" (*J*, V, 132). As in the womb, they rested in the "circumambient" unconsciousness of God (*J*, V, 385), becalmed on the ebbless sea of the Over-Soul[31] (*J*, V, 292, 490). And so when Emerson took his nightly walk, he felt that "nothing in nature has the softness of darkness . . . or the unutterable gentleness to the sense" (*J*, IV, 358). In darkness, as in sleep, he felt that he was falling back on God. "If I have weak . . . eyes," he wrote, "no looking at green curtains, no shutting them . . . are of certain virtue . . . but when at last I wake up from a sound sleep, then I know that he that made the eye has dealt with it for the time and the wisest physician is He" (*J*, IV, 143). In sleep and night were the restorative virtues of a return to the source of life; one ebbed or returned in the night only to flow with insight in the day. He copied from Sophocles

> *Dost thou behold the vast and azure sky*
> *How in its liquid arms the earth doth lie?*
>
> (*J*, IV, 285)

and saw in the protective maternity of Lidian for little Waldo a similar image of God's providential care of man (*J*, IV, 135). Darkness, then, far more than its usual associations with skepticism and atheism (*J*, III, 14), represented for Emerson a preparation — a night journey of sorts — for the day.[32]

In Emerson's analogy, night was the creator of day (*J*, IV, 469), just as in Thoreau's, silence was the *background* of sound.[33] For Emerson, day was the course of living the problems of life from their "uttermost darkness into light" (*J*, V, 74). Knowledge of God, he found in Scholastic philosophy, was *matutina cognitio*, morning knowledge (*J*, IV, 24–25 n.); and the self-recovery by which man regained insight and expanded beyond his previous limits he spoke of as *Easting* (*J*, III, 477). Man's mind, he wrote, by "his efforts at self-knowledge . . . will revolve so far that the increasing twilight will give place to the Sun, and God will appear as he is to his soul" (*J*, II, 303). He likened conversion to "day after twilight" (*J*, II, 298), and the self-evidence of its truth was its sun-like light (*J*, II, 516). In "Threnody" (ll. 201–202) he called it the "super-solar blaze." If this ecstasy of inspiration was a "new morn risen on noon" (*J*, VI, 14; III, 239–240), immortality was the "Day" following the long life of morning (*J*, X, 203).

But any change in the hodiernal cycle, suggesting the transitions of mind, represented the moment of inspiration.[34] Sunset as well as the dawn expressed for Emerson the qualitative feeling of influx (*J*, IV, 46). He believed "that no hour, no state of the atmosphere but corresponded to some state of the mind (*J*, III, 386). But even in the bright day of inspiration he felt that the sun needed shadow (*J*, VIII, 422). Realizing this polarity, he could accept the darkness and opacity of man and nature as the ground of light (*J*, VII, 61). He could extend the analogy by saying that sin was opaque and innocence transparent (*J*, V, 309), that society mistook darkness for light (*J*, V, 108), and that the problem of inspiration in writing was to make daylight shine through the word (*J*, V, 198). And in "Works and Days" he could contrast works and faith, "huckstering Trade" and the "deep to-day." His whole philosophy of the moment — of the time-transcending of the total response to nature — was expressed in this comparison: "Works and days were offered us, and we took works. . . [But] he is only rich who owns the day" (*C*, VII, 168).

Emerson experienced the day in his adverbial perception of nature, in his feeling of intimate union with the law in and behind the natural process. His awareness of law, of natural order and harmony, was expressed in its mental correlative, the Idea. And the possibility of representing a total feeling in a thought derived from the basic correspondence of the mental and physical spheres. "The crystal sphere of thought," he wrote, "is as concentrical as the geological globe we inhabit" (*J*, V, 555). This correspondence made possible a method of expression that seemed to him to unfold thought according to the method of nature.

He liked Plato's expression "that God geometrizes" (*J*, VII, 92). Plato, too, he found, geometrized, and this made him both a poet and a man who "at the same time [is] acquainted with the geometrical foundations of things, and with their moral purposes, and sees the festal splendor of the day" (*J*, VIII, 43; VIII, 37). Plato was the "great-eyed," and his second sight explained his stress on geometry (*C*, IV, 79, 84). His geometry of Ideas made possible the communication of inspiration and somehow preserved its splendor: "In his broad daylight things reappear as they stood in the sunlight, hardly shorn of a ray,

yet now portable and reportable" (*J*, VIII, 45). A similar "geo-
metric, astronomic morals" Emerson wanted for himself (*J*,
VIII, 418), and demanded earlier of the teacher he would become: "The Teacher that I look for and await shall enunciate
with more precision and universality, with piercing poetic insight those beautiful yet severe compensations that give to
nature an aspect of mathematical science" (*J*, III, 434).

In Emerson's geometry of morals, the circle was the basic
figure. He derived it, perhaps from his own sense of the bend-
ing horizon, from his own experience of the eye as the first
circle and the horizon as the second; and like the horizon, it
symbolized the Unattainable (*C*, II, 305) and the progressive
ascent by which one advanced on the chaos and the dark. As
the "primary figure," the "highest emblem in the cipher of the
world," the circle represented as well the unifying Idea (as he
adapted it from Coleridge), and its concentric expansion represented the process of ascending generalization, each step of
which, in man's moral progress, was his highest knowledge of
God. For God's creation of nature was also circular: "Nature
can only be conceived of as existing to a universal and not to a
particular end," he wrote, "to a universe of ends, and not to
one, — a work of *ecstasy*, to be represented by a circular movement, as intention might be signified by a straight line of definite length" (*C*, I, 201). By similar ecstasies and self-recoveries
man retraced in his own advancing circles of thought, the advancing circles of God in nature. And by taking up the angle
of vision, every man could become the center of the circle, at
one with God; for in Emerson's astronomy, as in St. Augustine's, God was "a circle whose center was everywhere, and its
circumference nowhere" (*C*, II, 301). God was the "centripetal force" in "the depths of the soul" (*J*, IV, 215), saving
man, in the unending antagonism of centripetal and centrifugal forces, from the circumferential ignorance. Man's life in
God began from the moment of ecstasy, and from "there the

Universe evolves itself as from a centre to its boundless irradiation" (*J*, III, 402). Again the circular growth of the self described this idea and god-seeking: "The life of man is a self-evolving circle, which, from a ring imperceptibly small, rushes on all sides outwards to new and larger circles, and that without End" (*C*, II, 304). And if God was the greatest circle, and the circle in its nature compensatory, Emerson could find in his notion of God as "the Great Compensation" a symbol of the Over-Soul as container and resolution of all antagonism; and the Over-Soul, as the circumambient atmosphere he felt overhanging him like the sky — a "heaven within heaven" — filled the intellectual circle with the content of his living experience (*J*, VIII, 567).

Like the Ideas they represented, circles were compensatory. In the dialectic of inspiration (and thought) they represented the limit of each expanding ebb and flow. Each Idea, by compensating for a multitude of observations, was an ascent; each Idea became a higher platform from which to survey the prospect for a still higher generalization looming on a still more distant horizon. Ascending to thought in this way was the intellectual equivalent of distant visioning; the synthesis was in the focus of ever widening vistas — and one's visual reach was best achieved in ascent (*J*, III, 373). Emerson described this intellectual visioning: "But now and then the lawless imagination flies out and asserts her habit. I revisit the verge of my intellectual domain. How the restless soul runs round the outmost orbit and builds her bold conclusion as a tower of observation from whence her eyes wander incessantly in the unfathomable abyss. I dimly scrutinize the vast constitution of being" (*J*, II, 223).[35]

This intellectual restlessness was the true compensation. Emerson said that his cardinal faith was "that all secrets of the less [the prudential] are commanded by the larger generalization [the spiritual]" (*L*, II, 344). And "ascent" was the proper word, because he always felt that the spiritual laws were *above* prudential concerns. The compensation of insight or self-recovery, then, lay in the power to press beyond the limits of a previous thought. When his center proved to be merely another circumference, he felt his powers decay (*J*, VIII, 102). He felt the heart's refusal to be imprisoned in an Idea, and he expressed this by saying "that around every circle another can be drawn . . . there is no end in nature." Or to return to the analogy of night and day, "There is always another dawn risen on mid-noon" (*J*, VIII, 239), and " 'He who contemplates hath a day without night' " (*J*, II, 478).

The possibility that with the returning life of influx he would regain a wider angle of vision seemed to him evidence in itself of God's presence in the universe. Unable to state the truth once and for all, unable to rest in an idea — these were signs to Emerson that in the harmony of man and the universe it was with man as it was with God: "There is no outside, no enclosing wall, no circumference to us" (*J*, VIII, 242). But the spasms of inspiration also showed him how humanly dependent he was, how fragmentary was the view from his angle of vision. He wrote that "a glimpse, a point of view that by its brightness excludes the purview, is granted, but no panorama. A fuller inspiration should cause the point to flow and become a line, should bend the line and complete the circle" (*C*, VIII, 273).

He could avoid the parallax of insight by a sympathetic correspondence with nature; in his own experience of distant vision and reflection he found that he could align himself with the axis of things. Whatever the magnetism of the universe was, for him, it directed his eye to the horizon and beyond to the "aboriginal self," to the "science-baffling star, without parallax." The deep force of "Spontaneity or Instinct" directed him, opened his eye in reflection to the source of being and light which he realized as Intuition. Beyond this his metaphysics of inspiration and self-reliance could not go (*C*, II, 63 ff.). For he knew that he could not willfully make his inspiration consecutive; it was like the coming of day, dependent on the law, and therefore to be awaited with assurance. But its coming always predicted night. An idea might at the moment of its conception bind a fragmentary nature within its circle, but in the total demands of an angle of vision come full circle, it could only serve as an arc. Emerson learned this more and more from the infrequency of his inspirational experiences; and when his early static conception of nature gave way to one of illusion and flux, he found that the arc again provided the only way in which his angle of vision could accommodate the ceaseless flow.

By joining the static and mechanistic circle of Newtonian astronomy (his debt to eighteenth-century science) with the dynamic science of Ideas or dialectic of Coleridge, Emerson made his circle an organic symbol capable of representing both the unfolding mind and the ascending natural chain of being. His circle united his two desires: the desire for fixity or centrality in the universe of the spirit, and the desire for change and growth and freedom in the organic universe of prudence. He wanted it to show both the "evanescence and centrality of things." He wanted a symbol for what the ancient myths taught him was still true in human experience, that "things are in a flood and fixed as adamant: the *Bhagavat Geeta* adduces the illustration of the sphered, mutable, yet centered air or ether" (*J*, VII, 29). The circle symbolized this sphered mutability, the growth that depended on a fixed center in being. As the center of the circle, God (through his sympathetic correspondence with Him) provided him the fixity and centrality he needed when nature became an ever-changing screen of "slippery sliding surfaces" (*C*, III, 48); the circumference of the circle, the human and natural limitations, receded in the ecstatic use of nature as the representative of law, whether that law was perceived directly in nature, or, later, through nature. That the perpetual *transformations* witnessed in the natural process expressed in their tendency the circular ascent of spirit were as much a miracle to Emerson as the mind's self-expansions.[36] For both were affirmations of the infinite, of the compensation of ascent, of the power of new prospects. Limited by his human angle of vision and the fitful light of self-reflection or intuition, Emerson still had for his own the arc of nature, and the arc perceived in the fullness of his ecstatic insight promised a corresponding circle and represented for him its portable and reportable truth.

4

The Arc of the Circle

*You must formulate your thought or 'tis all sky
and no stars.*
EMERSON, "Natural History of Intellect."

*Things admit of being used as symbols, because
nature is a symbol, in the whole, and in every
part. . . I find that the fascination [of na-
ture] resides in the symbol.*
EMERSON, "The Poet."

*I cannot myself use that systematic form which
is reckoned essential in treating the science of
the mind. But if one may say so without arro-
gance, I might suggest that he who contents
himself with dotting a fragmentary curve, recording only what facts he has observed, without attempting to arrange them within one
outline, follows a system also, — a system as
grand as any other, though he does not inter-
fere with its vast curves by prematurely forcing
them into a circle or ellipse, but only draws
that arc which he clearly sees, or perhaps at a
later observation a remote curve of the same
orbit, and waits for a new opportunity, well-
assured that these observed arcs will consist
with each other.*
EMERSON, "Natural History of Intellect."

The legitimate extension of the angle of vision was the
theory of expression — of symbol-making and symbol-using —
which Emerson represented in the arc of the circle. "We have

such exorbitant eyes," he wrote from his experience, "that on seeing the smallest arc, we complete the curve" (*C*, III, 225). This was the activity of intellect receptive, the mode of experience in which one achieved total sympathy or correspondence with the life in nature. By the process of distant vision, arclike objects fused themselves into the curve of nature; one achieved an angle of vision, an inspired centrality, in which one shared the currents of being. By receiving the pulses of inspiration, the angle widened into the ecstasy of merger and insight, and one ascended to higher platforms and new prospects from which the full circle, never fully realized, was dimly suggested in the bended horizon of thought. At this pole of the mind, a progressive ascent into unity was the only aim, and this Emerson expressed in the dialectic of ideas, the ever-widening expansion of circles in the sea of being. "The mind," he wrote of the receptive pole in "Plato," "is urged to ask for one cause of many effects; then for the cause of that; and again the cause, diving still into the profound: self-assured that it shall arrive at an absolute and sufficient one, — a one that shall be all" (*C*, IV, 48). This was the tyrannizing unity of the mind.

But this was only the activity of one pole of the mind — the mind, which we have seen, as a microcosm of the universe, had two poles, corresponding to the dualism of that universe. At the constructive pole, he wrote, "urged by an opposite tendency, the mind returns from the one, to that which is not one, but other or many; from cause to effect; and affirms the necessary existence of variety, the self-existence of both, as each is involved in the other" (*C*, IV, 48). A creature of two worlds, then, man could not rest at peace in either, but had to span the "whole space between God or pure mind" and man: "From one, he must draw his strength; to the other, he must owe his aim. The one yokes him to the real; the other, to the apparent" (*C*, I, 182). In the reconciliation of the one and the many, in the expression of the one in the many, one returned again to nature, to the chain of being in which diversity was expressed. For he found that "action tends directly back to diversity" (*C*, IV, 51). In the bipolar unity of perception, however, in diversity itself, one might see the unifying law and express it.

The complete circuit of the mind enjoined the publication of thought. In Emerson's description of the mind, one's "health" depended on "the fidelity with which he transmits influences from the vast and universal to the point on which genius can act" (*C*, I, 208–209). He wrote that "the moral sentiment never rests in vision, but wishes to be enacted" (*J*, X, 191). If intellect was an impartible essence, as he noted in Proclus, for him it was necessarily "impart*a*ble" and "communicable in the same proportion with its amount or depth" (*J*, VI, 199). His genius was not a mystic resting at the receptive pole, but a symbol-maker and user able to focus the fullness of his vision in the visible arc of the circle. For, as a transformer of vision, the mind at its constructive pole was actively expressive or outgoing.[1] The health of the mind required the release of efflux to balance its inspirational influx: "A man," Emerson wrote, "must pump up the Atlantic Ocean, the whole atmosphere, all the electricity, all the universe, and pump it out again" (*J*, IX, 294). Inspiration was only a preliminary state — the grasping of power — leading to spiritualized prudential action; and similarly, insight was only morally realized by its externalization: One gained on chaos and the dark by communicating the light. By focusing thought on objects, by showing the one in the many, one brought others, as far as expression admitted them, to the edge of darkness. Here, if courageous enough, they, too, might leap into sight. As the instrument of this communication, as the means of bringing others into their angles of vision or sympathy with being, correspondence was also a doctrine of expression. It followed from the way the mind came into and conceptualized its vision, from the mysterious symbol-making of the mind's constructive outlet.

That the mind should look through visible facts by making them symbols of invisible thoughts — this Emerson believed was not, as some scoffed, a "metaphysical whim of modern times," but a fact of experience "as old as the human mind" (*C*, VIII, 19). Language, the most revealing index of the mind's operations, testified to it. In the "primitive" beginnings of language, he wrote, "Words are signs of natural facts." Originally, for example, *spirit* meant *wind*. But having served to conceptualize an experience, that is, to locate a thing in the flux of one's impressions, it provided a way of making the thing itself a symbol of spiritual facts (*C*, I, 25). He knew the mystery of this process was hidden from him in the past. But the process was often repeated in his own experience, the process which we more fully explain today as a basic human need in the appropriation of experience — symbolic transformation.[2]

Emerson was aware of the verbal barriers to fresh experience. He knew that metaphors lost their living impact in the sterilization of overuse and generalization. "Language is fossil poetry," he said, recognizing what we today call "dead or faded metaphors": "language is made up of images, or tropes, which now, in their secondary use, have long ceased to remind us of their poetic origin" (*C*, III, 22). Originally, however, "each word was a stroke of genius," each word was a poem, "a brilliant picture" by which the namer symbolized the world (*C*, III, 21–22). And the poet or namer was able to name the thing "because he sees it, or comes one step nearer to it than any other." Naming, Emerson added, was not an art, but "a second nature," the expression of perception.

In the process of inspiration Emerson recapitulated the experience of the race in its development of language. In inspiration he freed himself from stereotypes and by dislimning objects regained the sense of fluid consciousness. "The wild fertility of nature," he wrote, "is felt by comparing our rigid names . . . with our fluid consciousness" (*C*, II, 138). The flowing of nature he achieved by inspiration gave him an almost primal sense of the original undifferentiated stream. And from this the genius, like early man, could again freshly conceptualize and name, fashioning metaphors that were immediate and alive with experience — that realized and added to consciousness (*C*, III, 14). This dissolving of stereotypes in fresh experience (inspiration) and the precipitation of new symbols was, for Emerson, the total process and fulfillment of the mind. The "primary writer" not only had come, like "primary man," into an angle of vision, but was enabled by his angle of vision to recreate the living reality in new symbols (*C*, I, 30). And this use of symbols, Emerson believed, "has a certain power of emancipation and exhilaration for all men." By suggesting the metamorphosis concealed by rigid words, the symbol-maker became a liberator, renewing man's sense of the ceaseless flow of divinity (*C*, III, 30).

The poet, then, represented the complete man and the complete mind. A "beholder of ideas," standing at the center of the universe, he was also the expresser: he stood for both halves of man — his need for living truth and for its (his) expression (*C*, III, 5). "The poet," Emerson wrote of his own ideal, "is the person in whom these powers are in balance, the man without impediment, who sees [contemplates], and handles [enacts] that which others dream of, traverses the whole scale of experience, and is representative of man, in virtue of being the largest power to receive and to impart" (*C*, III, 6). His function was expression: and because "thought seeks to know unity in unity" and "poetry to show it by variety; that is, always by an object or symbol," he became necessarily a symbol user (*C*, IV, 56). But knowing, too, both the fluidity of mind and of nature, he recognized that symbols had always to be recast to retain their highest service — the suggestion of transition.[3]

The metamorphosis of experience into symbol, the method of mind, Emerson believed could also be seen in the method of nature (*C*, I, 96). He expected from the correspondence of man and nature, from their identical God-given life, that the creative process of the mind, projecting itself on nature, would be represented in the method of nature. If nature — the fluid language of spirit creative — published its animating law in things, if in the ascending evolutionary flux old forms dissolved and new and higher forms emerged, then, he believed, "A deep insight making one acquainted with the flux and its law will always, like Nature, ultimate its thought in a thing" (*C*, VIII, 17). It followed, too, that if the mind continually externalized itself in natural objects, its method of unfolding ideas would also correspond to the method of nature in unfolding its various forms. As a naturalist of the mind, then, Emerson felt that he could best know the mind "by exploring the *method of nature*" (*C*, I, 197).

For nature, in his interpretation of Plotinian emanation, was "the memory of the mind," mind lapsed. "That," he wrote, "which once existed in intellect as pure law has now taken body as Nature. It existed already in the mind in solution; now, it has been precipitated, and the bright sediment is the world" (*C*, I, 197). Correspondence-as-expression was therefore possible because the things by which one symbolized the spirit were themselves "the last issue of spirit" (*C*, I, 34). "The visible creation," he wrote, "is the terminus or the circumference of the invisible world" (*C*, I, 34–35). By standing at the spiritual center, the world one dissolved in inspiration could be precipitated in the arc that symbolically expressed it — the many could represent the one. And because in both activities nature served as the means, the bridge to inspiration and its expression, he felt that "we may . . . safely study the mind in nature." Introspection, sometimes associated by Emerson with detestable subjectivism, was like looking directly into the sun. God's ways and the ways of the mind were best discovered indirectly in their expression in nature (*C*, I, 197).

If nature revealed the thought beneath by indirections, he discovered, too, that she remained opaque to system-makers whose "digested systems" falsified the truth and prevented its gleams (*C*, I, 70). A method like Cousin's eclecticism, he wrote Frederic Hedge, "has catalogued & classified all entities . . . & remains itself but one fact of the infinity of facts" (*L*, II, 123). A method could not rest in its application; neither could it detain the streams of nature and consciousness out of devotion to the sentiment of rationality. For nature's ways were as unpredictable as those of the mind. Like the mind, nature created by pulses, by "organic movements" that were "saltatory" and "impulsive," by a continual antagonism of ebb and flow (*J*, VI, 326). Nature falsified all methods of classification, and could only be expressed by an anti-method.

The anti-method Emerson chose to symbolize the unending ascent of creation and the unending ascent for more inclusive ideas was that of circles. By representing the process of inspiration, the circle, as we have seen, described the activity of one pole of the mind, of one plane of the universe: the dialectic of ideas Emerson adopted from Coleridge. And by representing the flux of nature, the circle also represented the other pole of the mind and the world of available forms — a world of appearance, of metamorphosis, through which could be seen the great chain of being. Emerson came to the knowledge of the dialectic of ideas before he appreciated its polar expression in nature's chain: the method he can be seen looking for in the 1830's (when his sermons, more or less, still followed the traditional pattern) had to be progressive, to express the great moral truth of nature, that all things ameliorate, benefit, ascend. The logic he wanted for his literary method had to be the silent logic of creation itself, and its symbols had to be fluid if expression was to be organic, "like the metamorphosis of things into higher forms" (*C*, III, 25).

When he visited the Jardin des Plantes on his first trip to Europe (1833), he saw for the first time the "natural" method of classification for which he had been seeking. Very early, it seems, Emerson had come into an awareness of the symbolic nature of things. His earliest journal entries reveal his wonder at the mystery to be read in nature, and his yearning after the laurels of eloquence sharpened in him his sense of the power of symbolic expression (*J*, I, 26, 105). If his father's generation used the trope more for decoration than penetration (and Emerson fell victim in his early verse), still he found a better guide in his Aunt Mary. More than anyone else, she represented the Calvinist legacy and opened to him its concrete spiritual language.[4] From her as well as from his early enthusiasm for the Swedenborgians, he might have learned that "everything is significant," that "an entire cabinet of shells would be an expression of the whole human mind" (*J*, II, 478). But in neither would he have found the symbol identified, as fully as he desired, with the process of nature. They spiritualized things, made the outer inner; but they did not see through the symbol, that is, by its means penetrate the flux and affirm its law.

He was probably all the more suspicious of Swedenborg's doctrine of correspondences as an applicable symbol-theory when he realized that Swedenborg himself had propounded a theory of forms, and then had failed to adjust his one-to-one correspondences to it (*C*, IV, 115). If Swedenborg had caught a glimpse of the natural metamorphosis of forms, summarized in Stallo's "The development of all individual forms will be spiral," he failed to see its relation to the *fluid* symbolic expression of dynamic perception. He never recognized, as Stallo again extracted the essence of Oken, Schelling, Laplace, and others, that "the configurations of nature are more than a symbol, they are the gesticular expression of Nature's inner life" (*J*, VIII, 77).[5] By failing to see this, he committed the "capital offence," as Emerson said, his "confounding of planes." Lacking a dynamic theory of symbols, he attempted to find in heaven a multiplicity of objects corresponding to those on earth (*C*, IV, 140); and by dogmatically interpreting symbols once and for all, Emerson felt that he was impeding the law of mind and things that he believed was both alive and immutable.[6] "Swedenborg," he wrote, "perceived the central life of each object and saw the change of appearance as it passed before different eyes. He does not seem to have seen with equal clearness the necessity of progression or onwardness in each creature. Metamorphosis is the law of the Universe. All forms are fluent . . . the thoughts of God pause but for a moment in any form, but pass into a new form, as if by touching the earth again in burial, to acquire new energy. A wise man is not deceived by the pauses: he knows that it is momentary: he already foresees the new departure, and departure after departure, in long series" (*J*, VII, 117).

The method of expression, therefore, if it were to parallel the method of nature, could not rely on a static interpretation of symbols any more than a static, merely accumulative, system of classification. Symbols not only had to reveal the essential dynamism of Reason and Nature, they had to express that flux when, as words, they could neither cover the multiplicity of things nor their life. What animated symbols was the vision itself of which they had become symbols — the correspondential world, the chains of thought and of being of which they were representative parts. For, as Kirby and Spence read organic nature, the chain of being was a chain of analogies; and analogy, as the tool of classification, relying on perception rather than accumulation, was itself progressive. "All science is transcendental, or else passes away," Emerson wrote, acknowledging his interest in natural science as exhibiting correct methods of thought and expression. "Botany is now acquiring a right theory. And how excellent is this MacLeay and Swainson theory of animated circles! Symbolic also, as in Kirby and Spence" (*J*, VII, 52–53). For what Emerson sought in scientific "schemes" was the hint that "Nature ever flows; stands never still" (*J*, V, 494). Classifications — even his own transformation of the Newtonian circle into the cipher of change — if accepted literally or for fact and content, without suggesting the living experience, was spiritually valueless. The greatest value of any method was its power to set the perceiver's world in motion, to set him thinking idealistically. He himself felt this at the Jardin des Plantes when he *saw*, in a "natural" classification (*J*, III, 161), the chain of being, the metamorphosis of forms, the worm aspiring to be man. The dialectic as a natural unfolding of thought — the science of ideas he discovered in Coleridge's *The Friend* — this, too, he saw *expressed* in the natural chain of forms in the Jardin des Plantes. It was the hint he needed. As he wrote much later: "One who has seen one proof, ever so slight, of the terrific powers of this organ [dialectic] will remember it all the days of his life. . . It is like the first hint that the earth moves, or that iron is a conductor of fluids, or that granite is gas. The solids, the centres, rest itself, fly and skip. Rest is a relation, and not rest any longer" (*J*, VII, 54–55).

He adopted the dialectic as a method of expression, then, because for him it was the only way to realize this antagonizing method of nature, and because it might furnish the proof needed to shock the unaware into fluid consciousness. It ordered his own analogies in such a way that others, to understand him at all, were forced to leap to their own. It conveyed more than a body of fact: it expressed a way of seeing and at the same time was designed to bring others into their angles of vision. This was the aim of poetic method, of true science.

And the true scientist was the poet, a perceiver who saw "the stability of thought" and "the accidency and the fugacity of the symbol" (*C*, III, 20). He aimed in expression to make things, once believed to be permanent, mere appearances, to use "forms according to the life, and not according to the form," to go beyond the facts by employing them as symbols (*C*, III, 21). And he knew that he could not rest his perception in a symbol, as Emerson believed Swedenborg had, for the life it temporarily caught flowed on and falsified it. Symbols, he knew, were "fluxional" and language "vehicular and transitive" — that is, symbols were only brief illuminations, and had to be reëmployed to convey new perceptions (*C*, III, 34). Perception, the pulses of insight, the life itself he sought — these made any available form their convenient symbol and an old symbol new. For only the life of fresh perception could keep the world in motion; it was the poet's power, and by it, Emerson wrote, "the poet turns the world to glass, and shows us all things in their right series and procession. For through that better perception, he stands one step nearer to things, and sees the flowing of metamorphosis; perceives that thought is multiform; that within the form of every creature is a force impelling it to ascend into a higher form; and, following with his eyes the life, uses the forms which express that life, and so his speech flows with the flowing of nature" (*C*, III, 20–21).

The dialectic with which Emerson chose to express the fluidity of the universe also represented the life of his perception, his many-sided penetration or ascent to truth. Symbols had to be fluid and their unfolding progressive, for the seer was like the surveyor who "goeth about taking positions to serve as the points of his angles [each symbol was a flitting angle of vision], and thereby afterwards he finds the place of the mountain. The philosopher, in like manner, selects points whence he can look on his subject from different sides, and by means of many approximate results [symbols] he at last obtains an accurate expression of the truth" (*J*, II, 523).[7] The accurate expression of the truth emerged as "a new and perfect and radiant whole"; it was the miracle in which the unity of life was glimpsed in its fragments (*J*, VI, 118). Only by placing things (thought) in their right series and procession — only by stretching out all the "sloven" length of his thought, and "by many fragments of thought to dot out the whole curve" (*L*, II, 29) — could Emerson make the parts the conveyancing of a living, flowing truth.

This preparation or leading up to truth was more important to him than the communication of fact in arbitrary classifications. "All our classifications are introductory and very convenient, but must be looked on as temporary," he wrote on his return from Europe and the Jardin des Plantes. "We have no theory of animated nature. When we have," he wrote, "it will be itself the true Classification [the 'pure, plastic Idea']. . . The way they [naturalists] classify is by counting stamens, or filaments, or teeth and hoofs and shells. A true argument, what we call the unfolding an idea, as is continually done in Plato's Dialogues, in Carlyle's *Characteristics*, or in a thousand acknowledged applications of familiar ethical truths, — these are natural classifications containing their own reason in themselves, and making known facts continually. They are themselves the formula, the largest generalization of the facts. . . Mr. Coleridge has written well on this matter of Theory in his *Friend*. A lecture may be given upon insects or plants, that, when it is closed, irresistibly suggests the question, 'Well, what of that?' An enumeration of facts without method. A true method has no more need of firstly, secondly, etc., than a perfect sentence has of punctuation. It tells its own story, makes its own feet, creates its own form. It is its own apology. . . The true classification will not present itself to us in a catalogue of a hundred classes, but as an idea of which the flying wasp and the grazing ox are developments. Natural History is to be studied, not with any pretension that its theory is attained, that its classification is permanent, but merely as full of tendency" (*J*, III, 293–296). Instead, his dialectic, like Plato's, was intended to be a self-affirming example of this method. Coleridge had explained in *The Friend* that if Plato had not presented the Dialogues as an exemplification of "the ART OF METHOD," "it would be difficult to exculpate the noblest productions of the 'Divine' Philosopher from the charge of being tortuous and labyrinthine in their progress, and unsatisfactory in their ostensible results." The dialectic as Plato used it, Coleridge said, never rested in truth, but ended by proposing a new problem: "The purpose of the writer is not so much to establish any particular truth, as to remove the obstacles, the continuance of which is preclusive of all truth." This — and it might apply as well to Emerson's essays — was its justification, "that the EDUCATION of the Intellect, by awakening the *Method* of self-development, was his proposed object, not any specific information that can be *conveyed into it* from without. He desired not to assist in storing the passive Mind with the various sorts of Knowledge most in request, as if the Human Soul were a mere repository, a banqueting room, but to place it in such relations of circumstance as should gradually excite its vegetating and germinating powers to produce new fruits of Thought, new Conceptions, and Imaginations, and Ideas." [8]

Margaret Fuller said as much in her review of Emerson's *Essays*. Those who "were accustomed to an artificial method whose scaffolding could easily be retraced, and desired an obvious sequence of logical inferences," she wrote, could not understand the method of the essays. "He really seemed to believe there were two sides to every subject," she continued, "and even to intimate higher ground from which each might be seen to have an infinite number of sides or bearings, an impertinence not to be endured!" Others, with enough experience in idealism, she added, were able to follow Emerson's "natural manner as a stream of thought." [9] For it was the natural method of idealism, especially when that idealism had been made dynamic and the life of the mind, like nature's, was felt to be a stream.[10]

Coleridge had argued, too, that this method was not visionary or mystic, "estranging the Mind from plain experience and substantial matter-of-fact." Instead it "dwelt in 'the sober certainty' of waking Knowledge." [11] And William T. Harris tried to show that this expression of waking knowledge was exactly what Emerson achieved by the dialectic in all his prose, and with greatest success in "Experience." [12]

Emerson, of course, glorified the dialectic as the science of sciences and the method of unity and progression in his essay on "Plato" (*C*, IV, 62). Plato, he said, was the representative of "the privilege of intellect, the power, namely of carrying up every fact to successive platforms, and so disclosing, in every fact, a germ of expansion" (*C*, IV, 81). He knew, too, that "all things are in a scale; and, begin where we will, ascend and ascend. All things are symbolical; and what we call results are beginnings" (*C*, IV, 68). And being a "balanced soul," "a more complete man, who could apply to nature the whole scale of the senses, the understanding, and the reason," he joined both planes of the world (both poles of the mind) and presented the key in his twice bisected line (*C*, IV, 68, 82). Here was the scale of knowledge spanning the visible world of objects and the intelligible world of ideas or being; here was the correspondential bridge by which one crossed from things to their spiritual meaning. "Things are knowable," Emerson said, "because being from one, things correspond. There is a scale: and the correspondence of heaven to earth, of matter to mind; of the part to the whole, is our guide" (*C*, IV, 62). The bisected line represented the "degrees in idealism" (*C*, II, 309), the stages in the transformation of the love of the particular into the love of the ideal, as Emerson used Plato's "The Symposium" to explain the ever-enlarging circles of thought in "the procession of the soul from within out" (*C*, II, 181 ff.), from sense and things to thought and spirit. It provided him a way to show how "interest is gradually transformed from the forms to the lurking method" (*C*, VIII, 5).

And for this reason the bisected line was also the model of Emerson's literary method. Walter Blair and Clarence Faust have shown this clearly enough in their analyses of Emerson's essays, "Art" and "The Poet," and the poems, "Each and All" and "Threnody." They suggest from these studies that Emerson "conceived of his own peculiar task in the way he ascribed to Plato. He was bound, as he saw it, to treat any subject in such a way as to relate it both to that which was above it and to that which was below it in the scale of being represented by the twice bisected line. The possibility of success in this enterprise he conceived as depending upon the comprehending powers of man's varied faculties. In considering any topic (say art, politics, poetry, manners or gift-giving) the movement of his discussion . . . resulted from his examining the subject first from one, then from another, level as its relations in one after another of the realms of being were explored." [13]

Emerson also executed this method in the organization of his early books. Although the dialectic was employed in each essay, the essays themselves balance each other, moving from the plane of sense to that of spirit. In the *Essays* (first series), "History" is set off by "Self-Reliance," "Compensation" moves beyond fate to "Spiritual Laws," "Love" informs the nature of "Friendship," "Prudence" and "Heroism" treat the laws of behavior from two vantages, "The Over-Soul" precedes as it necessarily includes all "Circles," and "Intellect" and "Art" less successfully balance the functions of mind. Emerson felt that the proportion of the book was weakened by the absence of the chapter he was then writing on "Nature," for not only would it have balanced "Art," it would have been, as the last chapter of the book, the proper antithesis of "History" and so a way of binding all together (*L*, II, 387).

The second series of *Essays* does not appear to follow the dialectic, but *The Conduct of Life* does rather successfully. For example, the first three essays consider the problem of power on the prudential level: "Fate" treats the limitary laws of nature; "Power," though unavoidably seeking its spiritual source, is for the most part midway to the "Wealth" its discipline produces. And all three are made preparatory to "Culture" and "Worship" which follow. "Considerations by the Way" reaffirms self-reliance, and although not especially organic in this series, is not out of tune with the rest. Perhaps it is needed to reinforce the polar essays, "Beauty" and "Illusions," for beauty is the result of seeing beyond illusions by means of one's spiritual center or reliance.

At any rate, Emerson was not without method. For the most part he was most successful in the individual essays, but whenever possible he seemed to balance one level with another, and the essays often come in pairs in his mind, as, for example, "The Conservative" and "The Transcendentalist."

But not only did the bisected line give him a plan of consecutive expression,[14] following what he believed was the true method of mind in knowing; it provided the basis of correspondence as a doctrine of symbol-using. For every object in the scale was a representative part, mirroring the whole. If the central belief of his ethics was that "virtue pervades the whole world, and none so poor as not to partake" (*J*, II, 7), its parallel in expression was that each thing partakes of the all, and so represents it. "Things admit of being used as symbols, because," he wrote, "nature is a symbol, in the whole, and in every part" (*C*, III, 13). Like Goethe, he believed that "a leaf is a compend of nature, and nature a colossal leaf" (*J*, IV, 22). And his faith in identity, in analogy, and symbolic correspondences, rested on the doctrine of Each and All. After the *Divinity School Address* he wrote to George Bush, in defense of his literary creed: "It is my habit to assume always as purely as I can, the attitude of an observer, & to record what I see. I am not responsible for the fact; for the truth of the record, I am. All that is out of my field of sight, I neither affirm nor deny; but I believe I am not unrelated to it; in good time, it may, it will come into sight & influence. But what I see now, — the feeblest intellection, rightly considered, — implies all the vast attributes of spirit, implies the uprising of the one divine soul into my particular creek or bay, & apprises me that the Ocean is behind. I think that the constant progress of the human mind is from observation of superficial differences to intrinsic analogies, &, at last, to central identity, in all things. The εν και παν I everywhere behold" (*L*, II, 156). If "all the laws of nature may be read in the smallest fact," then Emerson felt he needed only be "a faithful reporter of particular impressions" (*J*, V, 327). And to report the impression, he felt he needed only the available image which the mind itself spontaneously provided.

II

Emerson's image theory best described the way in which the mind naturally expressed itself. One's store of everyday experiences became significant only when, in the moment of inspiration, it yielded the image by which insight could be expressed. And truth was fulfilled as action only when the mind completed its circuit, joined past and present, sense and spirit, by making the image the portable power of its perception. Sampson Reed had pointed out in *Growth of the Mind* that "if we look merely at the truth, it will vanish away, like rays of light falling into vacancy." [15] In order to *use* the truth and to remember it, he added, we must dress it in the garments of God — find its natural imagery. Poetry, the corresponding expression of the imagination, was for him, then, "all those illustrations of truth by natural imagery, which spring from the fact, that this world is the mirror of Him who made it." [16] Truth, to be practical, had to be refracted by an object, for it was in an object that it acquired the mental materialism Emerson wanted for all abstraction: it was in the object that truth formed "a distinct and permanent image on the mind." [17]

Emerson found in his own experience of perception that the image was one with the insight — the thing to which he felt he had penetrated. A "true" inspiration, in this sense, was the complete activity of the mind, the bipolar unity in which man spanned the prudential and spiritual worlds. For out of the inspiration the garments of his thought were spontaneously provided. The idea he beheld seemed to unlock the store of his past experience and call forth the one best fitted to express it, to materialize it. This was the miracle of expression beyond which he could not go in his concern with the symbolism of the universe. But it seemed to him "a commanding certificate" of both his penetration to the truth (the reality) and the adequacy [18] of the image to freshly express it. When one is "exalted by thought," he wrote of his own creative process, "it clothes itself in images. A man conversing in earnest, if he watch his intellectual processes, will find that a material image, more or less luminous, arises in his mind, contemporaneous with every thought, which furnishes the vestment of the thought. . . This imagery is spontaneous. It is the blending of experience with the present action of the mind" (*C*, I, 30–31). The present action of perception "blended" by evoking a sensual image — on the plane of sense — from its resting place in the memory, and so made available the higher truth in a form which in turn could provoke both the sense and spirit of those who received it. He confirmed Oegger's doctrine that every step in thought involved a material symbol by recording his own experience: when he thought abstractly "that a man sees in the gross of the acts of his life the domination of his instincts or genius over all other causes," he noted that "while I thus talked, I *saw* some crude *symbols* of the thought with the mind's eye, — as it were, a mass of grass or weeds in a stream, of which the spears or blades shot out from the mass in every direction, but were immediately curved round to float all in one direction.[19] When presently the conversation changed to the subject of Thomas a Kempis's popularity, and how Aristotle and Plato came safely down, as if God brought them in his hand . . . and of the Natural Academy by which the exact value of every book is determined, maugre all hindrance or furtherance; then saw I, as I spoke, the old pail in the Summer Street kitchen with potatoes swimming in it, some at the top, some in the midst, and some lying at the bottom; and I spoiled my fine thought by saying that books take their place according to their specific gravity 'as surely as potatoes in a tub' " (*J*, III, 527–528).

This spontaneity was the natural life of the imagination, for, after all, as the poetic faculty on the plane of the Reason, imagination was an image-making faculty, a symbol-user (*C*, VIII, 17, 117). In some mysterious way imagination was connected with the memory — how, Emerson could not tell. But its function was "the nomination of the causal facts, the laws of the soul, by the physical facts" (*J*, IX, 127). One followed the creative ways of God, that is, imagination worked after the method of nature, for, as Emerson too briefly put it, "Nature makes flowers, as the mind makes images" (*J*, VIII, 9). Like the flowers, image-making was a spontaneous and natural creation only by sharing the circulations of being; it was never the artificial, manipulatory "creation" of fancy, but an organic creation of the life of inspiration.

Expressiveness, therefore, began by following one's instincts and culminated in the second inspiration or passion that alone could call forth the images and fuse them to "fluid obedience" (*J*, IX, 312; IV, 376). "No book is good," Emerson wrote, "which is not written by the Instincts": Lacking "animal heat," its "cold allegory makes us yawn" (*J*, VIII, 40). By the instincts, Emerson meant, as he said in "Spiritual Laws," "the soul's emphasis" (*C*, II, 145). To find what was appropriately one's own, one had to follow the "selecting principle" within, had to, as Emerson often expressed it, give "the reins to the horse," and seek "his safety in the instincts of the animal" (*J*, II, 426).[20] For instinct was the latent germ of inspiration, and pointed out the direction in which the faculties should be exercised for the fullest self-expression (and sincere communication) of man. "To coax and woo the strong Instinct⁻ to bestir and work its miracle," he said, "is the end of all wise endeavor" (*J*, VII, 98). Released from the misguiding will he knew that "the Instinct is resistless and knows the way" (*J*, VII, 99).

Instinct, then, was the germ of a man's genius that determined what things from "the multiplicity that sweeps and circles round him" were best fitted (corresponded) to his needs. By following the leading of the spirit, one unconsciously appropriated the garments or arcs of experience that in the moment of passion most truly and individually covered the thought. Of this tyranny of the objects that attracted his attention, Emerson wrote: "Those facts, words, persons, which dwell in his memory without his being able to say why, remain, because they have a relation to him no less real for being as yet unapprehended. They are symbols of value to him, as they can interpret parts of his consciousness which he would vainly seek words for in the conventional images of books and other minds. . . They relate to your gift. Let them have their weight, and do not reject them, and cast about for illustration and facts more usual in literature. What your heart thinks is great is great. The soul's emphasis is always right" (*C*, II, 144–145; *J*, V, 145). This reliance on instinct remained Emerson's working method of choosing what was nearest him and most worthy of *his* expression. As a young preacher constrained by the demand for weekly sermons, he gave over the reins: "I sit Friday night and note the first thought that arises. Presently another, presently five or six, — of all of these I take the *mean*, as the subject of Saturday's sermon" (*J*, II, 427).[21] And over thirty years later he recorded that "I told Alcott that every one of my expressions concerning 'God' or the 'soul,' etc., is entitled to attention as testimony, because it is independent, not calculated, not part of any system, but spontaneous, and the nearest word I could find to the thing" (*J*, X, 191).

By relying on instinct, the first condition of the mind's unfolding, Emerson felt that even though the images stored in the memory came as Locke said they did, still the mind-as-selector was free from the pressures of circumstance (*C*, II, 329 ff.). The root of the mind was merely using the senses to acquire its proper aliment. He always retained the Platonic notion of innate ideas in the mind awaiting the activity of life to call them forth; and he applied this idea to the mind's images, when, in his youthful enthusiasm to destroy Lockean sensationalism, he wrote his Aunt Mary Moody Emerson, "The images, the sweet immortal images are within us — born there, our native right, and sometimes one kind of sounding word or syllable awakens the instrument of our souls, and sometimes another. But we are not slaves to sense . . . but by fashion and imbecility" (*J*, I, 334). Even if he later recognized the mind's reliance on sensation to activate it, he reinterpreted the role of memory to give it the freedom from sense he desired. The senses, he knew, "collect the surface facts of matter." This was properly sensation; but "when memory came, it was experience," the uplifting of "brute reports" to the platform of intellect (*C*, VIII, 24). By storing the trifles of sensation, memory distanced them, gave them a perspective of time as distant vision had of space. It transformed a brute report by giving it its relations. "Any single fact considered by itself confounds, misleads us," Emerson wrote. But, "Let it lie awhile. It will find its place, by and by, in God's chain; its golden brothers will come, one on the right hand and one on the left, and in an instant it will be the simplest, gladdest, friendliest of things" (*J*, V, 79).

The reinterpretation of the powers of memory was especially important in Emerson's image theory when one considers that it was a reaction to Hume. For how could an image find its brothers in the chain of the mind, and so symbolically represent that chain, if the mind was the meaningless jumble of sensations to which Hume was believed to have reduced it? And how could the image symbolically correspond to the truth unless the memory were more than a repository, were itself allied to the selecting instinct that stored it? Because it emphasized what Hume had virtually eliminated, Sampson Reed's *Growth of the Mind* was one of the germinal books of Emerson's generation, and Emerson's source book for his treatment of the memory. It built the inner unfolding of the mind on the memory and restored the affections (a creative desire like instinct for what was truly one's own) as its storing principle. Memory thus became, as Emerson began his essay on it, "a primary and fundamental faculty, without which none other can work." It seemed to span both poles of the mind. It was — and the bogy of Hume stalks behind Emerson's words — "the cement, the bitumen, the matrix in which the other faculties are imbedded; or it is the thread on which the beads of man are strung, making the personal identity which is necessary to moral action. Without it all life and thought were an unrelated succession" (*C*, XII, 90). If the receptive pole of the mind was active only in the eternal present, if one escaped from time in inspiration, still the constructive pole had available for the continuity of expression the record of the past hived in the memory. "Perception," Emerson acknowledged, "though it were immense and could pierce through the universe, was not sufficient" (C, XII, 91). But the memory, like the journals in which transcendentalists filed away their thoughts, joined the past and the present, and provided the thread which made the present insight significant (C, XII, 92–93). Like the flowing chain of being, the flowing impressions in the mind formed a chain in which a new image took on the total significance of a progressively higher representative part. Memory ascended and generalized. Its record was "full of meanings which open as he lives on," Emerson said, "explaining each other, explaining the world to him and expanding their sense as he advances, until it shall become the whole law of Nature and life" (C, XII, 93). What did it matter if occasionally one forgot or a new impression effaced an old one? — "Yet we steadily gain insight; and because all nature has one law and meaning, — part corresponding to part, — all we have known aids us continually to the knowledge of the rest of nature" (C, XII, 101). Nothing significant was lost in memory. Just as Emerson found that the first word of a song recalled the whole line and then the stanza, so every new fact revived the past, found its place in the stream of experience, took its meaning from this context, and at the same time added "transparency to the whole mass" (C, XII, 94, 101).

In its alliance with the Reason, the memory supplied the connective thread making possible the analogical ascent of perception. "The mind has a better secret in generalization," Emerson wrote, "than merely adding units to its list of facts." Shallow thought, for him, was the result of short memory (C, XII, 99). Great thinkers had long and deep memories, and this determined, among other things, their intellectual rank. "A seneschal of Parnassus is Mnemosyne," he wrote, and "Thus, am I a better scholar than one of my neighbors. . . We read the same books a year, two years, ten years ago; we read the same books this month. Well, that fact which struck us both, then, with equal force, I still contemplate. He has lost it. He and the world have only *this* fact. I have that *and* this" (*J*, V, 167).

He noted Plato's insistence on the need for a good memory in genuine philosophers and twice praised St. Augustine's analysis of memory, especially the powers it had that were not sense-derived (*J*, VII, 528–529; VIII, 97). And in his inventory of his own powers, Emerson attributed a "strong memory" to his alter-ego, Osman (*J*, V, 433). One of the ironies of his life, certainly, was the failure of his memory, the aphasia or difficulty of finding the fit word for the idea, which grew worse with his declining health (*J*, X, 391–392). The lecture on "Memory," given in 1870–1871, was perhaps as significant to him as "Terminus," for he remarked, and summoned Newton as his example, that "defect of memory is not always want of genius" (*C*, XI, 100).

As an aid to the imagination, memory also served as the storehouse of images. It was, in a common metaphor of the day, "a kind of looking glass, which being carried through the street of time receives on its clear plate every image that passes." But unlike the mirror, Emerson continued, "our plate is iodized so that every image sinks into it, and is held there. But in addition to this property it has one more, this namely, that of all the million images that are imprinted, the very one we want reappears in the centre of the plate in the moment when we want it" (*C*, XII, 93).

In "Goethe" he explained that the mirror did not passively record the "print of the seal." Memory was active and alive, and although a looking glass, disposed of its images "in a new order." "The facts which transpired do not lie in it inert," he wrote, "but some subside, and others shine; so that soon we have a new picture, composed of eminent experience" (*C*, IV, 252). The images, then, when "domesticated" in the memory, took their own order, an order that Emerson assumed was the divine architecture of God (*J*, II, 446).

And the image arose spontaneously because the memory was not a "pocket, but a living instructor with a prophetic sense," collecting and reordering experience after the principle of affection (*C*, XII, 92). "The memory is as the affection," Emerson wrote, and followed with Sampson Reed's " 'The true way to store the memory is to develop the affections' " (*C*, XII, 104).[22] Reed had pointed to the possibility of connecting thought and image more organically when he wrote in support of an inner principle in the mind that "the reservoir of knowledge should be seated in the affections, sending forth its influences throughout the mind and terminating in word and deed . . . because its channels and outlets are situated below the watermark. There prevails a most erroneous sentiment, that the mind is originally vacant, and requires only to be filled up. . . The mind is originally a most delicate germ; whose husk is the body [senses]; planted in this world, that the light and heat of heaven may fall upon it with a gentle radiance, and call forth its energies. The process of learning is not by synthesis or analysis. It is the most perfect illustration of both. As subjects are presented to the operation of the mind, they are decomposed and reorganized in a manner peculiar to itself, and not easily explained." [23] Within the delicate germ of the mind, affection guided the appropriation of objects best fitted (corresponding) to the unfolding of its energies. In its narrow sense, intellect or mind was the faculty of analysis, separating the subject from its object; but affection, the power of the heart, as Emerson said, "blends," joining the perceiver and the thing perceived (*C*, XII, 44). Affection, therefore, was the "affirmative of affirmatives," the love or moral element which was antecedent to reason itself — the desire for merger which alone opened the circulations of being to reason (*C*, XII, 61). The dependence of reason on love explained why, for Emerson, memory was also called the seat of conscience, and why, therefore, to be an artist one had to be "good" (*Y*, 225).

Affection stored the memory by doubling the powers of attention, and only those images were stored and easily recalled which had come to the mind through a sincere devotion to one's objects. For this reason, one's expression was natural to him, and his imagery belied his character and preoccupations.[24] What one remembered, Emerson said, classified him, "one remembering by shop-rule or interest; one by passion; one by trifling external marks, as dress and money" (*C*, XII, 96). One's affection was easily seen in his method of classification, and how and how much a man had lived (on both levels of the universe) could be seen, as Emerson admonished the American scholar, in "the poverty or splendor of his speech" (*C*, I, 98). What affection had stored, it restored with its return as passion: in the heat of expression great men like Burke or Webster were able *to see wider* into their past and so found the sharpest tool for present use (*C*, XII, 98).[25]

Even if only for this vocabulary, the scholar was asked to follow Emerson's example, to become "covetous of action" (*C*, I, 98). "We can help ourselves . . ." he wrote, "only by coarse material experiences" (*C*, XII, 97). Because the language of spirit depended on the language of fact, an active life was necessary "to the end of mastering in all their facts a language by which to illustrate and embody our perceptions" (*C*, I, 98).[26] Burke's imagery, Emerson complained, was secondary or book-derived, but Webster's was "all primary," that is, natural. "Let a man make the woods and fields his books," Emerson early advised himself, "then at the hour of passion his thoughts will invest themselves with natural imagery" (*J*, III, 567). If Thoreau — Emerson's ideal of sympathetic correspondence and organic expression — occupied the long intervals between ecstasy with a naturalist's scrutiny of objects, he never did so in the interest of mere natural history but to advance his sympathetic union with nature and his command of her language. Similarly, Emerson preferred the "resources" of the country to those of the city. "The first care of a man settling in the country," he commented after a long life at Concord, "should be to open the face of the earth to himself by a little knowledge of Nature, or a great deal of knowledge, if he can, of birds, plants, and astronomy" (*J*, IX, 417).

Nature was, of course, of first importance to the scholar because it symbolized his spirit. But Emerson emphasized nature once more by making it a proper field of action (*C*, I, 84–85). It was, in fact, the primary field of action for man thinking and man symbolizing because, as the terminus of spirit, its symbols were not "ephemeral and local, but the universal symbols of thought" (*J*, IV, 180). He delighted in studies like the *Report of Herbaceous Plants in Massachusetts* and the *Fourth Report of the Agriculture of Massachusetts*, because the names of plants were metaphorical and image-evoking (*J*, VI, 193–194, 196). Natural symbols needed no translation, and, as he noted of Proclus's lusters, taught him to use them to "express his spiritual history . . . in such images as have a private significance to him" (*J*, VI, 159–160). For even though his symbols had private meanings, as the owl did for example (*J*, V, 82), he felt that just as he shared the eternal so they shared the universal. Furthermore, "The knowledge of nature is *most permanent*," he recorded; "clouds and grass are older antiquities than pyramids or Athens; then they are *most perfect*" (*J*, III, 284). And for this reason, in pursuit of images, life in nature was preferable to all others.

"Natural History," he added, "gives *body* to our knowledge" (*J*, III, 284). It was the archive of language, the dictionary of life. For, he wrote in *Nature*, all language in its beginnings was the naming of natural facts, and primary writers recreated the language by holding "primarily on nature" (*C*, I, 25, 30). By returning to nature the symbol-maker appropriated images that never lost their power to affect all men: his language became a language of things instead of words. No longer were books, essential to the scholar as the record of spirit in the past, to remain the source of life and of language. Men were to be educated to things not words (*C*, III, 257).

To do this the Platonists, he noted, used images where the Scottish Realists anatomized and analyzed (*J*, VII, 7); and in the literature of the seventeenth century, which he felt spiritually closest to him, the language of nature was the staple of every book. The use of the concrete, homely image to cover a principle so that the image carried the truth to both the sense and the intellect — this he found best represented in Thomas Shepard, whom, like Edwards, Emerson especially honored (*J*, III, 529; VI, 193). Shepard was an example of what Emerson (and Edwards, too, although unbeknown to Emerson) desired: the regeneration of language, and through language as the conveyancing of reality, of men [27] (*C*, I, 30). When he spoke of making the word one with the thing, he meant that the word had to follow a perception of the thing, and had, as the vehicle of that perception, to evoke the sensuously felt image of the thing in the mind. Words had not only to be intellectually entertained, they had to be felt, they had to elicit the total response which Edwards had rightly called "the sense of the heart" (*J*, IV, 169–170; VI, 29).

It was in this way that "a good word lets us into the world" (*J*, IX, 88). Correspondence as a doctrine of expression was not, as Emerson used it, the assigning of symbolic value to an object. It was, instead, the *perception* of the symbolic import of an object: a way to apprehend reality. To stand as realized symbols, objects had to recreate in others this perception of the reality behind things. The symbol's office was, as the vehicle of Reason, to lift the mind above the fact (the apparent) to its spiritual freedom (*J*, III, 492). But Emerson found that although images stimulated the fancy, they did not necessarily stimulate the Reason (*C*, I, 35). The unconscious truth he transformed for himself into a new weapon by defining in an object was powerless, unless the receiver, too, " 'interpreted it by the same spirit which gave it forth' " (*C*, I, 35). And this required for complete communication that men come into the poet's vision, share his angle of vision, and behold the universe with his eyes.[28] And this required the dialetic method as Emerson employed it, not to convey facts, but to lead others in the path of perception.[29] "What baulks all language," he wrote, "is the broad, radiating, immensely distributive action of Nature or spirit. If it were linear, if it were successive, step by step, jet by jet, like our small human agency, we could follow it with language; but it mocks us" (*J*, IX, 114). If, however, by following the fragments of perception one reached the circle of reality and discovered his own centrality, then any object rightly seen thereafter might become an arc of the circle and overcome the limitations of language. For although as a doctrine of expression, correspondence led others to insight, in the history of the mind it followed from the sympathetic correspondence with nature, which alone prepared the mind to see nature as the expositor of the divine mind. Only "a life in harmony with nature, the love of truth and virtue," Emerson affirmed from his own experience, "will purge the eyes to understand her text" (*C*, I, 35). Language was not its substitute. Only a life in nature supplied the images, the pattern of their unfolding, and the spirit with which they could be read.

5

Spheral Man

I don't like linear, but spheral people.

Every man's system should appear in his ascetic.

The only way into nature is to enact our best insight. . . Do what you know, and perception is converted into character.

EMERSON, *Journals.*

We value man's whole nature; man's whole nature is essential. . . We should retain and develop all our faculties, each in its place, so as to preserve unbroken harmony through the whole man.

ORESTES BROWNSON, Review of Benjamin Constant's *De la religion, considérée dans sa source, ses formes et ses développements.*

The brave man is a perfect sphere.

THOREAU, *The Service.*

In Emerson's natural history of the intellect, the mind was the transformer of experience, and expression was necessary to its health. To be complete, the process of thought had to end in action, the first stage of which was the publication of insight in symbolic correspondences. But once more this expression was only mediate: as the fruition of the poet's mind, expression for Emerson was often considered a terminal action; but it was a form of action only when it stimulated insight in others and led to a more thorough expression of ideas than words could provide: the act of language, unless heated in the character and transformed into eloquence, was not a whole act. Emerson was aware of the limitations of language. "Words," he wrote, "are finite organs of the infinite mind. They cannot cover the dimensions of what is in truth. They break, chop, and impoverish it" (*C*, I, 44–45). Language, preceding discipline in his account of the uses of nature, served best by unlocking the faculties, by making unconscious truth "a new weapon in the magazine of power" (*C*, I, 35). By providing the unconscious truth with its objective expression, it transformed it into an instrument of power, which in turn could be more completely expressed in action. For action, giving living form to the idea, was "the perfection and publication of thought" (*C*, I, 45). In action, insight found its most complete embodiment, and man, nature's highest form in the chain of being, was the most complete and living symbol of truth. Insight, then, was best realized in character, and insight in Emerson's vision demanded an active life (*C*, III, 105).

Experience, transformed into ideas by the symbolization of the mind, had to be enacted by informing the conduct of life. For Emerson the aim of life was to extend the inner order one achieved by his angle of vision to the outward, active order of character: on the level of the actual, the quest of reality became the quest of character; and inversely, the quest of character through action became the quest of reality. If expression was most naturally realized by unfolding ideas after the pattern of the chain of being, similarly man best developed character by living that unfolding, by rising through the chain, from sensually to spiritually directed behavior. "The excellence of men," Emerson noted, "consists

in the completeness with which the lower system is taken up
into the higher" (*J*, VIII, 45). The excellence of men was in
the supremacy of the higher faculties.

Emerson's conception of the hero extended his conception
of the genius — one who saw and expressed ideas — to the
plane of action, for the hero courageously applied ideas in
the arena of life. Unlike the man of talent and prudence,
cowed by conformity into the withering of his natural gifts,
the heroic genius ensphered the idea by making himself a
spheral man. He had the rare courage Emerson saw in John
Brown and Thoreau and Alcott (and, of course, in himself).
Such "courage charms us," Emerson wrote, "because it indicates that a man loves an idea better than all things in the
world, that he is thinking neither of his bed, nor his dinner,
nor his money, but will venture all to put in act the invisible
thought of his mind" (*J*, IX, 246). Ideas enacted — this was,
for Emerson, the most concrete and living correspondence, the
moral of biography, and the truly symmetrical expression of
a genuinely religious life (*Y*, 188).

Sympathetic correspondence with nature and its published
symbolic correspondences were, for Emerson, only the preparation for the conduct of life. The spiritual conduct of life
was his central theme; the ethics of identity preoccupied his
labors. In the course of one year's preaching, he devoted half
of his sermons to the problems of character (*Y*, 227); and all
through his life he affirmed the life in nature and the life of
vision only to help men crystallize what he thought they already knew but needed further assurance in knowing — "that
a man wants to feel himself backed by a superior nature"
(*Y*, 154).[1] Certain of this, like Emerson, they would leave off
the worship of historic personages and live to transform the
world into themselves. In their developing characters they
would more and more approximate the image of God and like
Jesus would become living divinities. For, to Emerson, Jesus

was the best image of God, because "he was a better man than any other," a *man* whose divinity was easily recognized in "the majesty of his character" (*Y*, 234).[2]

In this sense, character was the ultimate realization of life, just as, for Emerson, character was "the highest name at which philosophy has arrived." Such a character, the product of self-reliance and self-culture, provided the stable center of a world of illusion and flux. Allied to spirit, such a character lived in the moment and radiated its serenity in all the acts of life. In this centrality there was also the power to live by ideas and to withstand with genial indifference the pressures of society. Such a character, which Emerson apostrophized in "Works and Days," made life in the world bearable for him. "There are people," he wrote, "who do not need much experimenting; who, after years of activity, say, we knew all this before; who love at first sight and hate at first sight; discern the affinities and repulsions; who do not care so much for conditions as others, for they are always in one condition, and enjoy themselves; who dictate to others, and are not dictated to; who in their consciousness of deserving success constantly slight the ordinary means of attaining it; who have self-existence and self-help; who are suffered to be themselves in society; who are great in the present; who have no talents, or care to have them, — being that which was before talent, and shall be after it, and of which talent seems only a tool — this is character, the highest name at which philosophy has arrived" (*C*, VII, 183–184).

To create such characters, molded after his own representative needs, was the pragmatic reward of acting out the hypothesis of idealism as Emerson used it. In the desire to become a spheral man, to touch the universe on all sides, to merge with it and transform it into himself, correspondence provided the way to all experience. Even if one confronted the universe only in the limited arc of individual experience, still the faith in the doctrine of leasts — in representative parts and representative levels or degrees — guaranteed its circularity and universality. Read correspondentially, history, too, aggrandized the self (*C*, II, 38). Everything, the past of books and the present of nature, could be assimilated by the self; for the self became spheral in what George Herbert Mead has called "the reflexive mood of self-awareness," [3] in what we have already seen as the projection of the self in the forms of nature. Only by objectifying itself was the self knowable, and only by taking up all the world as itself, was its sphericity attained. This appetite for all experience as the realization of the self is nowhere better revealed by Emerson than in his record of a dream. Here, perhaps, he best represents the powers of assimilation he attributed to his alter-ego, Osman [4] (*J*, IX, 199). "I dreamed," he wrote, "that I floated at will in the great Ether, and I saw this world floating also not far off, but diminished to the size of an apple. Then an angel took it in his hand and brought it to me and said, 'This thou must eat.' And I ate the world" (*J*, V, 485).

Unfortunately, the world Emerson knew was not an apple and could not be so easily and deliciously eaten. The world he dreamed of eating in one gulp had to be assimilated piece by piece, in time, as the faculties developed through use and as his affinities widened. He had first to *domesticate* himself in nature, and by means of his humanly unique *adaptiveness* range widely in the world, mastering " 'the whole mass of reality in all its ramifications' " (*J*, VII, 103).[5] He had to find the objects that, because they corresponded, would unlock his faculties and admit him into the world. The world was not given to him by ministering angels, but seized by resisting circumstance, by the discipline of poverty and disease (*J*, VI, 309), and by the duration of life itself and the long battle to climb out of the chains of the senses into spiritual freedom. Character was formed by resisting circumstances, but action,

which alone repaired the character (gave it the force to resist),
was founded on Reality (*C*, III, 96, 101). Limited to his human share of gifts, and perhaps unaware of them, man still
had the compensation of his limitations: those he had,
prompted by the affections, by desire and instinct, found, by
an irresistible magnetism (the spirit working everywhere),
their appropriate objects and ways into the world. The faculties were the organs and channels of God, and the first step in
the conduct of life was their education by active life.

Emerson's theory of the faculties, like his theory of the
image, affirmed that the universe was fitted to fulfill man's
desires and growth. The images by which he expressed his
thought were adequate because both man and nature shared
the living spirit, and the faculties domesticated man in the
universe because they, too, were but modes of God's action.[6]
The faculties were the seeds planted in man in anticipation
of the nutrition they were to find ready for them in a universe
designed to call them forth. Every faculty man possessed, every
desire, however vague, was a promise that the universe would
answer to and fulfill them. The eye, for example, was an anticipation of the life of vision; it was part of man's equipment,
a tool that demanded use and was sharpened by use, and had
a corresponding world in which to exercise its powers. An
imperfect copy of God's perfection, every faculty was designed
for benefit (*Y*, 85). When only seventeen, Emerson wrote:
"We are not fashioned thus marvelously for nought. The
straining conceptions of man, the monuments of his reason
and the whole furniture of his faculties is [sic] adapted to
mightier views of things than the mightiest he has yet beheld"
(*J*, I, 74). And this faith that the faculties were guarantees of
benefit remained in the undiminished optimism of his later
thought. He called it "the doctrine of trusts" ("O believe as
thou livest that every sound that is spoken over the round

world which thou oughtest to hear will vibrate on thine ear"), and it was this deeper assurance that nothing he needed for his self-perfection was wanting in God's order that underlay his more individualistic assertion of self-reliance (*J*, V, 285).[7]

In his first sermon, "Pray Without Ceasing" (1826), he reinterpreted prayer as the petitioning of the desires in the heart, as the awakening of the faculties. Not in shallow verbal prayer, he said, but in "*every desire of the human mind*" men pray without ceasing (*Y*, 4). Ceremonial prayers, second-hand sentiments were mockeries: "The true prayers are the daily, hourly, momentary desires, that come without impediment, without fear, into the soul, and bear testimony at each instant to its shifting character" (*Y*, 5). These prayers, he was assured, were always granted, and propelled by his desire man achieved its object, because there "is a commission to nature, there is a charge to the elements made out in the name of the Author of events, whereby they shall help the purposes of man, (a preëxistent harmony between thoughts and things) whereby prayers shall become effects, and these warm imaginations settle down into events" (*Y*, 6). Emerson chose the hypothesis of idealism, because without it he felt that the petitioning of the faculties would go unanswered. He believed, as he preached in this sermon, that God had "furnished us with powers of body and of mind that we can acquire whatsoever we seriously and unceasingly strive after" (*Y*, 5). As he pointed out in another sermon, the whole universe ministered to the humble blackberry (*Y*, 207–208). And similarly the universe ministered to man: "For it is the very root and rudiment of the relation of man to this world, that we are in a condition of wants which have their appropriate gratifications *within our reach*; and that we have faculties that can bring us to our ends that are near neighbors to their objects; and our free agency consists in this, that we are able to reach those sources of gratification, on which our election falls" (*Y*, 5). Self-reli-

ance followed, and self-culture,[8] the discipline and active unfolding of the faculties, was enjoined by the constitution of
the universe. It was a practical doctrine, Emerson emphasized:
"Certainly, my friends, it is not a small thing that we have
learned . . . it cannot fail to elevate very much our conception of our relations and our duties. Weep no more for human
frailty, weep no more for what there may be of sorrow in the
past or of despondence in the present hour. Spend no more
unavailing regrets for the goods of which God in his Providence has deprived you. Cast away this sickly despair that
eats into the soul debarred from high events and noble gratification. Beware of easy assent to false opinion, to low employment, to small vices, out of a reptile reverence to men of
consideration in society. Beware, (if it teach nothing else let
it teach this) beware of indolence, the suicide of the soul, that
lets the immortal faculties, each in their orbit of light, wax
dim and feeble, and star by star expire. . . Weep not for
man's frailty . . . he is no puny sufferer tottering, ill at ease,
in the universe, but a being of giant energies, architect of his
fortunes, master of his eternity" (*Y*, 7–8).[9]

Man was the architect of his fortunes, because, like the tools
he invented and used, the faculties grew out of his structure
and needs (*C*, VII, 157). Self-culture began with the education
of the faculties, and education, for Emerson, was properly
"*e-ducation* or calling out of . . . faculties" (*J*, III, 276).[10]
Whatever attracted one, caught his attention, and evoked a
total response or enthusiasm signalized the direction of growth
(*C*, VI, 277). When Emerson admonished his congregation to
reconsider the education of children, he ended by saying what
Alcott confirmed in practice, "O quench not his hope, O do
not repress one impulse of enthusiasm" (*Y*, 52). For in hopes
and enthusiasms were the leading predictions of life.[11] He
gave this brotherly advice to Edward Emerson, reminding him
that although men rely on circumstances for the unfolding

of their faculties, he was not advocating "the cant of the
pupilage of *circumstances.*" By altering circumstances (the
Emersonian word for environment), New Harmony — and
later he would have included Brook Farm — did not necessarily transform the character. It might, however, provide an
increased scope for action which in turn might release some
latent gift. New occasions had this virtue and were not to be
foregone. He ventured this "ancient truism," and added, what
by now was another, for Edward's edification, "That the Mind
is something to be unfolded & will disclose some faculties
more & some less just in proportion to the room & excitements
for action that are furnished it" (*L*, I, 220). The corollary that
followed has sometimes been mistaken for laissez-faire indifference. But when Emerson disavowed circumstance, he was
saying, in effect, that all circumstances provide a beginning in
self-culture, that wherever one finds himself, there is the best
place to begin, and that one could safely be indifferent to
circumstance for whatever faculty was unlocked was a sufficient channel of the spirit. Edward, then, could begin his
career by lecturing at the Mechanics Institutes without any
regrets that he was not on a more advantageous platform.

Much of this doctrine of the faculties Emerson adopted
from Sampson Reed's *Growth of the Mind.* Like Emerson,
Reed believed that the highest use of nature was man's moral
discipline. Not only did nature provide nutriment (commodity) and language, but it "was precisely and perfectly adapted
to invigorate and strengthen the intellectual and moral man."
"It was intended," Reed wrote, "to draw forth the latent
energies of the soul; to impart to them its own verdure and
freshness; to initiate them into its own mysteries; and by its
silent and humble dependence on its Creator, to leave on
them when it is withdrawn by death, the full impression of
his likeness." [12] Emerson agreed that the world petitioned the
faculties (*C*, II, 62), that as the "shadow of the soul," its "at-

tractions are the keys which unlock my thoughts and make me acquainted with myself" (*C*, I, 95). But the world petitioned, because the faculties, anticipating their use, predicted the world: "Does not the eye of the human embryo predict the light?" he asked (*C*, II, 37). Assured that it did, he felt that the correspondence of faculty to object, of means to end, guaranteed the full use as well of the higher faculties.[13] The completion of the self — this the faculties promised in their marriage with nature, and they also promised immortality, because self-completion required "an interminable future for their play" (*C*, V, 239; *J*, II, 316; *C*, VII, 332, 338, 344).[14]

The theory of the faculties was, as the focus of Emerson's belief in man's correspondence to the universe, of great satisfaction to him in his need for an immortality that was an extension of his best moments. But the theory was also fundamental to his doctrine of compensation as he applied it to the transformation of limitations into benefits. Men — how well he acknowledged this himself! — were limited in their gifts and resources. But by discovering their limitations (another *use* of circumstances), they also discovered their unique gifts and directions. Like the mysterious powers of affection and attention which directed the mind to the objects whose images best expressed it, the internal principle of the mind unfolded by being drawn into those activities which were peculiarly fitted to its needs. Reed had stressed this again and again in the "Oration on Genius" and the *Growth of the Mind*, but nowhere better than when he wrote, "The mind must grow, not from external accretion, but from an internal principle. Much may be done by others in aid of its development; but in all that is done, it should not be forgotten, that, even from its earliest infancy, it possesses a character and a principle of freedom, which *should be* respected, and *cannot* be destroyed. Its peculiar propensities may be discerned, and proper nutriment and culture supplied; but the infant plant, not less

than the aged tree, must be permitted, with its own organs of
absorption, to separate that which is peculiarly adapted to
itself; otherwise it will be cast off as a foreign substance, or
produce nothing but rottenness and deformity" [15] Emerson
realized this in his long search for his best working attitude;
and in his frequent self-evaluations, especially when ecstasy
seemed remote, he recorded his determination to achieve it
once more. "The only condition," he wrote, "on which I can
expect a better sight is, that I put off all that is foreign. I am
still busy in that initial endeavor, I have not yet arrived at
virtue [complete self-realization]. I burn in purgatory still"
(*J*, V, 259). He was seeking what Reed had called the *peculium*
of the mind. Reed had enjoined men "to seek and to cherish
this *peculium* of our own minds, as the patrimony which is
left us by our Father in heaven — as that by which the branch
is united to the vine — as the forming power within us, which
gives to our persons that by which they are distinguished from
others; and by a life entirely governed by the commandments
of God, to leave on the duties we are called to perform the
full impress of our real characters." [16] Emerson appropriated
this notion of peculium and modified it to fit his astronomy
of imagination. Just as compensation for him was an extension
of the law of gravity, so peculium (which he variously named
"temperament," "bias," or, following Swedenborg, *probrium*)
was the extension of magnetism to the plane of moral action.[17]
The magnet in man, his bias or polarity, had its own true
north (*J*, X, 139–140) and responded to the moral forces, the
perpetual forces, of the universe (*J*, IX, 489). A mystery of
recent science and one of the spectacular demonstrations in
popular scientific lectures, magnetism early attracted Emerson
who saw in it, as he noted Goethe had, "a primary phenome-
non," the symbolic interpretation of which he especially
valued (*J*, X, 409–410). "I have seen a skilful experimenter,"
Emerson recorded in 1827, "lay a magnet among filings of

steel, and the force of that subtle fluid, entering each fragment, arranged them all in mathematical lines, and each metallic atom became in its turn a magnet communicating all the force it received of the loadstone" (*J*, II, 213). The loadstone exhibited the properties of the over-soul, and he entered John Adams' comment on it in his journal: " 'This substance is in the secret of the whole globe. It must have a sympathy with the whole globe' " (*J*, VIII, 229). Natural science, indeed, supplied him the basis of spiritual symbolism! (*J*, III, 192–193).[18]

Although he always felt that each individual had his own north, he found this confirmed in Professor Michael Faraday's researches in diamagnetism or cross-magnetism. Emerson recorded in "Greatness" that in 1848 he had heard Faraday lecture on this discovery — Emerson knew that in science was the stuff of correspondencies and on all of his European trips sought out the newest information in lectures. What he found in Faraday's discourse was another proof of the "adaptation of man to the world, and to every part and particle of it." For Faraday had shown "that whilst, ordinarily, magnetism of steel is from north to south, in other substances, gases, it acts from east to west." This was a tremendous "fact" for Emerson's use of magnetism in the spiritual attraction of character. The theory that Faraday advanced, "that every chemical substance would be found to have its own, and a different, polarity," made it clear to Emerson that "diamagnetism is a law of the *mind*," or as he expressed its spiritual interpretation, "that every mind has a new compass, a new north, a new direction of its own, differencing its genius and aims from every other mind." It made clear, too, that the private leading was in reality one's only sure road to spirit, that "whilst he shares with all mankind the gift of reason, and the moral sentiment, there is a teaching for him from within, which is leading him in a new path, and, the more it is trusted, separates and signalizes him, while it makes him more important and necessary to society" (*C*, VIII, 306–307).

Forty years later Emerson, still within the metaphor, completed the youthful passage by adding, "When we come into the world, a wonderful whisper gives us a direction for the whole road. . . This whisper wonderfully impresses us, and is temperament, taste, bearing, talent. 'Tis like the card of the compass, which arranges itself with the poles of the world" (*J*, X, 187). But by then he knew that even when the tendency was recognized and one had expended himself in seeking his spiritual north, the leadings were as nothing if the magnetic force withdrew. For all of his egotism, Emerson was never an Ahab who confidently aligned the compass of his ship by his own magnetic force. He knew that magnetism was the equivalent of spirit, not temperament, and that therefore "the needles are nothing, the magnetism is all" (*J*, VII, 67). Temperament was sensual, prudential prompting, and one could not safely follow it. Only when temperament (individualism) was properly overcome by spirit, that is, properly directed, was it a sure guide; and even then, because it seemed to be an intermittent force, one had continually to get his bearing and could not rest in its first attraction.

Like the flux of nature, temperament existed on the prudential level, and was something to be overcome (*C*, X, 73). The strait jacket of the hereditary self, it was comparable to the first circle of nature — a limitation, not to be rested in, but *used*, as a circumference was, for new views of the spirit (*C*, III, 50–55). If one limited himself to the mastery of one gift, if one specialized or made his gift a talent, then temperament was easily recognized in one's bias or preoccupation. In this way one's bias was a filter or lens unconsciously held before the eye, distorting one's vision. Without another bias (point of view), or without the influx that widened one's angle beyond the limitations of temperament, one was like any of the seven men Emerson moralized about in his parable. Seven men, he wrote, came into the same field: the farmer saw only the grass, the astronomer the horizon and stars, the physician a stagnant pond, a soldier the obstacles of the terrain, and so forth (*J*, X, 146–147). Each needed new biases, new perspectives and angles of vision to round out his limitations, and it was the office of the unfolding faculties, called into action by the demands of new scope, to provide them (*C*, VIII, 138). But even before action called out one's latent gifts, the self pointed out the way in the secret promptings of dreams.

In dreams one objectified his desires and prophesied his bias (*C*, II, 148). In the analogy of day and night, dreams were to the night of the mind — the preparation of repose — as their fulfillment was to the day of action. "The pictures of the night," Emerson wrote, "will always bear some proportion to the visions of the day" (*J*, IV, 323). For this reason self-culture neither overlooked nor overemphasized their importance. If, as he wrote in "Quatrains,"

> *Night-dreams trace on Memory's wall*
> *Shadows of the thoughts of day;*
> *And thy fortunes as they fall*
> *The bias of thy will betray.*

what they revealed was the "infirmities of our character." They were exaggerations of the *individual*, of the "Ego partial" or lawless will. Not quite certain of what proportion dreams had to day, he was certain that in them he saw his "evil genius" and that what they signified often bordered on the demonologic, unless the "Ego total" interpreted them (*C*, X, 20).[19] He was inclined to include dreams with coincidences, animal magnetism, omens, and sacred lots, to limit their prophecy by reducing them to the physiological level of life (*C*, X, 23–24). They were not properly the work of the spirit, and yet they had a spiritual value for self-culture by acquainting him with what the day omitted (*J*, VI, 179). They revealed the temperament, the house from which the spirit was to be freed (*C*, VI, 9).

But if "men are what their mothers made them," if one had *his* temperament and no other, if when man came "forth from his mother's womb, the gate of gifts closes behind him," if "he has but one future, and that already predetermined in his lobes, and described in that little fatty face, pig-eye, and squat form" (*C*, VI, 10–11), still his very limitations pointed out the compensatory ways in which he might become spheral. Temperament was fate, but, like fate, could be *transformed* into necessitated freedom, or character. What the squat form *became* mattered most, for the end of character was not a brute but an erect man.[20]

The beginning of transformation took place in the choice of calling one seemed necessarily to follow from the dictates of his *peculium*, the seedling planted in his temperament. Sampson Reed wrote what Emerson reaffirmed in "Find Your Calling" (*Y*, 163–169): "We should seek an employment for the mind, in which all of its energies may be warmed [an interesting word] into existence; which . . . may bring every muscle into action. There is something which every one can do better than any one else; and it is this tendency, and must be the end, of human events, to assign to each his true calling."[21] How difficult finding this calling was, Emerson knew from his own indirect course to Concord, and that it "may be hidden from him for years" (*Y*, 167). And he knew that, even though the diversifications of work in an advancing society opened up callings fitted to most men, one still had, if necessary to his best working attitude, to avoid falling too easily into the place society seemed to think his own. "Even now," he preached, perhaps preparing his congregation for his departure, "we occasionally see an individual forsake all the usual paths of life and show men a new one better fitted than any other to his own powers" (*Y*, 166). As the representative man of his times, Emerson's choice of calling was an experiment in finding the place best fitted to develop the man of vision. No oracle — church or institution — could pronounce on the necessary mode of life (*L*, II, 222); only the individual in his own self-reflection could determine the appropriate "ascetic" (*J*, III, 416–417). And because what the individuals discovered, when judged against the socially-approved callings, often appeared peculiar, he remarked that men hid their gifts and shriveled themselves to the awaiting mold. The very gifts society suppressed were their unique contributions: although the expression of the individual, these gifts were not individual in the temperamental sense alone. They were the impress of God, and when given voice spoke from the spirit of man. One's individual gift "called" him to the one thing he could do, and it was toward this goal that Emerson saw Christianity (and specialization) tending: eventually every individual would have a unique occupation (*Y*, 166). The perfect character was individual, the result of acting out the unique qualities one had. As Emerson wrote in "Trust Yourself," "I believe God gave to every man the germ of a peculiar character. . . And the more finished the character, the more striking is its individuality; and the better is the state of the world, the more unlike will be men's characters, and the more similar their purposes" (*Y*, 106). If men would cease striving "to hide all that is peculiar and would say [and act out] only what was uppermost in their own minds after their own individual manner, every man would be interesting." He wrote this to Aunt Mary Moody Emerson in 1827, and in it was the message of "Manners" and "Behavior" and "Culture," all the overt results of speaking out of the center of one's reliance. And he added the reason for the attractiveness (in the intercourse of men it was the irresistible magnetism of character) of such individual behavior: "Every man is a new creation; can do something best;

has some intellectual modes & forms or a character the general result of all, such as no other agent in the universe has; if he would exhibit that it must needs be engaging[,] must be a curious study to every inquisitive mind" (*L*, I, 207). In this individuality or originality of calling — "Let him scorn to *imitate* any being. Let him scorn to be a secondary man" — man was justified (*Y*, 108). His justification was in the "force of the feeling" (*Y*, 168), in the calling of the faculties themselves (*Y*, 166).

The faculty theory, then, was a convenient belief, that one's limitations or unique gifts *were* his calling. It transformed the individual concern with self-culture into a public duty, for one served best by making oneself an organ of spirit.[22] And, for Emerson at least, it rationalized the constitutional unfitness he felt in the demands of social life and made his removal to Concord the welcome call of the beckoning spirit. And after the fact, to judge by the results, who can deny that for Emerson it was?

For at Concord he found a calling in which he could express his love of nature and the perfect science of life and action (*J*, IV, 32). Here, as we have seen, he found his *habitat*, the conditions corresponding to the demands of his faculties (*C*, VI, 37). Here he found a way of life that he was doubly certain expressed his desires because it was the way of life corresponding to his first thought. He always felt in the similarity of first and third thoughts a special insistence, a verification of compensation. "Write about the coincidence of first and third thoughts," he began a sketch of a sermon, "and apply it to affairs." First thoughts were often distrusted because they seemed insupportable; they were indications of individual defect when compared to the opinion of society. But nevertheless these "defects" were the "shadows of our virtues." For first thoughts were God-given (*J*, III, 323): "God has the first word. The devil [society] has the second, but God has the last word.

We distrust the first thought because we can't give the reason for it. Abide by it, there is a reason, and by and by, long hence, perhaps it will appear" (*J*, II, 435–436). And this was what Emerson himself actually did in the long apprenticeship to his calling. In 1827, contemplating his thwarted ambition on the lonely wastes of St. Augustine, he reconsidered his early genius for the life of literature (*L*, I, 188). After his return to Boston, the Harvard Divinity School, and the Second Church — after his attempt to socialize his first thought — he heeded his third thought (*L*, I, 354).[23] In his famous letter to Edward Emerson, in which he elaborated on the Reason and Understanding, Emerson identified first thoughts with the "revelations of Reason" and saw in this distinction the key to literature, the church, and life. By then (1834), Ellen Tucker's death and her estate had made his third thought a practical one (*L*, I, 412–414), and he turned to nature for the freedom of action, the freedom to shape an "ascetic" by which he might live truly and see truly (*C*, II, 68). The insistent third thought made this his duty and called him to the country for the education of the higher faculties and the discipline of the active soul (*C*, I, 90). It was symmetrical expression he wanted — not the understanding of the city, but the reason of the country — and he felt in his own needs that the time had come, as indeed the literature of the day announced, to seek the life of his higher faculties in the life of Nature. The magnetism of the spirit was irresistible.

II

The search for symmetrical expression did not mean, as one might suppose from Emerson's choice of the life of reason in nature, that the higher faculties alone were to be exercised. Man was, the transcendentalists had above all else proclaimed, a creature of two worlds, equipped with two sets of faculties for an active life in both (*Y*, 113, 116). In their reaction to sensationalism and the dominance of the faculties of sense and understanding, they did indeed seem to cherish the life of reason as an end in itself.[24] But even a hasty reading of their journals shows that the largest measure of their lives was given over to the senses, that their problem was not so much a permanent merger with spirit, but its mediation in a life necessarily lived on a prudential level. Even when Alcott, with his amazing insight into his friends, elevated Emerson as "our best and almost sole example of the nobler type," he did not hesitate to add that he was "American in his understanding — dealing with affairs in a style quite mercantile, as if he were born within a wall and had a Threadneedle Street in his brain, as well as . . . a world of ideas." [25] And certainly Emerson, for all of his talk of heroism and living after the higher law, was a model of prudence; and this makes him, I think, all the more courageous and representative of the aims of transcendentalism. He and all his fellow transcendentalists, Jones Very excepted, were never guilty of the charge of mysticism to which their affirmations of reason opened them. In all their penetrating analyses of the two streams of Materialism and Spiritualism,[26] of sensationalism and intuitionalism, they recognized the ever-widening breach they believed they had to bridge once more for their generation. They sought a solution in the mediation of the two, for which, in every particular of their thought — language, character, theology — correspondence, as the way of mediation, was the most inclusive word.

The new life they proposed for themselves was, as Emerson named it for them, that of the mid-world (*C*, III, 64), the world where thought became one with action. Once again, thinking of the polar universe man was to span, Emerson wrote, "The middle region of our being is the temperate zone. We may climb into the thin and cold realm of pure geometry and life-less science, or sink into that of sensation. Between these extremes is the equator of life, of thought, of spirit, of poetry, — a narrow belt" (*C*, III, 62). Because it was a narrow line, Emerson knew that it was hard "to keep the middle point" (*J*, VI, 326). And even though the stupendous antagonisms between spirit and sense created the tensions of his thought and life, still the spanning of the worlds was his aim: in poetry to express the universal in the particular, the abstract in the concrete; in the total expression of character to give ideas their blood-warmth, to remain at once public and individual. On the level of action, then, correspondence was the mediation of the prudential and spiritual worlds, or perhaps more accurately, the prudential spiritualism which became the ethical goal of transcendentalism.

That man was a creature of two worlds was an obvious truth of the transcendentalists' insistence on double consciousness. In "Religion and Society," the title itself indicating the two worlds the Unitarians had failed to unite, Emerson said what George Ripley, Frederic Hedge, Brownson, and others were beginning to emphasize, that man was split within himself. "I recognize," Emerson said, "the distinction of the outer and inner self — of the double consciousness — as in the familiar example, that I may do things which I do not approve; that is, there are two selfs, one which does or approves that which the other does not and approves not" (*Y*, 200). Within man, the bipolarity of the universe was duplicated in the prudential self, acting after the needs of the senses, and the spiritual self, acting after the intuitions from its own infinite depths. Both promptings had to be followed — one for brute existence and survival, the other for human fruition and deification — but the spiritual, the more public and universal, had the higher claim, because it alone tapped the perpetual forces and gave wholeness to the partial acts of the senses. There was no equality of selves in man, no easy equilibrium: like the good and evil principles in the universe, they were forever at war. But this warfare was mutually rewarding and was, just as Emerson viewed the problem of evil, a perpetual antagonism between the partial and the whole. The "low" self was the partial but active self, and the whole self was the container or soul of man's entire being (*Y*, 182). The acts of the partial self had therefore to become symbolic acts, that is, acts in which the whole self could be seen and realized. And it was not only for the purpose of calling out the faculties that action was prescribed; it was necessary also to this expression of the soul. The soul or inner self was in Emerson's discipline a quiet center removed from the circumference of action, but as necessary to it as the center to the circle. The soul, in a description reflecting Emerson's own habits, was domestic. He said that it "sits at home, and does not learn to do things, nor value these feats at all." It was "a quiet, wise perception," retired from prudential time and living in the "great present" like the melon in *Nature* expanding in the sun (*C*, VII, 311). An intaking self like the receptive pole of the mind, it needed the balance of the active constructive external self for its publication.

The external self was active after the manner of the American stereotype: it left home and retirement ever mindful, as the American success was supposed to be, of the main chance. This was the self, Emerson said, that "is educated at school, taught to read, write, cipher, and trade; taught to grasp all the boy can get, urging him to put himself forward, to make himself useful and agreeable in the world, to ride, run, argue, and contend, unfold his talents, shine, conquer, and possess" (*C*, VII, 311). Such a self, obviously, followed a different law than that of the domestic self; and to bring them into harmony, Emerson knew, required rare skill. The degree of difficulty in balancing these selves drew from Emerson an illustration expressing uncommon nimbleness and balance. "A man," he wrote, "must ride alternately on the horses of his private and public nature, as the equestrians in the circus throw themselves nimbly from horse to horse, or plant one foot on the back of one, and the other foot on the back of the other" (*C*, VI, 47). He did not approve of those who rode securely on the horse of sense, for he knew that the senses carried the rider along the road of Fate to inevitable ruin. Occasionally, at least, one needed a less secure mount, needed to catch the spiritual steed, quickly distance the road, discover its obstructions, and see its terminus in freedom. Only then was the plodding of the senses bearable.

This awareness of the two worlds, two selves, or two platforms of life made it the transcendentalist duty to unite them in character. "Man," he wrote, "is not order of nature, sack and sack, belly and members, link in a chain, nor any ignominious baggage, but a stupendous antagonism, a dragging together of the poles of the Universe" (*C*, VI, 22). None of the transcendentalists — perhaps because their Puritan heritage remained in a sense of duty and prudence — ever felt justified, as Emerson noted of Plotinus, in living united with God and separate from the actual world of events. Because of the difficulty of maintaining the soul in a world of trade, the quiet mystical removal to God appealed to them, but they were not sufficiently free of the sin of ambition or the desire for social usefulness (and prominence) to make it their salvation. For all their contemplation, they were active, but in their action they scorned the other alternative, even with its great rewards, of uniting with the world and having "no communion with the Divine" (*J*, IV, 149–150). Whatever the occupation, their ideal man joined Reason and common sense, was yoked to the Real at one end and at the other to the apparent. In the two areas of life in which they found callings best fitted to harmonizing the poles, their representative men were Jesus and Shakespeare. Jesus was great, according to Emerson, because he dwelt "in mind with pure God" and dwelt "in social position and hearty

love with fishers and women." And Shakespeare drew "direct
from the soul at one end" and pierced "into the play-going
populace at the other." And interestingly, when Emerson
spoke of spanning the two poles, he indicated that the activity
of transmitting spirit to the prudential pole was to be socially
useful. The great man, he wrote, "should occupy the whole
space between God and the mob" (*J*, IV, 149–150).[27]

Prudential action in itself was not the great difficulty. Living on the prudential platform, where the law of compensation quickly punished and educated one to virtue, one soon
enough felt the rough edge of matter, its inescapable laws,
and, if only for survival, abided by them. One was sufficiently
prepared for life on this level by society — by church, school,
and trade — and needed only the common sense to accommodate himself to and rest his success in the expediency of prudential laws. The difficulty came with the awakening of the
whole self to the spiritual law and with the awareness that the
laws of the partial self were expedients not absolutes. Spirit
often announced its presence by freeing the partial self from
the restrictions imposed on it by society, and for this reason it
was considered lawless and enthusiastic by the decorous Unitarians. In fact, the sense of restriction, growing from the desire of the instincts[28] for release or expression, was the first
sign of the spirit. In its first manifestation it was often exces-
sively individualistic and willful, unmindful of prudential
laws and their social warrant. In this form, spirit was welcomed by young transcendentalists, who found in its release
and expansive joys an unprecedented self-realization and sense
of power. It shook them free from the society they felt paralyzing their wills and sent them in search of solitude and nature
and the calling of self-culture.[29] Here they could let out all the
length of the reins, as Emerson said, and revel in their instinctive force. And in the desire to do this they expressed their
kinship with the romanticism that the Unitarians (and later

Irving Babbitt) abhorred. Emerson, too, especially before his public chastisement for the *Divinity School Address*, glorified this sense of power and emphasized man's private nature or individual absorption of God instead of the public falling back on God of the remainder of his work. His essay on "Heroism" was really his valediction to the heroic pose he had adopted and in which he had identified himself with Byron. His first trip to Europe was in many ways a pilgrimage in which he followed Byron;[30] and however mild it seems, his removal to Concord in search of the resources he needed was in his *sturm* and *drang*, the assertion of self he had to make before he could freely accept the shackles of society.

But although he never forsook heroism, realizing that the calling out of the faculties needed this scope, his essay on "Prudence" made clear that he was done with unharnessed power. He was not quite certain that impulsive action was good *for him*; at least he could not follow it, whatever its compensations, as Byron had, into vice. In November 1838, probably because the *Divinity School Address* was more self-revealing than he desired, Emerson entered the following self-evaluation in his journal: "I should not dare to tell all my story. A great deal of it I do not yet understand. How much of it is incomplete. In my strait and decorous way of living, native to my family and to my country, and more strictly proper to me, is nothing extravagant or flowing. I content myself with moderate, languid actions, and never transgress the staidness of village manners. Herein I consult the poorness of my powers. More culture would come out of great virtues and vices perhaps, but I am not up to that. Should I obey the irregular impulse, and establish every new relation that my fancy prompted with the men and women I see, I should not be followed by my faculties; they would play me false in making good their very suggestions. They delight in inceptions, but they warrant nothing else. I see very well the beauty of sincerity, and tend that way, but if I should obey the impulse so far as to say to my fashionable acquaintance, 'You are a cox-comb, — I dislike your manners — I pray you avoid my sight,' — I should not serve him, nor me, and still less the truth; I should act quite unworthy of the truth, for I could not carry out the declaration with a sustained, even-minded frankness and love, which alone could save such a speech from rant and absurdity.

"We must tend ever to the good life" (*J*, V, 113–114). Certainly, in the conduct of his life, there was nothing extravagant or flowing. He had a dread of the extravagant and impulsive, just as he did of mysticism, because he felt they would consume his powers (*J*, IV, 213). He knew that there were "certain risks" in inspiration, and these he sought to control (*C*, VIII, 279).

In "Prudence" he studied the problem of control, which for him was the question of how to plant the genius in the earth without destroying his correspondence with the heavens. He pointed out that the genius is not a genius by disobeying the laws. Byron had done this, and even if he had his justification in the higher law of self his action made evident in time, his lawlessness ended in self-consumption and death. Instead the prudent genius obeyed the laws, for he saw in them the divine order operating in matter: he could obey them willingly and acknowledge their beautiful necessity because he saw them correspondentially. By using them as discipline, by transforming their compensations into new powers by discovering his faculties, he transcended them and used them to enrich his perceptions. In this way he accommodated himself to necessitated freedom. Like the shipwrecked men struggling in the sea of Fate, the only freedom Emerson recognized was their "right to their eye-beams," that is, the freedom of perception (*C*, VI, 19).

In the conduct of life, one had to go in the direction of law

(to some extent even social law). One could no more free himself from his reliance on matter than from his need for society;
power required form, thought required objects, and the forms
or objects, whether of expression or action, were at the prudential pole. Emerson's mysticism, then, could not be lawless
or, as he put it, subjective. Its control was in seeking the objective, and it pointed away from the center of self, just as the
self in its self-culture developed from the inside out. As the
highest fulfillment of spirit, character, too, was not self-cen-
tered culture, but the culture in which character joined with
event — in the broadest sense, socially-useful culture.[31] This
was part of the message of "Literary Ethics" — that the writer,
believing "in the presence and favor of the grandest influences," must deserve that favor by learning "how to receive
and use it, by fidelity also to the lower observances" (*C*, I, 178).
The aim of prudential spiritualism or controlled insight was,
"by the mutual reaction of thought and life, to make thought
solid, and life wise" (*C*, I, 181). The genius could not slight
common sense for Reason. "If he be defective at either extreme of the scale," Emerson wrote, "his philosophy will seem
low and utilitarian; or it will appear too vague and indefinite
for the uses of life" (*C*, I, 182). The prudential level, then, like
matter, was not to be despised; just as the faculty theory made
good use of the prudential in calling forth the latent spiritual
germ, so, once more, when the self had attained its spiritual
power, the prudential provided the rudder by which it could
be controlled.[32]

The necessity of controlled insight was, therefore, forced on
Emerson by his conception of a polar universe, and even when
control made inspiration more difficult to achieve, by the demand that it be communicated or made useful. When Emerson spoke of inspiration as power, he was always thinking of
power *to transform*, of power *realized* and concentrated in an
object. Realized in language, invention, possessions, and espe-

cially character, power was concentrated for use on the prudential level. It was stored and usable power, just as character stored the never failing power of virtue. In discussing the "ascetic" of controlled insight, Emerson said that the "one prudence in life is concentration; the one evil is dissipation" (*C*, VI, 73). By "concentration" he meant the accumulation or focusing of force which could only be had by taking "the step from knowing to doing." Inspiration was necessary, and there was a kind of "sublime prudence" in which one postponed the doing in the interest of greater influx, but ultimately inspiration served as the spasm by which man collected and swung "his whole being into one act" (*C*, I, 256; VI, 74). On the level of action, spiritual force was often recognized in this total response, in the fusion of mind and heart in outgoing activity. And as necessary as it was in making the partial whole, inspiration did not eliminate the need for the partial act or efface the partial self. Part of the common sense of genius was to "keep sight of his biographical Ego, — I have a desk, I have an office, I am hungry, I had an ague, — as rhetoric or offset to his grand spiritual Ego, without impertinence, or even confounding them" (*C*, XII, 62).

The cost of this "ascetic" of controlled insight was felt by Emerson in what he called the "health" and "decay" of his powers. "Our health," he wrote, "is our sound relation to external objects; our sympathy with external being" (*J*, V, 63). Health was the vitality and expansion of sympathetic correspondence; it was the feeling he had in tapping the "wild" powers of spiritual energy, in the dawn of perception, in the awakening of the faculties and in the urging of them to fulfill their powers in action and use. How to acquire this health, this frolic of the faculties, was itself a major concern of his "ascetic" (*J*, XII, 98). He was always looking for whips for his top, for ways to preserve his sensibility (*C*, XII, 43). "Every reasonable man," he wrote, "would give any price of house and land, and

future provision, for condensation, concentration, and the recalling at will of high mental energy" (*C*, VIII, 269). One
means he emphasized more and more as he grew older was the
physical health and acuity of sense he identified with youth. In
youth one had the "heat" or animal vigor and freedom from
care with which to facilitate communion with nature (*C*, VIII,
276, 280). But age, too, if youth had not been wasted, was not
without its rewards. For *use* of inspiration was as important
as its availability. "Being," he said, "costs me nothing." In the
ecstasy of insight he could "despise city and seashore, yes, earth
and the galaxy also." It was "the organizing" that taxed his
strength (*J*, VI, 6). Decay followed the waning of bodily energy, but it also followed from inaction or lack of release.[33]
One's powers increased or were maintained and strengthened
by use, and this was another reason for action and the wise
selection of a calling. Even in old age, one was rewarded with
this health, the accruement of faithful labor after the spirit. It
showed itself in virtue and character, both products of discipline and time, and was therefore an achievement of age *(C*,
VII, 320). In character, one maintained his spiritual height;
one had ready the total accumulation of spiritual power he
had brought to realization in affairs. In this way character was
the best adjustment of the alternations of life — of health and
decay (*J*, VII, 13).

Another resource of youth as well as of age and closely related to the development of the faculties and character was
concentration, which could only be gained through the discipline of work on the prudential level. The doctrine of work
was a doctrine of concentration in which dissipating demands
— things foreign to the self — were put off. Work was the secret
of control, and Emerson wrote its catechism and revealed the
taunts he felt in applying it: "To every reproach, I know now
but one answer, namely, to go again to my own work. 'But you
neglect your relations.' Yes, too true; then I will work the

harder. 'But you have no genius.' Yes, then I will work the harder. 'But you have no virtues.' Yes; then I will work the harder. 'But you have detached yourself and acquired the aversion of all decent people. You must regain some position and relation.' Yes; I will work harder" (*J*, VIII, 171). He could say this because he believed that by doing the work of self-culture he was making the need felt which only he could supply, that by unfolding himself he was creating as well the proper reception of his gifts. He felt that he had to justify his calling, and he did this over and over again in his lectures by affirming that the true vocation was the communication of himself "to others in his full stature and proportion." Character, like reason, had a self-affirming justification (*C*, II, 141–142), for true character was public — the loss of individuality in the divine, God acting through man. But he added that character could not be achieved in a deliberate preoccupation with self. Anything man did could be done "divinely," anything that drew man away from himself was best for his culture (*C*, II, 142). By joining man and matter, labor was thus a necessity of the spirit, and whether or not he practised what he preached, Emerson believed in the spiritual rewards of manual labor: "We must have a basis for our higher accomplishments, our delicate entertainments of poetry and philosophy, in the work of our hands. We must have an antagonism in the tough world for all the variety of our spiritual faculties, or they will not be born. Manual labor is the study of the external world" (*C*, I, 236). He glorified the farmer as the natural man, the man closest to nature. But not up to the rigors of the farm, Emerson found his equivalent for manual labor in keeping his senses alive in nature. Recourse to nature, as the habits of Thoreau and W. E. Channing testify, was often a labor in itself. On one level, it was an example of the modern majesty of work, of fitting means to end (*C*, I, 179), but there were few — and even the more socially active Parker and

Brownson, who knew hard labor in their youth did not appreciate it — who recognized this labor after language and spirit as more than self-gratification. Even today, how many realize the cost Thoreau paid for what they think his sentimental withdrawal to nature? There, he was the fulfillment of Emerson's "ascetic" — as Emerson was acutely aware — a man who could without the slightest misgiving make the experiment of character the aim of his life (*C*, X, 356).

But Thoreau was not Emerson's ideal man. In him, Emerson felt a wasted leadership (*C*, X, 449 ff.). His life was not sufficiently active in the social sense. As character there was perhaps no one more self-reliant than Thoreau, but as the spheral man he failed to measure up to Emerson's ideal, an ideal which in itself was a self-projection of his own failures. What constituted greatness was a lifetime problem which Emerson tried to answer out of his own progress from society to solitude and from solitude to society. In his youth all he meant by eloquence shaped his conception of the great man, and he was never able to free himself from the belief that writing was a closet performance. "There is a limit," he wrote, "to the effect of written eloquence. It may do much, but the miracles can only be expected from the man who thinks on his legs" (*J*, V, 6). Apart from the sense of public activity he felt in eloquence, he found it the best way of exhibiting the force of his character. "Eloquence," he said, "is the appropriate [corresponding] organ of the highest personal energy" (*C*, VII, 81). He wrote that the true orator was the true hero, and what was more important to Emerson, that "his speech is not to be distinguished from action. It is the electricity of action. It is action, as the general's word of command, or chart of battle, is action" (*C*, VIII, 115). For Emerson, action, like creative power, was masculine. He identified it with creative power (*J*, VI, 361) and could not rid

himself of the notion that poetry was a feminine trait.[34] He
liked Aristotle's comparison of lectures to battles well enough
to record it (*J*, VII, 6).

This antagonism of thought and action runs throughout
his journals. In his retirement (1836) he wrote: "You must
exercise your genius in some form that has essential life now;
do something which is proper to the hour, and cannot but be
done" (*J*, IV, 38–39). Later in the same year he added: "Moral
sentiment must act, or there is no self-respect. The most
brilliant achievement of the intellect would not reconcile me
to myself, or make me feel that there was any stability and
worth in human society. But if I command myself and help
others, I believe in and love man" (*J*, IV, 111–112). For awhile
he was able to reconcile himself by equating the written word
with action. He did this by making literature the end of previous action, a spiritual act of *transformation* which gave
literature its moral sanction. But even though art was "an
outlet for his proper character" and a symbol of his character,
it did not bring with it the life by which it was fully appreciated (*C*, II, 260). Literature was less communicative than
action because it was "the conversion of action into thought
for the delight of the Intellect" (*J*, III, 286). In the pursuit
of self-culture it was an indispensable discipline and, as he
advised Thoreau, a method of self-therapy by which he
released what more normally would find outlet in action (*J*,
V, 128; *J*, VI, 94). But he preferred spoken to written eloquence — as Alcott preferred the conversation — because it
made public the heat of activity in which this transformation
of experience (or publication of self) took place. Not only
did Emerson need the public occasion to call forth his own
heat (perhaps one of the few times he was genuinely warmed),
the heat made the word an act of character by reaching the
affections as well as the intellect of his audience (*C*, VIII,
118–119). His emphasis on tone as the expression of character

was proper only to the spoken word. The fact converted into speech, "all warm and colored and alive, as it fell out," was the "true transubstantiation" (*C*, VII, 68). With the spoken (or acted) word he not only showed his magnetic force, his true alignment with the spiritual pole, but discharged its power by electrifying the listener (*C*, VII, 90). This was the total circuit of thought as the conversion of power that he never felt satisfied he achieved in the written word. The desire for action was thus in a way the need for an audience, for social response.

The desire for action was always present because Emerson felt that he was constitutionally unequipped for it.[35] He knew, as he wrote his brother William, that the leprosy of the Emersons was "ill-weaved ambition" (*L*, I, 233). None of the Emersons had the vigor needed to carry out his promise. For them, decay was a normal condition because, like Emerson, they always took too seriously the gulf between the Idea and the Act (*J*, V, 46). They never lost the drive for greatness their early rivalry and Aunt Mary Moody's urging had instilled in them. And of them, only Emerson achieved a control that saved him from the fate of Edward and Charles. He learned early the uses of patience and inactivity and had the willingness to give his gifts the time and conditions they needed. He wrote William to adopt the remedy he had found for his own "narvous" difficulties — "he who would *act* must *lounge*" (*L*, I, 233). He might have added that he follow his example and leave the pressures and forced growth of the city for the less ambitious country.

But even in the country he could not escape his own desire for action, for it was not so much action as sympathy he needed. When he was petitioned by reformers and philanthropists (and his age was alive with good works), he confessed that he felt guilty of his own inaction. He could escape his guilt, however, by interpreting it correspondentially: "I cannot do all these things," he wrote, "but these my shames are illustrious token that I have strict relations to them all. None of these causes are foreigners to me. My universal nature is thus marked. These accusations are part of me too. They are not for nothing" (*J*, IV, 371). But nevertheless, his journals reveal that he could not dismiss them so easily. He knew, as he wrote of Osman, that idleness was necessary to his mode of vision (*J*, VI, 50), and he tried to make his idleness availability. At the end of "Manners" he spoke of Osman, who "had a humanity so broad and deep," a great heart "so sunny and hospitable in the centre of the country, — that it seemed as if the instinct of all sufferers drew them to his side." But he followed: "I shall hear without pain, that I play the courtier very ill, and talk of that which I do not well understand" (*C*, III, 154–155). For his inaction was also identified by himself and by others (Brownson, Ripley, Margaret Fuller, Alcott) as coldness and lack of sympathy. Here was one more reason why he tried to fuse himself with men by eloquence, by social action. He needed action for his completion: his defect pointed that way. He could write, and frequently in the same vein, that "my life is optical, not practical" (*J*, VI, 158), and he could try to justify himself to Alcott by saying that he "was created a seeing eye and not a useful hand." [36] But he knew that "I speculate on virtue, not burn with love" (*J*, VI, 158).

He advised the American scholar to subordinate his books to action and to learn instead from rough experience, and he believed he had his share of poverty, illness, and exile, but books served him as much for vicarious experience as for signs of the spirit in the past. In a delightful sketch of a day in the Athenaeum, he selected from his day's reading the excitement and action of Himmaleh ascents, tiger hunts, and duels. He projected his inaction to the others in the reading room and remarked, "Secluded from war, from trade, and from tillage, we were making amends to ourselves by devouring the descriptions of these things, and atoning for the thinness by the quantity of our fare." Fully aware of this compensation, he went on: "Yet I read with joy the life of Hampden, Pym, or Penn, of men conversant with governments and revolutions, and dilate in the swelling scene. Is not the delight I there find an intimation that not always in speculation, not always by Poetic imagination alone, shall the scholar, the private soul, be great, but one day in action also?" (*J*, IV, 319–320). Just as he had seen a phophecy of his own creative powers in his ability to respond to great literature, so again by responding to the lives of great men he could at least acknowledge at the same time that he postponed the need for action. The intimations of the faculties had this compensation. And he preferred to read history in the biographies of great men.[37]

His preoccupation with greatness and with action, like that with the representative man, was an attempt to provide a scale by which to measure himself (and his contemporaries). Beginning with the sermon on "The Genuine Man" (*Y*, 180 ff.), he drew many portraits of the ideal man — the hero, the genius, the poet — and utilizing the perspectives of six biographies, published the composite picture in *Representative Men*. Apart from the application of correspondence — ideas embodied in men — he tried to affirm his theory of virtue, that the only true help is "through the intellect and affections," the only positive good, "mental and moral force" (*C*, IV, 13). His picture was of the representative *mind*, his scale the degree of perception great men had, especially "the perception of identity and the perception of reaction [compensation]" (*C*, IV, 18). He wanted to show, too, that there were no symmetrical men, that men "are tendencies . . . and none of us complete" (*C*, IV, 19). He admitted that he admired men at both poles, "those who stand for facts, and for thoughts," and he described the gentleman of "Culture" and "Manners": "I like a master standing firm on legs of iron, well-born, rich, handsome, eloquent, loaded with advantages, drawing all men by fascination into tributaries and supporters of his power." [38] But he certified that the man of Reason was greater (*C*, IV, 23) for having abandoned his private individual nature, for having chosen to do the work of reason by the only means by which it could be done (*C*, IV, 23). And the man he probably meant was either Socrates or Jesus.

Of all the representative men, Montaigne seemed to maintain best the balance of the spheral man. Plato and Swedenborg, both system-makers, were defective in mystical feeling or enthusiasm. Shakespeare was only a poet of beauty whose symbols fell short of their mission of truth and being.[39] Napoleon, the "head" of the nineteenth century, lacked the moral sentiment or conscience, but Emerson was intrigued by his power of execution, and he frequently evoked Napoleon as the image of a power in which he was weak. Goethe was the genius of the nineteenth century, but not the "heart." He sought truth, Emerson said, only to aggrandize the self, not to help society. He was too cool, and it is understandable that in the privacy of his journal Emerson could acknowledge himself the Goethe of America (*J*, VIII, 62). But in *Representative Men* he seemed to have identified himself with Montaigne, with the earthy and actual. He described the abstractionist-scholar with enough vehemence to exorcise him from himself: "The studious class are their own victims; they are thin and pale, their feet are cold, their heads are hot, the night is without sleep, the day a fear of interruption, — pallor, squalor, hunger, and egotism. If you come near them, and see what conceits they entertain, — they are abstractionists, and spend their days and nights in dreaming some dreams; in expecting the homage of society to some precious scheme built on a truth, but destitute of proportion in its presentment, of justness in its application, and of all energy of will in the schemer to embody and vitalize it" (*C,* IV, 155–156). And he tried at least, in what was — as biography — the thinnest of all the biographies, to root himself in the intelligent common sense of the skeptic (here defined as the mediator of the abstractionist and the materialist) before showing the absorption of skepticism in the ascent to Reason.

Emerson confessed that he was incapable of drawing a portrait of Jesus.[40] As an ethical teacher Emerson considered Jesus beyond comparison, but he did not think him a complete man. He said that he was "a very exclusive and partial development of the moral element, such as the great Compensation that balances the universe provides to repair accumulated depravity" (*L,* I, 451; *J,* III, 532). He was not sufficiently intellectual. To him he preferred Socrates because he exhibited "all the traits of humanity" and especially of "intellectual nature." Socrates was the "complete, universal man, fulfilling all the conditions of man's existence" (*J,* III, 532). What he said of Newton and Jesus in "Trifles" he might have said of Socrates, that he was "not distinguished by any singularity, natural or affected, from any other individual" (*Y,* 51). For what he particularly prized in Socrates was his common humanity, the want of all signs of vulgar greatness. But he prized, too, the very things he sought for himself and early expressed in his Bowdoin Prize essay on "The Character of Socrates": his "chastised enthusiasm," "the plain good sense" with which he investigated his character in others, the fact that he was not a poet but dwelt "on earth, dealing plainly and bluntly with men and men's actions, instructing them what to do and to forbear . . ." and especially his fortitude, self-denial, and control which exempted him from the influence of circumstances.[41]

But the man in the present — the living ideal he needed — with whom he identified his unsatisfied ambition, was

Webster. Even after Webster had betrayed the higher law, even after Emerson had publicly shamed him, he could not prevent his pen from writing its usual adoration when Webster died. There was no sign, Emerson wrote in his journal, "that America and the world had lost the completest man. Nature had not in our days, or not since Napoleon, cut out such a masterpiece. He brought the strength of a savage into the height of culture. He was a man in *equilibrio;* a man within and without, the strong and perfect body of the first ages, with the civility and thought of the last. '*Os, osculosque Jovi par.*' And what he brought, he kept. Cities had not hurt him; he held undiminished the power and terror of his strength, the majesty of his demeanour" (*J,* VIII, 335–336). And what expressed this character was its eloquence.[42]

Emerson preferred to call the fulfillment of the natural tendency in man "greatness." He meant "completeness," for the natural tendency of the faculties was to develop the spheral man. But completeness or sphericity he knew was "adjourned for ages." Only in perspective (*C,* VIII, 301) — for the sake of character he was willing to lean on time — could one find symmetry (*J,* VI, 20). "Our exaggeration of all fine characters," he wrote, "arises from the fact that we identify each in turn with the soul." Each for the moment was the ideal he would execute out of himself (*C,* III, 226–227). But each was partial, like any fragment only momentarily whole in its representative capacity. There were no finished souls, and one had to be content, as he was when he came to accept the partiality of Thoreau, Alcott, and Newcomb, to judge men by their tendency, by the length of the chain of experience they had traversed (*J,* IX, 341) and by their ability to become the link, through whatever faculty they had, between the "two craving parts of nature" (*C,* I, 207).

The whole man was an ideal like the spheral man in

Plato's *Symposium* who had two faces, four hands and legs, and whom God divided, as Plutarch later rationalized the fable, to make man more helpful.[43] This fable of the divided man helped Emerson reconcile himself to his limitations and to find compensation in the best use of his faculties by following his bent. "Action and idea are man and woman," he wrote, "both indispensable" (*J*, VII, 544). And in expressing the geniuses' unfitness for society, he spoke biographically: "They want either love or self-reliance" (*C*, III, 228). He was wanting in love — in action. He was sufficiently self-reliant and feminine — Alcott was attracted by his feminine traits.[44] But unable to marry the two sexes in his own person, unable to mix the two elements in every act, he was not Hermaphrodite, "the symbol of the finished Soul" (*J*, VI, 378). He had, nevertheless, the guarantee of correspondence that the "powers I want will be supplied me as *I* am supplied," and he could resign himself without losing his optimism because he believed that "the philosophy of waiting is sustained by all the oracles of the Universe" (*J*, VII, 521; III, 403–404). And time seemed to bear him out.

6

Friendship

We must be warmed by the fire of sympathy to be brought into the right conditions and angles of vision. EMERSON, "Inspiration."

It occurs that the distinction should be drawn in treating of Friendship between the aid of commodity which our friends yield us, as in hospitality, gifts, sacrifices, etc., and which, as in the old story about the poor man's will in Montaigne, are evidently esteemed by the natural mind (to use such a cant word) the highest manifestations of love; and secondly, the spiritual aid, — far more precious and leaving the other at infinite distances, — which our friends afford us, of confession, of appeal, of social stimulus, mirroring ourselves.

EMERSON, *Journals.*

The world hath many centres, one for each created being, and about each one it lieth in its own circle. Thou standest but half an ell from me, yet about thee lieth a universe whose centre I am not but thou art. . . [But] our universes are not far from each other so that they do not touch; rather hath God pushed them and interwoven them deep into each other.

THOMAS MANN, *Joseph in Egypt*
(New York, 1944) vol. I.

The frequency of Emerson's journal entries on friendship reflects his awareness of his failings to measure up to his own ideal of the complete man. When he wrote of the geniuses' unfitness for society, he was speaking from his deepest need: "They want either love or self-reliance" (*C*, III, 228). When he evoked the androgymous man of Platonic myth, he knew he was only the feminine half — the passive, receptive "observer." By his estimate he was both unsympathetic (in the spiritual sense of sympathy as outgoing) and inactive, and, as we have seen, he saw both failings as one: as an unwillingness to enter into society and make social amelioration the end of the democracy of transcendental intuition. This trait had been recognized very early in his public career. Orestes Brownson, whose transcendentalism was socially oriented like George Ripley's and Theodore Parker's, quickly sensed in Emerson's "Literary Ethics" (1838) that Emerson was preaching a self-culture too remote from the arena. He was making, as Frederic Hedge enthusiastically welcomed it in *The Dial*, the scholar's calling of self-culture an end in itself — an art of life to be "made a distinct aim, or wholly abandoned." [1] Brownson could not admit that "the scholar must be a solitary soul, living apart and in himself alone; that he must shun the multitude and mingle never in the crowd." And he warned Emerson that his words would live only when he put by his "scholastic asceticism" and truly prepared himself for his calling "by loving his countrymen and sympathizing with them." [2]

When Emerson drew his own portrait, he seemed to accept the truth of Brownson's censure. In "Character" he described himself as the "uncivil, unavailable man" (*C*, III, 100), and more than once he defended his lack of symmetry by asserting: "I was born a seeing eye, not a helping hand" (*J*, IV, 208). "Always the man of genius dwells alone," he recorded in 1837, "and, like the mountain, pays the tax of snows and silence for elevation" (*J*, IV, 202). He was willing to pay this tax for the spiritual elevation (or isolation) he needed for the concentration of his powers. Like Thoreau, who escaped to Walden as much for solitude as for economy, Emerson's isolation was a working necessity, a condition of inspiration. Before the social implications of transcendentalism were raised in Brook Farm and Fourierism and hardened him into a resolute individualist, he sought in solitude the isolation he needed when "the whole world seems to be in conspiracy to invade you, to vanquish you with emphatic details, to break you into crumbs, to fritter your time." There was in solitude a calm that would not "scare away the Muse" (*J*, V, 188), and he did not so strenuously oppose solitude to society until its primacy as the habitat of self-culture was questioned by social organization. Then, the possibilities of the fulfillment of the faculties in associated life were vigorously denied, and Emerson took up the pose of the solitary genius even though society was what he wanted most. At the time of Alcott's persecution for his conversations in the Temple School, Emerson noted that he was only the seeing eye and added, "I can only comfort my friends by thought, and not by love or aid" (*J*, IV, 208). But this admission, like many more, hardly fits the Emerson who in this instance was one of the few to come to Alcott's defense — publicly — and who was, for so many people, a sheltering tree.[3] Nor does the pose of the solitary genius fit the Emerson who was a club-man from college to death or who spent a great part of his life in the social aura of the lecture hall. Emerson's admission goes deeper: to his inability (which he excused on temperamental grounds) to make self-culture as he saw it the legitimate end of the transcendental social ethic that was clearly shaping in the early 1840's. His admission had little to do with friendship between individuals — although his ideal of this relation made him a hard friend and a willing one only on his terms — but with the whole democratic ferment and the associationism of the period which his "ascetic" never quite accommodated.

For Emerson, friendship was a way of discussing both the relation of man to man, a wholly personal relation, and the relation of man to society. This range is understandable because a subjective-individualistic philosophy such as Emerson's would try to reduce social problems to problems of friendship, and, ultimately, to problems of the spiritual life. On this level society was easily eliminated: one merely chose as friends those who best fitted his personal needs. The question of what kind of society corresponded to the faculties of the erect man — the problem Ripley tried to solve at Brook Farm, and Alcott at Fruitlands, and negatively, Thoreau at Walden — was painlessly answered by the self-reliant man who made his own world and determined his affinities. It was easier to transform the self than society, and when the responsibility for melioration terminated in the self, easier to bear. And until Ripley, Brownson, Parker, and even Alcott thrust the social burden on Emerson, he was unquestionably content with the responsibility of the self.

For Emerson first considered friendship from the perspective of individual need. Only those friendships were to be undertaken and maintained that contributed to the life of insight, that helped him toward inspiration and angles of vision. Personally considered, the mutual responsibility of friendship was to keep the receptive pole of the mind active. Socially considered, however, like the constructive function of the mind, friendship inescapably led to social benefit: vision had to be applied, what the self received had to be repaid, self-culture had to be socially useful. In the attainment of vision, in the attempt to remain pure and uncontaminated, society perhaps might be shunned; but the possession of vision called for a society to receive it (*C,* VII, 16). When Emerson said he was feminine, he meant that he was receptive but incapable of the masculine action that fully — that is, socially — communicated the insight. He believed that self-culture would be socially useful as example, that character might replace active participation in reform. He admired the "useful egotism" of his Puritan great-grandfather. "The minister," he wrote, *"experienced* life for his flock." Transforming his experience after the fashion of Emerson's, "he gave prominence to all his economy and history for the benefit of the parish. His cow and horse and pig did duty next Sunday in the pulpit. All his haps are providences. If he keeps school, marries, begets children, if his house burns, if his children have the measles, if he is thrown from his horse . . . all his adventures are fumigated with prayer and praise — he improves next Sunday the circumstance, — and the willing flock are contented with this consecration of one man's adventures for the benefit of them all, inasmuch as that one is on the right level and therefore a fair representative" (*J*, VII, 339). It was enough to transform one's own experience, to be a representative man, let alone to transform society. It was enough — one can see it in his nostalgia for Everett's eloquence — if one opened the eyes of others to new perceptions (*C*, X, 330–335). After all, weren't the reformers he knew "gentle souls, with peaceful and even genial dispositions," so unlike the "fiery souls" of their ancestors? (*C*, X, 346).

"The problem which life has to solve is," Emerson wrote in 1836, "how to exist in harmonious relation to a certain number of perceptions, such as hunger, thirst, cold, society, self, God; — it is a problem of three bodies" (*J*, IV, 22). By 1836, as *Nature* shows, he had been able to solve the problem of the self and God, leaving the problem of society and the self-and-God (as one he placed them in opposition to society) [4] to the aftermath of the depression of 1837. In 1836 it seemed sufficient to affirm the self-and-God: the transcendental awakening was still arguing the nature of man and the miracle of Reason. Men had first to repossess their souls. The quest was for the Real, for selfhood, not for the Actual. And friendship, in "Friendship" and "Love," was subordinated to this personal spiritual need. In the search for inspiration or merger with God, what could society offer? Prudential society, Emerson found, offered an imperfect union: "I am led on from month to month with an expectation of some total embrace and oneness with a noble mind, and learn at last that it is only so feeble and remote and hiant action as reading a Mirabeau or Diderot paper . . . This is all that can be looked for. More we shall not be to each other. Baulked soul! . . . man is insular and cannot be touched. Every man is an infinitely repellent orb, and holds his individual being on that condition" (*J*, IV, 238).[5] Perhaps he was demanding too much from friendship: at least, by this standard, he had no misgivings in making the union of merger with God its substitute. As long as inspiration was easily attained in nature, its human stimulus in friendship could be foregone. But the willingness to turn from society to solitude was more the result of an exceptional self-awareness of his own needs, of his personal requirements for vision. Even though the correspondence of souls — the desire to discover one's self in others — was the proper extension of correspondence (*J*, III, 341), still it was a superhuman ideal, and, as such, a barrier which Emerson erected for his own protection.

He needed the protection of an impossible ideal because he never satisfied himself in the demands of personal relationships. He knew he demanded too much of friendship when he himself — as he prefaced so many letters — had "not health or constitution enough to bear so dear demanding a relation" (*L*, III, 459). What could he do, knowing that he was cold because he was warm at the heart — "cold at the surface only as a sort of guard and compensation for the fluid tenderness of the core . . . ?" (*J*, V, 411). He was acutely aware of both his coldness and his desire for sympathy. He asked God to defend him "from the vice of my constitution, an excessive desire of sympathy" (*J*, III, 221), perhaps because it was not a virtue of the self-reliant man. One of the annoying forms of egotism, he said in "Culture," was "a craving for sympathy" (*C*, VI, 133). But at the same time that he wrote, "I am full of tenderness, and born with as large hunger to love and be loved as any man can be," he knew that "its demonstrations are not active and bold, but are passive and tenacious." "My love," he confessed, "is always there under my silence, under displeasure, under cold, arid, and even weak behavior" (*J*, V, 565).

He accepted the fact that he was cold and that this contributed to his low estimate of social relations. Faced with Margaret Fuller's exuberant social reporting, he could only answer that "I delight from my corner to know that such society is no fable . . ." and that "such rare pictures as you paint, make me suspect my own habitual skepticism in respect to the stimulus of society to be merely mine springing from want of organs which others have" (*L*, II, 163). He recognized, too, that self-reliance did not mean self-sufficiency, that solitude was a curse "when mother, wife and child are gone" (*J*, IV, 366; *J*, IV, 398). And he admonished himself: "Let him not wrong the truth and his own experience by too stiffly standing on the cold and proud doctrine of self-sufficiency" (*J*, IV, 366). For, earlier, the deaths of his brothers Edward and Charles had shown him how much his life had been lived in others (*J*, III, 347; IV, 39 ff.), and especially in Charles he had found the forever afterward unrealizable friend. Coldness and self-reliance, like his personal doctrine of gifts, [6] were his shields, warding off the injuries of relationships that entered into too deeply and then severed might bereave him of part of himself.

He also saw something heroic in the impassive, cold public exterior. If coldness (that is, the lack of the heat of the heart) were fatal to eloquence, still a cold surface was admirable. "Give us," he wrote, "the rare merits of impassivity, of marble texture, against which the mob [7] of souls is broken like crockery falling on stone: the endurance which can afford to fail in the popular sense, because it never fails in its own" (*J*, VII, 152–153). And when he looked back in "Historic Notes of Life and Letters in New England" (1880), he dwelled at length on the models of his youthful devotions, on Everett whose magic was in form and manner and on Dr. Channing who was privately of cold temperament but publicly an irreplaceable spokesman of the history of the times (*C*, X, 334, 339–340). In them he saw the ministerial pattern which, like the clerical garb, he never abandoned, and his manner was accordingly lofty and aristocratic. As much as he admired Father Edward Taylor (Melville's Father Mapple,) he himself never adopted the abandonment of this "life philosopher" who was "profuse of himself" and never remembered "the looking-glass" (*J*, III, 431). The priestly fit Emerson's needs too well: he could never see himself only as a poet; he needed to be the priest through whom the private poetic heat could find a decorous, controlled, and undefiled expression. As the priest he could have society on his own terms; from the platform he would never have to descend to meet, to compromise, or accommodate himself to lowest. His coldness could be accepted as part of his office (*C*, III, 136–137).

But if coldness passed as a public virtue, it could only impede the personal uses of friendship that Emerson needed to implement the inspiration of nature. He recognized, even before he saw it working itself out in Thoreau, that the vigor of "natural" inspiration was the reward of youth, that by thirty nature was less friendly, and that he had to find other whips for his top. His doctrine of friendship expressed an ideal relationship in which the friend supplied the deficiency of nature and provided the possibilities of the fullest self-culture. Like nature the friend was both a source of inspiration and a mirror of the self.[8] By the time he wrote "Society and Solitude," the ideal (actually, the terms on which he would engage in friendship) was still visible but genuinely humanized. Then he readily admitted, " 'Tis hard to mesmerize ourselves, to whip our own top; but through sympathy we are capable of energy and endurance" (*C*, VII, 11). It was hard because the little heat he had to fuse the facts was slowly ebbing, because the "capital defect of cold, arid natures is the want of animal spirits" (*C*, VII, 11). He needed the friction of the society of others to generate his enthusiasm. Some perceptions ("The permanent and controlling ones" — he thus maintained his self-reliance) one had to find for himself, but "others," he wrote, "it takes two to find" (*C*, VIII, 292). Between two, selfless abandonment and confession were possible. With another he could melt before the fire of sympathy and "be brought into the right conditions and angles of vision" (*C*, VII, 293).

As Emerson described friendship in "Friendship," it was a relationship of souls above the commodity level of society. "I hate," he wrote, "the prostitutions of the name of friendship to signify modish and worldly alliances" (*C*, II, 205). He knew the ebb and flow of friendship, and how much he contributed to its decay by "mining for the metaphysical foundation" of the relationship (*C*, II, 196). But for him, friendship had to provide the capital of other people's experience and the environment of the self: it was only truly friendship when correspondentially conceived. To Emerson a friend was a paradox of nature because, unlike nature, the friend became the perfect mirror of the self. "I who alone am," Emerson wrote, "I who see nothing in nature whose existence I can affirm with equal evidence to my own, behold now the semblance of my being, in all its height, variety, and curiosity, reiterated in a foreign form; so that a friend may well be reckoned the masterpiece of nature" (*C*, II, 204). The corollary, which again made self-reliance and coldness defensible, was that "love is only the reflection of a man's own worthiness from other men" (*C*, II, 212). The service of friendship thus worked two ways: a new friend (Emerson always wanted to keep his friends "strangers") mirrored a latent idea and provided its embodiment, but a new idea also created new relationships and attracted new friends (*J*, VI, 25). "Friends," he said in "Character" where he was upholding the magnetism of self-reliance, "also follow the laws of divine necessity; they gravitate to each other" (*C*, III, 112).

But, for Emerson, the magnetism of the relationship was useful chiefly for self-culture; and, understandably, Alcott found Emerson's views of social relations faulty. Alcott wrote in 1838: "Men are too purely ideas with him. He makes affection an idea, and despoils it of all its life. Men are uses, with him. Like Bacon, he slurs the affections. He loves his Ideals, and, because these have not actual life, contemns the men who live around him as unworthy.

"This is the vice of his theory, but not of the generous, friendly theorist. He plays the seer alone in his theories, and will have no need of heart, while in life the fair and noble affections thereof belie his philosophy. The *man* will, by and by, find full acknowledgement in this." [9] Criticism and prophecy well-taken! Alcott had, of course, got to the heart of Emerson's personal dilemma. Love — affection, instinct, sympathy — was the central idea and condition of transcendental insight. As Emerson had shown in "Love," this was a perpetual force in the universe, the force that carried man from material to spiritual objects, from human warmth to ideas. Love was the great blender and fuser, the cement of the split universe, as Whitman later magnified this Emersonian emphasis. But unlike Whitman, Emerson seemed able only to express his love intellectually, that is, on the level of ideas. To this level, he desired to raise human relationships. He was cold at the surface where human beings touched, but warm at the core where ideas had their being. And by interpreting the warmth of the core as truly "public" (as the absence of all individuality), Emerson tried verbally, at least, to overcome both his preoccupation with men as ideas and the imputation of coldness and social indifference that followed this example of self-reliance. By giving "public" the meaning of inspirational transcendence, that is, the falling back on the Over-Soul, the loss of "individualism" in the merger of the private self, the usual connotation of "public" seemed to cover with social utility this central act of self-culture. "Every sensual pleasure is private and mortal," he wrote, "every spiritual action is public and generative" (*J*, VI, 6). And this saved him from his own self-accusation. For he hoped his spiritual action (and isolation) would make him in time an irresistible friend. "The most private is," he wrote, "the most public energy . . . The reason I am not is because I am not real. Let me be a lover, and no man can resist me. I am not united, I am not friendly to myself, I bite and tear myself. I am ashamed of myself. When will the day dawn, of peace and reconcilement, when, self-united and friendly, I shall display one heart and energy to the world?" (*J*, VI, 198–199). Until he could eradicate the private sensual self — the self that made friendship on his terms unsatisfactory — he would not admit others. And again, he was willing to postpone the relationship until he was a finished man (*C*, II, 213).

Tormented by the need for friends to help him towards completion, still Emerson never overcame his belief that in Idealism "friends become ideas" (*J*, IV, 25). Even when

Waldo died, the service of Newcomb's friendship was its spiritual consolation. Reading his manuscript, Emerson was raised above grief: "I felt for the first time since Waldo's death," he wrote, "some efficient faith again in the repairs of the Universe, some independency of natural relations whilst spiritual affinities can be so perfect and compensating" (*J*, VI, 214). Like the embodiment of men as ideas, this relationship cost him nothing: "Persons are fine things, but they cost so much! for *thee* I must pay *me*" (*J*, VI, 367). And in all relations he tried to reduce the cost. His most ardent friendships were carried on by letters or by the exchange of journals, manuscripts, and diaries. Not only did this give Emerson the distance he wanted and the privacy he needed for sympathetic response, it gave him the *thoughts* of his friends, not their persons (*L*, II, 342–343, 441). It made him the master of the occasion, as he seldom was in the group. It made possible the only society he could face, and the profession of love an experience he could properly worship. He was, as he told Margaret Fuller, who demanded so much of him even in her letters, "diffident, shy, proud of having settled it long ago in his mind that he & society must always be nothing to each other" (*L*, II, 351). Pressed too far even in a letter, he would terminate their relationship (*L*, II, 352). "I knew," he wrote, "that if I would cherish my dear romance, I must treat it gently, forbear it long, — worship, not use it, — and so at last by piety I might be tempered & annealed [10] to bear contact & conversation as well mixed natures should" (*L*, II, 351).

The pleasure he experienced in writing "Friendship" was the result of having successfully experimented with and found sufficient this form of thought-exchange (*J*, V, 415). The background of that essay, which Emerson first pondered in January 1840, was an experiment in letter-friendship carried on in the summer and autumn of that year (*L*, II, 336–350).

He wrote his brother William that getting his essays ready for print was "hard & mechanical compared with my writing romances of letters which I have done all this idle happy summer" (*L,* II, 348). In these letters to Margaret Fuller, Caroline Sturgis, Sam Ward, and Anna Barker, he satisfied his inner warmth and reached the limit of his intimacy. And it was in these letters that he most fully used his friends for confession and sympathy. He was especially excited by the courtship of Sam Ward and Anna Barker, and with the help of Margaret Fuller and Caroline Sturgis, lived that relationship vicariously — so fully that their marriage upset him. Anna Barker was the hidden concern of many of his letters, and even in his old age he took pleasure in recalling *his* American Madame Recamier.

But "Friendship" was more than his experimental findings. Given the background of Emerson's domestic life (best seen in the letters of 1840–1842) and his conflicting needs for solitude and social participation, the essay becomes a manifesto to both the reformers and his correspondents. He would be tied to neither. Lidian Emerson, who Emerson knew had paid the price of his experiment (*L,* II, 402), had responded eagerly to the idea of community life and represented the demands of the reformers in his own sanctuary. Ripley's plan was as much a part of the family conversation as the latest word of Margaret Fuller in that idle summer. And if a later letter, showing Emerson still contending against association, can be used to indicate the domestic climate, Emerson was probably frequently taxed with "egotism" by his wife (*L,* III, 20). Again, his solution, suggested as a possibility of the unprecipitated future, was a community on his own terms, an extension to the group of his personal ideal: "a circle of godlike men and women variously related to each other, and between whom subsists a lofty intelligence" (*C,* II, 206). By embodying ideas, he would make his own community. "In whatsoever thought of God I live," he as much as warned Caroline Sturgis, "I must find the inhabitant of that thought. I see not how any alliance can have any security or any other foundation" (*L*, II, 338). The community he proposed was to embody *his* ideas and serve his needs. He wrote in "Friendship" that "we weave social threads of our own, a new web of relations; and, as many thoughts in succession substantiate themselves, we shall by and by stand in a new world of our own creation" (*C*, II, 194). His relations with Thoreau and Alcott were of this order: he saw in them the living symbols of his thought. The "best of all external experiences" he found was in the assurance "that magnanimity walks & works around us . . . " that Alcott, for one, provided (*L*, II, 344). He could call them "his" men because they were *his* ideas. He could draw them into his orbit by his unfailing loyalty and personal kindness: he felt he owed them something. But they knew that without a second thought he could write Lidian: "Perhaps I will bring home with me Charles Newcomb to show him some of my men & things" (*L*, III, 13).[11]

II

Today, the signs marking the approaches of Concord tell us that here was the home of Emerson, Thoreau, Hawthorne, and Alcott. In 1840, Emerson would have appreciated this announcement and might have added to the list (he made innumerable lists of men) the candidates he had selected to live with him in his ideal Concord community. For at one time or another, especially in the formative years of Brook Farm, he had urged his friends to make their residence in Concord. By the response he unwillingly gave to the social reformers, he knew that in his self-reliance he was not immune to the social ideas of the times: his faculties showed him his affinities. And he felt the guilt of his idle happy summer. In December 1840 he wrote his brother William, "We are absorbed here at home in discussions of George Ripley's Community." He added — what amounted to a confession — "I am very discontented with many of my present ways & bent on mending them." And after relating the details of Ripley's project, especially the union of manual and intellectual labor, he asked, "Can I not get the same advantages at home without pulling down my house? Ah my dear brother that is the very question we now consider" (*C*, II, 365).

Within two weeks he had given Ripley his answer: "I have decided not to join it & yet very slowly & I may almost say penitentially." Although the general grounds of his refusal were his own social shyness and self-reliant determination to mend after his own fashion, Emerson stressed the advantages of Concord.[12] "I am in many respects suitably placed in an agreeable neighborhood," he wrote, "in a town which I have many reasons to love & which has respected my freedom so far that I may presume it will indulge me farther if I need it. Here I have friends & kindred. Here I have builded & planted: & here I have greater facilities to prosecute such practical enterprizes as I may cherish, than I could probably find by any removal." And he continued by countering his own experiments with Ripley's: "The principal particulars in which I wish to mend my domestic life are in acquiring habits of regular manual labor, and in ameliorating or abolishing in my house the condition of hired menial service. I should like to come one step nearer to nature than this usage permits. I desire that my manner of living may be honest and agreeable to my imagination. But surely I need not sell my house & remove my family to Newton in order to make the experiment of labor & self help. I am already in the act of trying some domestic & social experiments which my present position favors. And I think that my present position has even greater advantages than yours would offer me for testing my improvements in those small private parties

into which men are all set off already throughout the world."
To the plan for the Brook Farm school and the "concentration
of scholars in one place" he genuinely warmed, and hoped
that in time this would make the community attractive to him.
But he added — and time, perhaps, has justified him — "According to your ability & mine, you & I do now keep
schools for all comers, & the energy of our thought & will
measures our influence. In the community we shall utter not
a word more — not a word less." But his refusal — what were
all his reasons but a defiant I-can-do-better-here? — was hard to
give. He had to admit that he was not robust enough for reform, that he was not skillful in conversation, that "new
methods" might hinder his habits of literary composition, and
that what he was called to do "I must do alone." He preferred
the "secretest improvements" he could nurture and hide in
solitude, and so refused an active part in Ripley's company.
But nevertheless, he said, "I shall regard it with lively sympathy & with a sort of gratitude" (*L*, II, 368–371).[13]

A community of his own was agreeable to Emerson's
imagination, especially a loosely linked group of Concord
residents bound by the same interests, but pursuing them
each in his individual manner. Such a community expressed
his own belief in the magnetism of character and rewarded
his private literary ethics with a social setting. Its compact was
not an associative document and share holding plan, but the
idea of self-culture and the mutual need for representative
men. He knew, as he preached in "Self and Others," that "improvement is from a selfish to a social life — a development
of power to act with and for others" (*Y*, 130). But constitutionally unable to serve in a social way, he had to make self-
culture itself a social good. He had need to find his own self-
sufficiency and work a defense against reformers who might
think him useless and parasitic. In the essays that were written
after the depression of 1837, when reform was seriously getting

underway, and Brownson and Parker were castigating the oppressors of the laboring classes, Emerson had to show that his inactivity was not disapproval. He welcomed Edward Palmer, who had renounced the use of money, and thought with him, "I have a perfect claim on the community for the supply of all my wants if I have worked hard all day, or if I have spent my day well, have done what I could, though no meat, shoes, cloth, or utensils, have been made by me" (*J*, V, 88). But he was aware that there might seem to be a contradiction in postulating both direct relations with the universe and the educative good of labor, as he did in "Literary Ethics," especially when one labored as a scholar. A bustling reformer at least appeared to be doing something to repair the collapsed society, but what good did the scholar do? Was it appropriate to tell the young men of Dartmouth College that their true callings as scholars were to be found in solitude? If he told them this, then, he had to ask them to answer the question he had posed many times to himself: "How can the man who has learned but one art, procure all the conveniences of life honestly?" (*C*, I, 245). If the scholar made self-culture his aim didn't he have to strive for self-sufficiency? What other way was there for him honestly to maintain his self-reliance? "What right, cries the good world, has the man of genius to retreat from work, and indulge himself?" (*C*, I, 248).

Emerson answered that self-culture *was* the Reform of Reforms, that self-help was the beginning of self-reliance, and that the economy he practiced was "be rich to great purposes; poor only for selfish ones" (*C*, I, 245). The true economy which underlay his doctrine of work was to do as much for oneself as one could, or go without. Like Thoreau, he preached, if he did not as thoroughly practice, simplicity: "It is better to go without, than to have them at too great a cost" (*C*, I, 245). And in Thoreau he acknowledged that he saw his ethic enacted (*J*, VIII, 303 ff.). But he was not equipped to take this step himself: he had an uneducated body. He said that he did not "wish to be absurd and pedantic in reform" — neither compelled to suicide nor "absolute isolation" (*C*, I, 247). Life would be impossible, he said, if we did without the commodities of society and social life, however corrupt they were. These had to be accepted on the condition that "we must clear ourselves each one" by asking "whether we have earned our bread to-day by the hearty contribution of our energies to the common benefit" (*C*, I, 247). In self-culture as he explained it, he believed he had.

In self-culture one worked with the only means that could truly reform: perception. He was willing to acknowledge the reforming ferment of his time, but he raised the issue to the spiritual level where he was competent to handle it. Reform was good, but only if men *saw* in it "that the world not only fitted the former men, but fits us," and then cleared themselves "of every usage which has not its roots in our own mind." And lest he be misunderstood when he said that a man is born "but to be a Reformer, a Re-maker of what man has made," he widened the meaning of reform to accommodate his own preoccupation: "the effort to re-attach the deeds of everyday to the holy and mysterious recesses of life." In this reform one raised himself by "the power of principles" and transcended "the power of expedients." And this was the blow with which he hoped to shatter the practical reformers (*C*, I, 248–251).

"These reforms of our contemporaries," he pointed out in "Lecture on the Times," "they are ourselves; our own light, and sight, and conscience; they name only the relation which subsists between us and the vicious institutions which they go to rectify. They are the simplest statements of man in these matters; the plain right and wrong. I cannot chose but allow and honor them" (*C*, I, 276). He recognized them as a *sign* of the times, but disowned any responsibility to help them succeed. He admitted that the impulse and theory behind them were good; he parted company over the practice — the means: "The Reformers affirm the inward life, but they do not trust it, but use outward and vulgar means." The soul of reform, he said, was not reliance "on men, on multitudes, on circumstances, on money, on party" — all prudential means — but the "love which lifted men to the sight of these better ends . . . the disposition to trust a principle more than a material force" (*C*, I, 276). And just as he criticized the use of exaggeration in the linear writing of his day, so he saw in the expression of reform the exaggeration of "some special means." Reform lost the "purity" of the idea: "They are quickly organized in some low, inadequate form, and present no more poetic image to the mind, than the evil tradition which they reprobated" (*C*, I, 277). This was the extension of Emersonian correspondence to the politics of the day: the idea had not been adequately embodied, reform had not gone beyond prudential expedients.

Then, too, the work of reform was done "profanely, not piously." Reformers acted partially, and reduced "man to a measure." In whatever work man was called to do, Emerson wanted the total act of the whole man, acts that represented the whole spirit. If he could not "act with truth," that is, with the whole force of his character, he could not act with "effect." And this was the logic of his essay: "I must consent to inaction." He would be inactive *not because* he disapproved of reform in itself, but because the reformers themselves had forced him out of their own insufficiency to the task! They, not he, had repudiated the Reform of Reforms; they had forced his consent "to solitude and inaction" by proposing schemes to which he could not agree because of "an unwillingness to violate character" (*C*, I, 278). And out of his "respect and joy" in the reforms of the day, he urged "the more earnestly the paramount duties of self-reliance" (*C*, I, 278–279).

Because of his unwillingness (inability?) to face the public varieties of action, he made these lectures a public rationalization of his own method of action. He was driven back to assertions of self-reliance that, removed from the context of his needs, have seemed the naïve expression of a sentimental liberal. By shifting the ground from actual reforms to reforms of spirit, he seemed once more to avoid the problem of evil. And the political realist, mistaking the level of Emerson's discourse, has never been able to make sense out of statements that most succinctly apply Emerson's literary ethics to reform:

The man of ideas, accounting the circumstances nothing, judges of the commonwealth from the state of his own mind.

If I am just, then there is no slavery, let the laws say what they will.

Give the slave the least elevation of religious sentiment, and he is no slave (*C*, I, 278–280).

His aim — and correspondence was its instrument — had been to nullify circumstances. How could the "benefactors" who hoped "to raise man by improving his circumstances," who hoped by "combination of that which is dead . . . to make something alive," understand that only by the influx of spirit could *man* be remade? (*C*, I, 281). And if they understood, as Ripley did, hadn't *they* shifted the reform to things, not men?

With this Emerson could turn from the "actors" to the "students" and reaffirm the utility of his literary ethics. A new method of life and "new modes of thinking" were needed more than a tampering with laws and manners (*C*, I, 283, 285). Men of genius chose the life of intellect, not because they shunned action, but because the "inadequacy of the work [reform] to the faculties is the painful perception which keeps them still." And this, he remarked, "happens to the best." This "contrast of the dwarfish Actual with the exorbitant Idea" alone compelled the genius to decline the deed for a "beholding" (*C*, I, 283–285). Was inadequate action to be compared with the spiritualist's inaction when that inaction signified a "greater Belief," a "piety which looks with faith to a fair Future, unprofaned by rash and unequal attempts to realize it?" (*C*, I, 285). He had strategically moved from reformers to the spiritual needs of poets. The issue was no longer inaction but whether society could recognize the high service of inaction represented in the poet's calling. Poets served best by "affirming the need of new and higher modes of living and action"; they alone abstained, in an age too full of activity and performance, from recommending "low methods" (*C*, I, 286). They stood aside and surveyed the thousands of "sides and signs and tendencies" of the age and saw "the great spirit which gazes through them" (*C*, I, 287). They served by standing for reality, for the whole beneath the partial aspects of prudential life and its reforms.

The Concord Community he proposed was to be dedicated to this end, to the augmentation of the self-reliant life of his literary ethics. Essentially, it was to be a literary community (*J*, V, 113, 173–174), in which the "beholders" were to have available the sympathy they needed. It was to provide the part of education that solitude prohibited: the sympathetic and social (*C*, VI, 149). Domestic life was to be its center (*C*, VII, 129). It was to duplicate the only attraction Emerson saw in Ripley's proposed community, that, as he wrote Margaret Fuller in December 1840, "it may bring friends together conveniently & satisfactorily." "But perhaps," he added, "old towns & old homes may learn that art one of these days, under the kingdom of the New Spirit" (*L*, II, 364).

Meanwhile, he had more immediate mending to do in his domestic reforms. He had to try the experiment of intellectual and manual labor on which his self-reliance depended. He felt that society would consider him a dreamer and fanatic unless he made his "fine words good" by a "brave demonstration to the senses of their [the reformers'] own problem." "The pure," he wrote, "must not eat the bread of the impure, but must live by the sweat of their own face & in all points make their philosophy affirmative" (*L*, II, 374–375).[14]

In December 1840, he wrote his brother William that, having refused Ripley, "I am quite intent on trying the experiment of manual labor to some considerable extent & of abolishing or ameliorating the domestic service in my household" (*L*, II, 371). He was a little impatient, he said, of inequalities, and, "an agrarian at heart," wished he had a smaller house or that someone — he suggested Alcott — would share it with him (*L*, II, 371–372). But although Alcott was willing, Mrs. Alcott refused (*L*, II, 389); and his other domestic reform met a similar refusal. The cook herself thought it unfitting to sit at the family table (*L*, II, 389). He was successful, however, in getting Thoreau to live with him, to work with him, and to teach him gardening (*L*, II, 394). But believing manual labor a "whimsy . . . which infects us all like an influenza," he was never as serious a laborer as Alcott was in his own garden or Thoreau in his bean field (*L*, II, 387). He delighted in his apple and pear trees all his life, but gardening for him was never more than relaxation; by June, he had experimented enough to know, as he reported to Margaret Fuller, that "when the terrestrial corn beets onions & tomatos thrive, the celestial archetypes of the same in the gardeners head do not" (*L*, II, 410).

What really attracted him in Ripley's proposal was the concentration of friends, and in the early years of Brook Farm he tried to persuade his friends to make a similar experiment at Concord. In May 1842, he gave one of the few hints in his journal that one of the most searching problems of these years had been his community: "Here is a proposition for the formation of a good neighborhood: Hedge shall live at Concord, and Mr. Hawthorne; George Bradford shall come then; and Mrs. Ripley afterward. Who knows but Margaret Fuller and Charles Newcomb would presently be added? These, if added to our present kings and queens, would make a rare, an unrivalled company. If these all had their hearth and home here, we might have a solid social satisfaction, instead of the disgust and depression of visitation. We might find that each of us was more completely isolated and sacred than before. You may come — no matter how near in place, so that you have metes and bounds, instead of the confounding and chaos of visiting" (*J*, VI, 207–208). In August 1843, Emerson was still trying to realize his "Concord Socialism," now as a stay against the almost wholesale removal of his friends to Europe. Many, oppressed by "social disadvantages," had taken flight to Europe. "They fancy," he told Elizabeth Hoar, "that by living within reach of each other's society they could work & suffer better, & very reasonably anticipate from the instructions of sympathy an unlimited benefit." But he knew that travel was only a postponement, that if they could realize a society at home, their work would be advanced. He said that there was no other way "to stop the perpetual leakage of the continent" except by "concentrating good neighborhoods." And he pointed to flourishing Brook Farm as a valuable example of "the possibilities & eminent convenience of living in good neighborhood." He was willing to accept that part of Ripley's scheme and was even willing to make a "Sacred Phalanx" at Cohasset or Berkshire if Concord was unsatisfactory. If only a "half a dozen rare persons" would "by the slightest concert . . . choose one place" (*L*, III, 203–204). In time Hawthorne and the Ellery Channings moved to Concord, and Margaret Fuller remarked that "Your community seems to grow" (*L*, III, 72 n.). But that was its peak. He was never able to get Henry James, Ellen Hooper, Margaret Fuller, Caroline Sturgis, Charles Newcomb, Frederic Hedge, or George Bradford to settle near him (*L*, III, 50, 51, 72–72 n., 206; V, 299). But the concentration of scholars he desired was soon made possible by the opening of the Boston and Fitchburg Railway, first agitated in January 1842, and in successful operation by June 1844 (*L*, III, 4, 256; *C*, VI, 148). The desire for a literary society to augment his powers, which was the constant aim of his reforms, was now possible in another form; and in his later years, as much for conviviality as for inspiration, Emerson became as enthusiastic a club man as he had been in his college days.[15]

Even if Emerson's Concord Community and domestic reforms had failed, for him Brook Farm still remained an unsatisfactory alternative. From the start he had opposed Brook Farm over the question of organization. In spite of all its claims after the change to Fourierism in 1844 that it offered the best (and only) social organization corresponding to the faculties of man, it was still disagreeable to him. What he had attempted in his domestic experiments — which the social pressures forced him to undertake — had only strengthened his conviction that any organization imposed from without before the organism felt the need for it and provided it of itself was doomed to failure. He was certain that outward social forms had to develop and vary with inner individual needs: they had to express, not repress, life. And the adoption of the Fourier Phalanx seemed to him a more rigid scheme than the idyllic carefree life, however inefficient, the early Brook Farm admitted.

In introducing Albert Brisbane, America's foremost Fourierist, to the readers of *The Dial*, Emerson wrote a short note on "Fourierism and the Socialists" that genially ridiculed the system.[16] Three months earlier he had been besieged by Brisbane in New York and personally given an explanation of Fourierism, and he was so put upon that his essay reflected an attempt to better that occasion. He had written Lidian that "they [Brisbane and Greeley] are bent on popular action: I am in all my theory, ethics, & politics a poet and of no more use in their New York than a rainbow or a firefly." Their enthusiasm prompted him to ask: "One of these days shall we not have new laws forbidding solitude; and severe penalties on all separatists & unsocial thinkers?" (*L*, III, 18). He had been taxed so far that, he wrote Margaret Fuller, he was driven at once to say, "I must unfold my own thought. Each man must build up his own world, though he unbuilt all other men's, for his materials. So rabid does egotism, when contradicted, run" (*L*, III, 20). In the essay, he reported that "as we listened to his [Brisbane's] exposition, it appeared to us the sublime of mechanical philosophy." He called the system "Ptolemaic," even though he alone might appreciate the disapprobation of the term. And without the benefit of Parke Godwin's *A Popular View of the Doctrine of Charles Fourier*,[17] he quickly saw the "strange coincidences betwixt Fourier and Swedenborg." Then he attacked the system with the same derision that he later found serviceable for Swedenborg's static correspondences: "The hyaena, the jackal, the gnat, the bug, the flee, were all beneficent parts of the system," he wrote; "the good Fourier knew what those creatures should have been, had not the mould slipped, caused, no doubt, by these same vicious imponderable fluids. All these shall be redressed by human culture, and the useful goat, and dog, and innocent poetical moth, or the woodtick to consume decomposing wood, shall take their place."[18] He could not curb his humor and elaborated the details of the system in the same vein: "It takes 1680 men to make one Man, complete in all the faculties; that is, to be sure that you have got a good joiner, a good cook, a barber, a poet, a judge, an umbrella-maker, a mayor and aldermen, and so on."[19] Now fancy, he said, and sketched the system of phalanxes established throughout the world: a sight fit for

Aladdin and Scheherazade. "Genius, grace, art shall abound, and it is not to be doubted but that, in the reign of 'Attractive Industry,' all men will speak in blank verse."

When he became serious, he attacked Fourier's system for the conduct of life on the same grounds that he attacked Swedenborg's symbols. As applications of correspondence both were static, both instituted forms that restricted perception and new forms: "Our feeling was, that Fourier had skipped no fact but one, namely, Life. He treats man as a plastic thing, something that may be put up or down, ripened or retarded . . . at the will of the leader; or, perhaps, as a vegetable, from which, though now a poor crab, a very good peach, can by manure and exposure be in time produced, but skips the faculty of life, which spawns and scorns system and system-makers, which eludes all conditions, which makes or supplants a thousand phalanxes and New-Harmonies with each pulsation." An instituted insight, however good, had still to correspond in a higher way; it had to permit the method of nature — life and growth. And it was from the level of this higher correspondence that Emerson found the application of correspondence in social organization a confusion of means for ends. He was too acutely aware from his own experiments in the socialization of correspondence to deny that "there is an order in which in a sound mind the faculties always appear, and which, according to the strength of the individual, they seek to realize in the surrounding world." No doubt Fourier, like Swedenborg, deserved his fame: both had valuable insights. But, as he said of Swedenborg's private associations, "Could not the conceiver of this design have also believed that a similar model lay in every mind?" The mistake both made was their "rigid execution," their failure to see that "what is true and good must not only be begun by life, but must be conducted to its issues by life." [20] And he was sure that by following life, by living in perception, "that no society can ever be so large as one man" (*C*, III, 265). Whether or not his personal magnetism drew a community to him, in the freedom of perception, the individual was not "dwarfed" by a social "mortgage" to others. He had in his friendships and "natural and momentary associations" a natural means for multiplying himself (*C*, III, 265). In friendship he had new life and inspiration and the only society that truly expressed the faculties and their incessant demands for new objects and affinities. Once more the problem of social organization resolved itself into friendship as a fluid relationship of the self and others. And in the hydrostatic paradox he symbolized "the relation of one man to the whole family of men": the self-reliant man became the column of water that balanced the ocean (*C*, III, 280).

III

The issues of friendship and social reform were more fundamentally parts of a larger problem Emerson faced throughout his life: solitude and society. In his search for sympathetic correspondence, he had discovered that the proper habitat of the (his) soul was nature. Nature alone provided the scope and objects required for the calling forth of the faculties, and it was chiefly in terms of nature that Emerson postulated his doctrine of the faculties and character and affirmed the possibility of self-reliance. His doctrine of the educative effects of labor was subordinated to the need for vision, as were the self-culture and self-sufficiency one reaped from contact with the coarse stuff of life. Like literary expression, self-expression had to follow the method of nature, living by its pulsations, creating new forms, and terminating in affirmative, socially useful action. But again, for Emerson, vision was the highest form of action embodied in the highest organization and form that nature provided. In the ideal man — the complete, self-sufficient man his literary ethics were in-

tended to create — in the ideal man whose character best expressed him, the hydrostatic paradox was easily explained. If
the individual created his own world and lived only to represent its worth to others, the calling of self-culture was socially
justifiable: Such a man could support the world. And come
full circle, the intellectual ends of his doctrine met in solitude
and society, in the perfect adjustment of the man to the society
he needed both for audience and for inspiration. Thus the
circle of Emerson's thought was circumscribed around his
needs for vision.

Solitude, for Emerson, described his entire "ascetic," and
because the conditions of that "ascetic" varied, solitude meant
many things to him in the course of his life. At times, especially in his early years, solitude was equated with elevation,
with nature as the primary place of inspiration, and accordingly became the antithesis of a linear and artificial society.
But apart from its congenial surroundings, solitude also afforded protection, and in the early years of his adjustment
from preacher to poet, he needed this most (*C*, III, 41; VI,
159). During the first of his European travels, he felt the desire for solitude, even before he had seen Wordsworth and
Carlyle living it (*L*, I, 394–395). The cities oppressed him, and
he wrote with a nostalgia characteristic of the romantic emphasis on solitude but genuinely reflecting his needs: "Sometimes I would hide myself in the dens of the hills, in the thick-
ets of an obscure country town. I am so vexed and chagrined
with myself, — with my weakness, with my guilt. Then I have
no skill to live with men, that is, with such men as the world is
made of; and such as I delight in I seldom find." But even here
he was hesitant, too well-nurtured in the desire for greatness
that the city alone could fulfill: "But would it not be cowardly
to flee out of society and live in the woods?" (*J*, III, 131). When
he had fled society, he accepted solitude as penance for worldly
ambition. "I think," he wrote of himself, "he had better live

in the country, and see little society, and make himself of no reputation" (*J*, III, 459).

This, too, was the message of "Literary Ethics." If, he pointed out, one accepted his views of the resources and subjects of the scholar, then these considerations must guide "his ambition and life." To possess the world, to put "himself into harmony with the constitution of things," one had to "embrace solitude as a bride" (*C*, I, 173). And he had done this himself, fortified, perhaps, by one edition or another of Johann Georg von Zimmermann's *Solitude*.[21] Throughout Zimmermann's treatise, full of the sentiment of the eighteenth century, solitude was extolled as the cure for almost every worldly disease from the unrewarded ambitions of youth to the renewal of energies in old age. But the heart of the treatise was Zimmermann's own need for solitude after the loss of his wife. This, undoubtedly, was one of its attractions for Emerson, whose loss of Ellen Tucker precipitated his own removal from society. And what Emerson made of solitude can hardly be divorced from the effects of this loss: his doctrine of compensation and desire for immortality were fulfilled in the practice of vision.[22]

By the time he wrote "The Transcendentalist" (1842), he had projected this way of life — a sign of the times — to all transcendentalists, affirming that "this part [the solitary life] is chosen both from temperament and from principle." Solitude was the better of two evils, and its choice did not indicate melancholy, unsociability or pitilessness. Transcendentalists may, he said, "betake themselves to a certain solitary and critical way of living," but — and he spent more than a page to elaborate — "they have even more than others a great wish to be loved" (*C*, I, 341–343). But, then, he was defending himself from the reformers.

Like Zimmermann, he claimed everything for solitude. But he never made the solitary life a hermit existence or complete withdrawal from society. Solitude, for both, was best achieved by adopting the country life, a slower, freer society in which reflection [23] or the withdrawal of the mind into itself could more easily be attained (*J*, VI, 197). By 1840, when the elevation of solitude had become a disposition of his character, Emerson was eager to effect the mediation of country solitude and the society of the city; even in society, he learned from Zimmermann, this solitude was possible. For solitude was no longer circumstance, but character. It was the self-containment reaped in the severe discipline of self-reliance, and it made possible the great man, "who in the midst of the crowd keeps with perfect sweetness the independence of solitude" (*C*, II, 54). As an attribute of character, solitude was another way of using or transforming society for the purposes of genius. Zimmermann had suggested that society could be used as "the great scene of our observations" and that it was the appropriate place to amass the materials that one arranged in solitude.[24] And Emerson-the-observer used society in this way. Solitude remained the working condition of his mind, the correspondential attitude raising him above the impact of prudential affairs to the platform from which these affairs could contribute to the life of his intellect.

A solitude of this kind *in* society was Emerson's aim, not, as he earlier noted, the alternation and surfeit of each (*J*, IV, 473). When he came to write "Society and Solitude" (1870),[25] he had experimented enough to know that between these poles (which, in effect, represented sociologically the poles of the mind) "our safety is in the skill with which we keep the diagonal line." "Solitude," he concluded, "is impractical, and society fatal." With a wisdom that spoke for all of his own attempts to make solitude sociable or the life of genius bearable, he noted after Hawthorne's death the tragic element in his life, "the painful solitude of the man, which, I suppose, could not longer be endured, and he died of it" (*J*, X, 39–40). Such a solitude, like the mysticism that all but destroyed Jones Very, was not for him. "We must keep our head in the one," he wrote, "and our hands in the other" (*C*, VII, 15). He was no longer content to let others "represent all courtesy and worldly life" or "do the great and resounding actions" for him. To "lie close hid with nature" had its costs and penalties, too (*C*, III, 41). In time he saw that "some allowance" had to be made for "the poor Whiggish facts" of social evils and that the "stoical thesis" of his youth — not "to degrade our life by the trivial measures of practice" — was a "faith without works" (*J*, VIII, 162). And when Webster shattered his ideal, to save it Emerson himself, more than ever before, became a public man. The courageous John Brown, enacting the ideal without considering the inadequacy of the means, became his new representative man; and in the whirlpool of the Civil War, Emerson was willing to cast off his theoretical restraints and take what for him was an active role. Henceforth he was social and could write: "The conditions [of society and solitude] are met, if we keep our independence, yet do not lose our sympathy." The readiness of sympathy became the one social virtue he could not sacrifice to solitude, and although he wrote that "a sound mind will derive its principles from insight, with ever a purer ascent to the sufficient and absolute right," he was now able to add, "and will accept society as the natural element in which they are to be applied" (*C*, VII, 15–16). But by this time his force was ebbing, and nature was no longer restorative. Now the dead issues of social reform in the 1840's could be wistfully retold, and the warmth of fame that had spread around him could melt the chilly solitude of the early man (*C*, X, 325–370).[26]

7

Prospects

The new prospect is power.
EMERSON, "Circles."

There arises a pleasant prospect to pay us for our labour as we ascend; and as we continue our labour in ascending, still the pleasantness of the prospect grows.
JONATHAN EDWARDS, *Images or Shadows of Divine Things.*

Be an opener of doors for such as come after thee, and do not try to make the universe a blind alley. . . Do let the new generation speak the truth, and let our grandfathers die.
EMERSON, *Journals.*

However uncritically Emerson read the philosophers, he recognized that in the long history of speculation men were driven by the need for security and certainty to system building in which they split (or united) their metaphysical universes according to their temperaments. By temperament, men and nations were either nominalist or realist — either sense-bound and strong in their possession of details, like the English of his day; or spirit-bound in the quest of the really real, like the essence-seeking German transcendentalists (*C*, III, 231). Although he knew that "the nature of the Great Spirit is single," he knew as well that by temperament men often preferred the many to the one. He knew from his own experience, which he attributed to the polar structure of the mind, that in speculation men tended to unity and in action to diversity; and this antagonism of the mind he tried to control by correspondence, by joining the one in the many. He found this polarity of the mind expressed in all the endeavors of thought and action, in the life of men and nations. Unity and diversity were everywhere, and in "Plato" he summarized their manifestations: "One is being; the other, intellect: one is necessity; the other, freedom: one, rest; the other, motion: one power; the other, distribution: one strength; the other, pleasure: one, consciousness; the other, definition: one, genius; the other, talent: one, earnestness; the other, knowledge: one, possession; the other, trade: one, caste; the other, culture: one, king; the other, democracy: and, if we dare carry these generalizations a step higher, and name the last tendency of both, we might say, that the end of the one is escape from organization, — pure science; and the end of the other is the highest instrumentality, or use of means, or executive deity" (*C*, IV, 50–52). Obviously, this balance sheet suggested the necessity of mediation; for if democracy were the expression of diversity (of the senses and affectionless intellect) and genius of unity (of Reason and sympathy), then his role as the representative American was shaped by the need for their reconciliation.

As he read the history of thought, Emerson also found the corresponding temperaments or partialities in nations. Asia, for example, was the "country of unity, of immovable institutions, the seat of a philosophy delighting in abstractions, of men faithful in doctrine and in practice to the idea of a deaf, unimplorable, immense fate." On the other hand, Europe was "active and creative," used philosophy as a discipline, and so became "a land of arts, inventions, trade, freedom." The

West, he said, "delighted in boundaries," and the East "loved infinity" (*C*, IV, 52). But the two partialities sometimes interpenetrated, and especially when the love of infinity and unity reawakened in the West, it seemed to Emerson that faith was also reborn. For, at least to him, the alternations of temperament reflected the cycles of faith in history. When the high tide of "Divine Presence" ebbed, men lost the upward glance, turned to things, and respected only the "performance, not the power" (*C*, V, 221–222). Nations became spiritless and were preoccupied with the commodities of life. When the tide of faith was at its full, when "heats and genial periods arrive in history," the human spirit renewed itself, saw the symbolic grandeur of the universe, and genius and piety flowered once more (*C*, V, 220). These alternations of temperament were the "silent revolutions in opinion" that marked the progress of culture. They were the correspondencies in nations of man himself, equipped with two sets of faculties, now living by one and absorbed in the particular, now living by the other and the universal (*C*, III, 229). One, he said, could be called the conservative, the other a transcendentalist. One stood on "man's confessed limitations" and on circumstance or "negative fate," the other on man's "indisputable infinitude" and principles (*C*, I, 298–299). They represented the poles of the mind and the perpetual counteraction of the centripetal and centrifugal forces in the spiritual history of men and nations.

He knew, too, that men were forever challenging the old assumptions they felt restricting their advance. He believed that truth was prospective and that new symbols were always needed to catch and glimpse it. Thus, new symbols were evoked, new ideas generated, new conceptions of truth proposed, and new metaphysical projections of the sentiment of rationality erected. At the points of conflict and transition — whether men were mired in materialism or buoyant with spiritualism — the need to keep alive the sense of a living relationship with both levels of the universe, the need to be a whole man, was strongly felt. Especially in these critical periods, men felt both the wide gulf between the "worlds" and the difficulties of achieving their union. Unwilling to put on metaphysical blinders that limited human aspiration to either the material or spiritual alone, they adopted or revived some assumption of correspondence to assure themselves that the two worlds (the two modes of the mind), though two, were not unrelated, and that life included both. For if there were two worlds, as the spiritual experience of man testified, they felt — as Emerson expressed his own need for correspondence — that "without identity at base, chaos must be forever" (*C*, XII, 20).

The bringers of the metaphysical relief of identity, Emerson called the reconcilers, the balanced souls (*C*, IV, 54). They alone saw the good of both conservatism and transcendentalism: they had respect for both facts and ideas, for the prudential life that could not be completely divested of poetry and for the spiritual life of ideas that rounded and ennobled "the most partial and sordid way of living" (*C*, III, 231). They made their mission and the mission of their age, like the mission Brownson summoned the nineteenth century to perform, the uniting of the infinite and the finite.[1] They came as mediators. They came in that moment in the history of every nation (and the history of a nation corresponded to the growth of the individual mind), "when proceeding out of . . . brute youth, the perceptive powers reach their ripeness, and have not yet become microscopic: so that man, at that instant, extends across the entire scale; and with his feet still planted on the immense forces of night converses, by his eyes and brain, with solar and stellar creation" (*C*, IV, 46–47). When they came, myth served as poetry and science and united both projections of the mind.

Looking for the original reconciler, the first balanced soul and metaphysician of correspondence, Emerson returned to the youthful age of the world's history, to Greece, and to Plato, her representative man. Plato, Emerson said, had the excellence of Europe and Asia in his brain and came "to join" and "to enhance the energy of each." "This exhausting generalizer" had mounted the highest platforms of thought and had united the worlds of East and West, which Emerson used to characterize the two poles of the mind: otherworldliness and worldliness, infinite expansion and definition, intellect receptive and intellect constructive.[2] In Plato, Emerson projected his own aims and methods. As the balanced soul, he was "perceptive of the two elements," saw the upper and under sides of nature, and united them in the consciousness of man (*C*, IV, 54). "If he loved abstract truth," Emerson continued, "he saved himself by propounding the most popular of all principles, the absolute good. . . If he made transcendental distinctions, he fortified himself by drawing all his illustrations from sources disdained by orators and polite conversers; from mares and puppies; from pitchers and soup-ladles; from cooks and criers. . . He cannot forgive in himself a partiality, but is resolved that the two poles of thought shall appear in his statement. His argument and his sentence are self-poised and spherical. The two poles appear; yes, and become two hands, to grasp and appropriate their own" (*C*, IV, 55). Thus, for Emerson, Plato was the fountain of unity from which all subsequent thought flowed, and all the followers hereafter in the search for identity were Platonists. The history of thought — once Plato had shown the possibility of union — was a departure and return, like the ebb and flow of the mind, an oscillation from his normative ideal, from faith to skepticism.

But unity was as fleeting as a perception of the mind. Over and over again, when nations departed from their youthful health and sanity of unifying perception and lapsed into the decay and old age of the senses, a new reconciler had to come with his "armed perception" to affirm, and so lead men back to, the wonders of harmonious existence. This was all the more difficult when an original perception, in the process of its enunciation and appropriation, solidified into the system built to advance it. As a system (or institution) it became — as for Emerson, Swedenborg's vision had — arbitrary, abstract, and limitary, chopping experience or withholding its full realization.[3] To be effectively living, the vision of unity, therefore, had to be reborn in every age, in every generation, colored by all the peculiar demands and knowledge of that age, just as perception was colored from moment to moment in the history of the mind by the mood and experience of the perceiver. Even Plato, Emerson said, lost something of the enthusiasm of the East by becoming too much a "definer" or philosopher, and to serve later generations had to be enriched by the mysticism of the Plotinians (*C*, IV, 76).

Similarly, new reconcilers were needed when the silent revolution of science effaced the many centuries of religion, and, as Emerson described the waning of the seventeenth-century religio-scientific genius, the "spirit . . . glided away to animate other activities" (*C*, V, 220). The century of physics, urged apparently by the spirituality of the century of genius, turned from cause to effect (*C*, IV, 48), and its limited concept of Reason and mechanically conceived universe hemmed in the soul. It forced the next mediator — and the tremendous obstacle was the fact that the eighteenth century had substituted science for the deity — to spiritualize the physical description of the science that had even penetrated the celestial universe. The reconciler had to question the sufficiency of the science mankind had only begun to accept. He had to balance physics with mind, mechanism with life, and had to show (which the language of science and Lockean Reason could not serve to express) that, although the universe of secondary causes was mapped and ordered, the mind, ever aware of the spirit of life, was impatient with its limitations. No one more than Emerson appreciated the design and lawfulness of the universe science revealed: It seemed the handiwork of the deity and, Emerson approvingly acknowledged, made all men, at last, believers in the necessity of law. But like all systems — like Fourierism, for example, which claimed to be scientific — the cost of neatness was too great to pay, especially when the expense was life. The mystery and wonder of the universe eluded the system because the enigma of life could only be experienced: perception alone gave the fullness of life; what remained in the system was skeletal and lifeless. The missing life of science, then, had to be sought in consciousness. The present revolutionary age, Emerson wrote, as opposed to the traditional age of the eighteenth century, was the reflective period, "when man is coming back to consciousness" (*J*, V, 214, 306). The war of his generation, he said in "Historic Notes," had been between intellect and affection and to bridge the "crack in nature" men had become aware of the mind itself. "Men grew reflective," he said; "There was a new consciousness" (*C*, X, 225–226). Science, too, he noted, had become introversive (*J*, V, 94). Therefore, the reconciler of the nineteenth century had to be a psychologist. Not the psychologist, however, with whom we are familiar: the manipulator, experimenter, and statistician. Rather, he had to be the poet of the mind, a reporter of the natural history of the intellect, one for whom the mystery remained after the search and for whom knowing was a religious experience of being and becoming. His genius had to be a sensitivity to life.

By his own definition — one who held the stupendous antagonism of the universe together — Emerson was one of the reconcilers of the nineteenth century. In his private list of American representative men, he compared himself with Goethe, the man who, he felt, was most important to the cul-

ture of the nineteenth century (*J*, VIII, 62, 214). He wrote
Margaret Fuller, whose enthusiasm for Goethe was equal to
her enthusiasm for Emerson, that Goethe had both the common sense and genius "which enabled him to be the interpreter between the real & the apparent worlds" (*L*, II, 202–
203). Goethe was by his own definition an *Augenmensch* — an
eye-man who saw, as Emerson put it, out of every pore of his
skin. He was the "Argus-eyed" philosopher of multiplicity,
"able and happy to cope with this rolling miscellany of facts
and sciences, and, by his own versatility, to dispose of them
with ease" (*C*, IV, 271–272). He drew his strength from a full
communion with nature and thus had the power "to unite the
detached atoms again by their own law" (*C*, IV, 271, 273).
"Amid littleness and detail," Emerson wrote, "he detected
the Genius of life." He had the earnestness to "outsee" other
men of greater talent, and proved in his scientific pursuits that
"eyes are better . . . than telescopes or microscopes" (*C*, IV,
274, 283). That is, for Emerson, he vindicated the role of the
scholar as the man of insight, ideas, poetry, and expression,
and made him the peer of the wise masters of the ages, of the
"old philosophers" who did not lose the poetry and humanity
of life in "tabulation and dissection" (*C*, IV, 274).

As a reconciler — apart from his demonstration of the literary uses of correspondence — Emerson was chiefly a scientist
of the mind. He was an explorer of consciousness and the natural historian of its ebb and flow; and for this reason his insistence on self-culture as the true calling of the scholar, even
when it led to solitude, was justified. In the mind he had experienced a power enabling him to "resist the contracting influences of so-called science" (*C*, III, 52). So-called science, he
had learned from Coleridge, lost sight of the indispensable
help of ideas and did not pause in its search for facts to reflect
on the mind's contribution in perception of unifying and life-
giving ideas. But for all of his disgust for unrelated fact-find-

ing, Emerson recognized and, in his way, glorified the mechanical physics and burgeoning researches that supplied him
the terrestrial map for his spiritual explorations.

As early as 1830, he preached in a sermon on "Providence"
that "the discoveries of science, not the instructions of revealed
religion but the discoveries of science, have compelled men to
believe that nothing is made without a purpose" (*Y*, 220 n.).
This was the great spiritual benefit of science that he ever
afterward praised and that prompted him to study in natural
history the behavior of the mind. Unlike later science — "the
narrow and dead classification" — the science he approved,
and even found worth while in pseudoscientific fads like mes-
merism and animal magnetism, affirmed the "unity and connection between remote points" (*C*, X, 337). Summing up the
revolution of his generation in "Historic Notes," he said that
the "paramount source" of the revived faith of his generation
had been "Modern Science" (*C*, X, 335). By verifying the purposiveness and lawfulness of the universe, science, when used
correspondentially, provided the basis of ethical law, that is,
the laws of mind and of the conduct of life. In this way science
"affected an imaginative race like poetic inspirations"; he was
speaking of the progress of culture in America (*C*, VIII, 211).
In this way, "The axioms of physics translate the laws of ethics," and the laws below answered to the law above: thus nature became a moral fable (*C*, I, 33; VIII, 223). At one time,
Emerson even approved Paley's analogy of the world-machine,
because it was an early attempt to extend Newtonian physics
to morals (*Y*, 220 n.). Of course, he realized the spiritual in-
adequacies of a watchlike universe, which, like the science
that "murders to dissect," abolished the miracle of life or
creation by removing the necessary presence of God (*Y*, 41).
He was not opposed to science-as-science but to science-as-
scheme, the science which had forgotten the poetry of ideas in
the assurance that the sensible fact was sufficient and that ac-

cumulation would give the universe meaning. And he was not so much opposed to Paley's analogy-as-analogy, but to its implications of determinism. Emerson also built his moral analogies on the Newtonian astronomy, but he restored the creative function of perception as the guarantee of freedom, life, and unity. By making perception a communion with the source of life and law, he necessarily altered the analogy of design from that of the mechanical watch to that of the dynamic organism of nature.

By emphasizing perception, Emerson humanized science; and for him, science was always secondary to the moral insight it helped to awaken. Science dealt with an "inferior" nature which helped — if there were to be a reconciliation of science and faith — the possession of the world by man in the moral "excursions of Poetry into lower nature" (*J*, V, 57). Like Herder, whom Ripley had popularized, "his favorite wish" was the "discovery of the laws of nature, and of their union and harmony with each other and the universe, even in a moral point of view." And he believed with Ripley that " 'the germ of all human knowledge . . . must become to us the germ of new life and new virtue.' " He believed and made it his mission to " 'cultivate this germ, according to our present modes of conception, and the knowledge and power which we have acquired from the past; so that every truth, of which we become certain, may lead us more freely to the great spiritual objects of our being. As physical science receives new light, the operation of spiritual powers is confirmed, and the soul of man is elevated in reverence and love towards the Supreme Creator.' " [4] For "something is wanting to science," Emerson said in preparation for his description of the office of the great man, "until it has been humanized" (*C*, IV, 10). The "higher advantages" of science were lost until the fact was taken up and interpreted by man in character and in symbol (*C*, IV, 10). "A great deal of God in the universe," he wrote, "but not

valuable to us until we can make it up into man" (*J*, VII, 50–
51). Thus, he urged the young scholars in "Literary Ethics,"
there was an "extreme need of the priests of science," of spiritual seekers to "explore, and explore" (*C*, I, 186). If one of the
features of the age was the "paramount place of Natural History," then the role of the scholar or reconciler was to make
Natural History pious — poetical (*J*, VIII, 35, 122). Sampson
Reed had made the "soul of science" the poetic response in
which one felt "the power of creation." Only the poet, by reviving the sense of the divine presence in nature, properly
humanized the sciences; for without the "exact agreement
with the creative spirit of God," science, for Reed, remained a
"fiction." [5] This was true for Emerson, too, who also saw that
what the silent revolutions had brought about could not be
put aside: science could not be forgotten in a devotion to
ethics, for without its natural basis moralism was also insuffi-
cient.[6] Science and poetry, fact and value, had to be joined —
this was the mission of the age — and the union was possible if
the facts of science became the "verge of today," the new center from which the poet gained his spiritual prospect (*C*, II,
315 ff.). "The moral of science," he said, "should be a transference of that trust which is felt in Nature's admired arrangements in light, heat, gravity, and so on, to the social and moral
order" (*J*, VII, 101). Poetry, in its transcendental function,
was the means of transference.

Like many idealists of the day, Emerson was eager, therefore, for the newest discoveries of science. In his European
travels, he sought out the scientists, visited the museums of
natural history, and attended scientific lectures. At home he
maintained a friendship with Louis Agassiz and Dr. Holmes
and read the latest books on science. He began his career as a
lecturer before the Boston Society of Natural History. In four
of the five lectures he tried to explain the lesson he had learned
at the Jardin des Plantes, how the highest advantage of the

study of natural history was its help in explaining man to himself, its revelation of "that correspondence of the outward
with the inward world, by which it is fitted to represent what
we think." And to use science in this way, he said, one had to
remain "a poet in his severest analysis," that is, one had to
subordinate the naturalist to the man.[7] As a poet-priest of
science, Emerson never lost his early interest in what he later
called the "*zymosis* of Science" (*J*, X, 264). For science provided the stimulus of new perceptions and the material of new
analogies and correspondences in the poet's advance on the
frontier of the mind. "The good augury of our larger dedication to natural science in this century is," he wrote, "not so
much for the added material power which it has yielded
(though that is conspicuous and we cannot have too much) as
for the intellectual power it evokes, and, shall I say, the sublime delight with which the intellect contemplates each new
analogy appearing between the laws of Nature and its own
law of life" (*J*, X, 204–205). And better than the attempt to
find an "exact" analogy for each law of nature, as Swedenborg
had, was "the spasm (shall I say) of pleasure which pervades
the intellect in recognizing, however dimly, the instant perception of its equal holding through heaven, as well as through
earth" (*J*, X, 206). Life was in seeing, not fashioning, the analogy, and Emerson was willing to keep his perception alive by
new symbols as well as by the reperceiving of old ones. It was
with this necessity of vision in mind that he wrote in "The
Poet" that "the fascination [of nature] resides in the symbol"
(*C*, III, 15). And it was with the sensualism of linear science
in mind that he affirmed that "there is no more welcome gift
to men than a new symbol" (*C*, VIII, 13).

Science provided the material of new symbols and therefore
the vehicles of perception. In the reconciliation Emerson
sought, science supplied an accurate map and an exact physical language, which, when used symbolically, helped in the

exploration of the spiritual territory of the mind. His theory of language, like Horace Bushnell's, was an attempt to make language the instrument of mediation between matter and spirit. What Emerson briefly outlined in *Nature*, Bushnell elaborated in his preliminary dissertation on language in *God in Christ*.[8] Emerson wrote in *Nature* that "the use of natural history is to give us aid in super-natural history: the use of the outer creation, to give us language for the beings and changes of the inward creation." Words, he said, were originally "signs of natural facts" — or, as Bushnell wrote, words as signs were merely pointers in a language of physical things. The name of the natural fact or sign became a symbol of "particular spiritual facts," and all of nature became the "symbol of spirit" (*C*, I, 23 ff.), because, for both Emerson and Bushnell, their correspondence was already assumed in the metaphysical constitution of man. When Emerson said that all men were analogists, he was saying in effect what Bushnell said when he wrote that man was framed for language by God.[9] Analogy (or the spiritual use of language) was only reliable if, as Bushnell said, "there is a logos in the outward creation, answering to the logos or internal reason . . . there is a vast analogy in things, which prepares them, as forms, to be signs or figures of thoughts, and thus, bases or types of words. Our bodily mechanism [here he described the faculty theory: 'the body is a living logos, added to the soul, to be its form, and play it forth into social understanding'], and the sensible world we live in, are in fact made up of words, to represent our thoughts and internal states." [10] By this logic the fact that language could be used symbolically to suggest the spiritual realm proved the correspondential design of the universe, and analogy, according to Emerson, became the key to the universe (*J*, IX, 176; VIII, 271–272).[11]

The importance of this theory, however, was the fact that nature (science) was given a spiritual *use*. "The Mind," Emerson knew, "must think by means of Matter; find Matter or Nature the means and words of its thinking and expression" (*J*, X, 236). Appropriated by the analogist, science was no longer opposed to religion and metaphysics, but served as an "index of our self-knowledge." [12] If the discoveries of science seemed only to bring darkness, the fault lay in the "observer" whose "corresponding faculty" had not yet become active. The discoveries of science, then, provoked new perceptions, and in this way, far from hindering man's spiritual conquest, kept "abreast with the just elevation of . . . man" (*C*, III, 14–15). For this reason the scholar, even if poorly schooled, was justified in his interest in science, and felt the need to prepare himself, as the elderly Emerson noted, at "the college or the scientific school which offered [the] best lectures on Geology, Chemistry, Minerals, Botany." These sciences, Emerson added, gave the scholar his alphabet, and every secret the new science opened helped "to authorize our aesthetics" (*J*, X, 393). These sciences "waked and tested every faculty of thought" and made possible the perception and expression of "finer distinctions" and the correction of metaphysics (*J*, X, 455).

This theory warranted the optimism and faith in science of the transcendentalist. Even if, as the elder Henry James recalled the fault Emerson's generation found with science, "Science has no eye for truth, but only for Fact, which is the appearance that truth puts on to the senses, and is therefore intrinsically second-hand, or shallow and reflective," [13] still science remained as the reliable instrument for penetrating the spiritual world by setting the world of appearance in order. Bushnell expressed this faith in the mapping function (and limitation) of science and made it the preliminary tool of the poet-psychologist: "It is, that physical science, leading the way, setting outward things in their true proportions, opening up their true contents, revealing their genesis and final causes and laws, and weaving all into the unity of a real universe, will so perfect our knowledges and conceptions of them, that we can use them, in the second department of language [as symbols of spirit], with more exactness." [14]

Faithfully written, transformed by perception, science became poetry or myth: the humanized science of Reason. For Emerson, Plato was the preëminent myth-maker. He domesticated the soul in nature — this was the aim of transcendental vision — by representing "the circles of the visible heaven" as the "circles in the rational soul." He was a discoverer of "connection, continuity, and representation everywhere," a "Euclid of holiness" who married "the two parts of nature" (*C*, IV, 85–87). All humanizers of fact for Emerson, all "those who delight in giving a spiritual, that is, an ethico-intellectual expression to every truth, by exhibiting an ulterior end which is yet legitimate to it," were Platonizers and myth-makers. Only they admitted light into the recesses of nature and repaired the lack in science of a "human side" by seeing the universe from its center in man (*C*, VI, 282–283). They announced "the good of being interpenetrated by the mind that made nature" (*C*, IV, 63). They followed the original motive of science, "the extension of man, on all sides, into Nature, till his hands should touch the stars, his eyes see through the earth, his ears understand the language of beast and bird, and the sense of the wind; and, through his sympathy, heaven and earth should talk with him" (*C*, VI, 284). Sympathy became their method, not the linear logic of mathematics and contrivance. As Thoreau wrote in the "Natural History of Massachusetts" and exemplified in practice more than any other transcendentalist, "The true man of science will know nature better by his finer organization; he will smell, taste, see, hear, feel, better than other men. His will be a deeper and finer experience. We do not learn by inference and deduction, and the application of mathematics to philosophy, but by direct intercourse and sympathy. It is with science as with ethics, we cannot know truth by contrivance and method; the Baconian is as false as any other, and with all the helps of machinery and the arts, the most scientific will still be the healthiest and friendliest man." [15] But to communicate the findings of sympathetic exploration, they had to have the "cosmic imagination" of the Greek mythologists (an "astronomic imagination" like Emerson's), the power "of expressing in graceful fable the laws of the world, so that the mythology is beautiful poetry on one side, at any moment convertible into severe science on the other" (*J*, VIII, 360–361). Not only did they point to the fact, they became one with it, and colored it with the fullness of life. Seers and perceivers, they got within the veil and so their words embraced the thing. And even though Emerson was aware, and Bushnell too, that the symbol could only suggest and never cover the spiritual thing, still he believed that the poetical use of language gave the "most accurate picture" (*J*, IV, 244, 266). The poetic symbol of the fable and the myth served by suggesting, as "hints, or images," according to Bushnell, "held up before the mind of another, to put *him* on generating or reproducing the same thought." [16] Emerson would have added, "the same perception."

For Emerson glorified the myth because it illustrated as well as stimulated the perceptive powers. Myth, he said, depended on the perception of degree; it was fashioned by men who were devoted to ideas and who employed ideas to raise the facts through the full extent of the bisected line, from the visible to the intelligible platform. Myth followed the Coleridgean method of science. Unlike the linear method of natural history, building up, Emerson wrote, "from oyster and tadpole . . . mythology gives us down from the heavens" (*J*, VIII, 525). Myth assured him that the method of ideas was superior, because myth never lost the power to "speak out clearly ever and anon the noble sentiments [what the literal word "transformed" expressed] of all ages" (*J*, X, 154). Furthermore, myths seemed to express the same archetypes. From his wide reading in the scriptures of the Orient, the Near East, and Scandinavia, he discovered that there was a "singular correspondence . . . in the fables themselves" (*J*, III, 412). All spoke with the voice of the divine and hinted the same abiding truth. Like their miniatures, the proverbs, myths, for him, were "the literature of reason" (*C*, II, 108–109).

But what was the myth that the humanizer should create for his own age? What should characterize the nineteenth century's literature of reason, the permanent as opposed to the transient literature? Emerson was unable or unwilling to say, because he had come to realize that time was needed to distance the representative men and ideas of history. Time was needed to efface the forms and faces of men, to see the ends for which they strove and to recognize the tendency. Nevertheless, he was aware of the "mythologic names" of the scientific, commercial, and industrial age in which he lived. By simply listing Watt, Fulton, Arkwright, Stephenson, Fourier, and so forth, he revealed that he was acutely aware of "the direction of the march" (*J*, VII, 383). The applications and benefits of science characterized the age. And the age, Emerson said when speaking of the superstitions of the times, had too great a faith "in the steam engine" (*J*, VII, 317–318), too great a faith, as Henry Adams finally symbolized it, in the dynamo. The faith of the age was in power, mechanical power, the power of things, not spiritual power. And although he tried to gloss this faith in the machine by showing the spirit needed to invent, he had his misgivings: the stuff of myth was there, but he wanted, before he subscribed to it, to propose his own way of using it.

Unlike the myth of the understanding taking shape in his age, Emerson's was the myth of the reason. He tried to vindicate by means of the lesser myth of science the spiritual power of mind. "No other imaginative writer," John Burroughs wrote, "has been so stimulated and aroused by the astounding discoveries of physics . . . there is hardly a fundamental principle of science that he has not turned to ideal uses." [17] The most momentous contemporary scientific achievements shaped his vision: his doctrine of compensation was the moral equivalent of Newton's law of gravitation, and his spiritual interpretation of the correspondence of the faculties to both levels of the universe (his theory of the growth of the mind) was supported by Faraday's findings in magnetism. He found the warrant of his method and his sublime confidence in correspondence and ideas in the Newtonian astronomy and in the pre-Darwinian evolutionary science of the day. One provided the basis of his astronomy of the imagination, the other helped make it dynamic. Growth, benefit, progress, interrelatedness, and unity — and innumerable examples of design in details more suggestive of analogies than the mathematical grandeur of the Newtonian heavens — all these were everywhere to be seen in the chain of being. With these he felt equipped to sketch the natural history of intellect and to make his metaphysics, as it was pragmatically for himself, one of use. He was searching for the larger law the nineteenth century needed, a law "embracing mind and matter" (*J*, VIII, 102). Although he knew that Kant, Hegel, and Schelling had made the initial surveys, he still awaited "the Copernicus of our inward heaven" (*J*, X, 53). "There is no use in Copernicus," he wrote, "if the robust periodicity of the solar system does not show its equal perfection in the mental sphere — the periodicity, the compensatory errors, the grand reactions" (*C*, VIII, 223). He felt with Parker the need for some genius to "devise the 'novum organum' of humanity . . . and with deeper than mathematical science, write out the formulas of the human universe, the celestial mechanics of mankind!" [18] But he knew that he was not equipped to provide the *system*: he had too great an abhorrence of system to do more than report his moods and insights in what became his most philosophical presentation, "Natural History of Intellect." Nevertheless, in its way, his vision was one attempt to chart the inward heaven.

And this, perhaps, is his lasting value. Even if, as Joseph Warren Beach has demonstrated, Emerson read his science in popularization, impatient with logic, indiscriminate of details, for the most part for lusters,[19] still, as a naturalist of the mind, his description of the processes of imaginative perception has an undiminished authenticity and contemporary worth: too few have reported the adventure of the spirit. After a century of scientific progress, it is more difficult to find in science itself the source of faith in correspondence that Emerson found — more difficult to believe, as he did, that the chief value of science is metaphysical, "the test it has been of the scholar" — more difficult to feel that "immeasurable nature" gives "clear answers" and that, therefore, the human mind is equal to the universe (*C*, VIII, 221). Even Emerson saw the new difficulties Darwin had created for the poet. "Natural Science," he wrote, "is dimming & extinguishing a good deal that was called poetry. These sublime & all-reconciling revelations of nature will exact of poetry a correspondent height & scope, or put an end to it" (*L*, VI, 63). Emerson's faith in the ability of men to use science, therefore, and his own attempt to imaginatively understand the universe science was then extending, more than the temporary symbols in which he achieved this, has its significance now. He was doing what the silent revolutions had made the work of an age of science: he was reconciling one projection of the mind with another, humanizing science by interpreting it in terms of the aspiration of whole men. With the equipment and ideas his age provided, he was the "critic of abstractions," "harmonising them by assigning to them their right relative status as abstractions, and . . . completing them by direct comparison

with more concrete intuitions of the universe." [20] He was re-
affirming the creative functions and freedom of the mind in
order to give both man and nature the wholeness of which the
age of commodity and skepticism had robbed them.

Mechanical physics had revealed the operation of law in the
universe, but it was incapable of revealing the law to mind, as
experience or idea. Its description did not prepare the way —
was inadequately conveyanced — for the perception of law
which alone gave it human significance. This was the function
the poet performed. He perceived, felt the fullness of which
the abstraction was the skeleton, and he expressed his insight
in a way to make others realize the full immediacy in *their*
perception. His concern both initially and terminally was
with perception, with how to keep it alive for himself, and
with how to convey and stimulate it in others. The mind,
therefore, was his province. But in his devotion to mind and to
ideas, which expressed his deepest desire to overcome circumstances, Emerson did not cast aside the achievements of mind
in science. After all, science was another manifestation of the
polarity of the mind, representing — at least in its eighteenth-
century applications — the human concern with commodity
and limit. For the mediator it had to be included, but balanced with the organic vitality of the other pole of the mind.
To reassert correspondence for his time, Emerson had thus to
attribute it to the structure and function of the mind and had
to describe as best he could how the life of the universe flowed
into and from the mind, making its symbolically realized perceptions adequate expressions of its own desire for harmony.
The mind itself, then, had to be conceived of as the instrument
of identity. Made in the image of the universe, its structure
was polar, its functioning the ceaseless antagonism of expansions and contractions, of watching and doing, that marked its
natural history in the search for balance or unity.

The power of the mind to merge with the life of the universe and to perceive relatedness and feel the continuity of experience — these were the attributes of mind or the modes of its operation that the eighteenth century minimized and that therefore especially concerned the reconciler. To overcome the mechanically conceived mind, the contriving mental machine of Locke, Emerson refashioned the mind after the pattern of organic nature. His description of the mind followed that of the method of nature — a pulsating, creative organ, living from moment to moment with the tides of the spirit. Even when he likened the mind in its relations to the universe to an angle of vision, he retained its living and creative aspects by making the metaphor one of perception. Perception was the way into the universe. As a metaphor of the mind, the angle of vision (and circles of thought) was indebted to the Newtonian astronomy, but the dynamism it represented for Emerson was added from the post-Kantian reassertions of intuition. The metaphysical poets Emerson admired would have appreciated this fusion of astronomical-mathematical design with the demand for insight rather than observation, for the conceit itself was an example of mediation. The angle symbolized the most important change that Emerson made in man's relation to the universe: now placed at the center of the universe and aligned with its axis, man became the focus of nature. His world was as much as he could see, as much as his sympathetic correspondence and perception created for him to see. The angle, therefore, was a visual means of conveying the fact of the centrality of the self (of the equality of the self and the universe) and the fact that the world existed to be, or morally only when, converted into the self. "Through him," Emerson wrote, "as through a lens, the rays of the universe shall converge, whithersoever he turns, on a point" (*J*, V, 20).

But at the same time that the angle of vision signified the infinite scope of the mind's activity, it also represented the inescapable restriction of the mind at its constructive pole. As the unifying center of experience, the mind could penetrate the recesses of being, and, ideally, it could come full circle — but only in the moments of its release from its earth-bound pole. In communicating the fullness of life, however, it was limited to a fragment or arc of the life of the actual world. It was through the actual world that it saw the real. What science contributed, then, was essential to the advance on chaos and the dark: it charted the actual and thus provided the basis of spiritual communication. Ultimately the metaphor expressed the antagonism of the mind itself, its refusal to be contained even when the container was its own self-made perspective. And it pointed directly to the problem of symbolization: that only perception — fresh perception and return to the sources of life — could prevent the solidification and limitation of formulation, that by failing to *use* his perceptive powers man made the world a blind alley.

Emerson still turned to more organic metaphors, even though the visual-spatial metaphor was closest to his constitutional preference for visual stimulus and, as we have seen, the eye and light were his equivalents for mind and consciousness. He likened the mind and its mysterious unfolding to the growth of a plant, and, perhaps anticipating William James who marked the passage in his edition of Emerson, to a self-made flowing stream.[21] The mind-as-plant had its organic attachments and could not be explained mechanically. It suggested the friendly dependence on the life of the universe with which Emerson tried to replace (as he also did with his use of climate, atmosphere, and Over-Soul) the fatalistic environmentalism of the time. He learned the lesson of Reed's *Growth of the Mind*, that the mind-as-germ, for all of its dependence, still had the self-determination of selecting and absorbing the things peculiarly fitted to its growth. Like James's, his mind was given the freedom of selection. Furthermore, the mind-as-

plant transformed matter into its own life (that is, image-form-
ing in a creative memory), and like one of Emerson's favorite
images of man — the tree — stood rooted in the earth but aloft
in the higher air.

Like the stream,[22] the mind flowed and made its own channels, deepening down to the ocean of life, compelled by perpetual forces as constant and as irrevocable as gravitation.
Emerson wrote in "Natural History of Intellect," "In my
thought I seem to stand on the bank of a river and watch the
endless flow of the stream, floating objects of all shapes, colors
and natures; nor can I detain them as they pass, except by run-
ning beside them a little way along the bank. But whence they
came or whither they go is not told me. Only I have a suspi-
cion that, as geologists say every river makes its valley, so does
this mystic stream. It makes its valley, makes its banks and
perhaps the observer too" (*C*, XII, 16). The life of the mind
was continuous and fluid, and its experience cumulatively
rich and heavy. If, as Emerson tried to express it again, "we
figure to ourselves Intellect as an ethereal sea, which ebbs and
flows, which surges and washes hither and thither, carrying its
whole virtue into every creek and inlet which it bathes," then
the stream was but an opening to the divine mind, a way of
picturing mind in its outward course through nature to the
inward sea of being (*C*, XII, 15).

Emerson did not go beyond these metaphors in his analysis
of the mind. In all of them he acknowledged both the mind
implicated in space, time, and matter, and the mind free to
control, use, or transcend these limiting circumstances. Mind,
for Emerson, was but another way of talking about the "un-
solved, unsolvable wonder" of "to be." The wonder of "to be"
was his constant affirmation, the experience which shaped his
vision and which the vision itself was intended to express.
Wonder was the emotional enlargement that prevented the
pressures of the actual universe from making him unequal to

the real universe. Mind was *all* the universe, the all-containing Over-Soul, the "hidden source" of both nature and man. "The Intellect," he said, "builds the universe and is the key to all it contains" (*C*, XII, 16, 5). If science had reduced the wonder of the physical universe, wonder still remained in the mind's self-reflection, in the perception that built and rebuilt the universe after the heart's desire. This was the fundamental assertion of Emerson's vision, that human faculties and desires exist only to prove the existence of their objects, that man was made to find the universe morally meaningful, and would do so, even at the expense of the reigning science that seemed to be the foremost, all-sufficient projection of his spirit.

II

Retrospectively in "Historic Notes of Life and Letters in New England," Emerson summed up the silent revolution of transcendentalism in New England culture. The age, he said — and his perspective was the post-Civil War America — had been marked by "a certain sharpness of criticism" and "an eagerness for reform." As he had signalized the demands of transcendentalists in the first number of *The Dial,* so now he repeated that the criticism and reform had been "a reaction of the general mind against the too formal science, religion and social life of the earlier period" (*C*, X, 337). The age had been — and from our perspective Emerson had been its representative man — a revolt against formalism. Its result had been "a return to law," by which he meant the higher law above the expedients of prudential regulation, a law of self-affirming individual perception. The age, therefore, was an age of faith, or as he said, "The age was moral" (*C*, X, 338). By choosing vision, or by heeding it, it had chosen the path of regeneration; even its Brook Farms were a sign. But even more, the choice of vision characterized a new hope in the power of men (partaking of the fullness of God) to overcome fate itself. The compelling faith, the compelling need, had been the will to believe, as Emerson expressed it for himself, that though "I am *Defeated* all the time; yet to Victory I am born" (*J*, VI, 190).

As he read the history of the times or traveled in England and Europe, America became in Emerson's mind the place in which this vision was being enacted. His vision had its roots in America; and even the materialism of later day America seemed to him superficial, for in reality he saw it as an expression of the spiritual destiny of a nation armed with a faith in man's power to overcome fate. America, he said in a course of lectures on "American Life," "inspires large and prospective action. . . America means opportunity, freedom, power" (*J*, X, 84). Perhaps because he could only compare the prospective power of America with the colossal power of England, he preferred to read the praise of Englishmen as praise of the Americans. For the Englishmen he saw, that is, the typical products of English civilization, were already too devoted to commodity. The genuine Englishman was, in fact, the American whose path was westerly, away from European worldliness toward the spirituality of the East. Reading his map of the universe of spirit (and in his desire to mediate East and West in the nation), he said of the Americans, "We are the Englishman, by gravitation, by destiny, and the laws of the universe" (*J*, VIII, 317). In this, he joined his vision of the newly spiritually awakened individual with the manifest destiny an open continent had always inspired and which had become one of the spurs of prospective action in the mission of America he inherited. From Crevecoeur to Whitman, the westering spirit moved with divine approval. "Americans," Crevecoeur had rhapsodized, "are the western pilgrims, who are carrying along with them that great mass of arts, sciences, vigour, and industry which began long since in the east; they will finish the great circle." [23] They would finish the circle, because for Emerson the western course was spiritual: it was easting, a return to the source of light and the everlasting now. American civilization would produce the whole man, because here was a continent large enough to call forth or correspond to the needs of many individuals. This belief in the correspondence of the expanding nation and the spiritual man fired the transcendental vision. Early in the revolt, Brownson wrote: "We [the Americans] are, in fact, turning our attention to matters of deeper interest, than those which relate merely to the physical well-being of humanity. We are beginning to perceive that Providence, in the peculiar circumstances in which it has placed us, in the free institutions it has given us, has made it our duty to bring out the ideal man, to prove, by a practical demonstration, what the human race may be, when and where it has free scope for the full and harmonious developement of all its faculties. In proportion as we perceive and comprehend this duty, we cannot fail to inquire for a sound philosophy, one which will enumerate and characterize all the faculties of the human soul." [24] Frederic Hedge, too, like all those who called for the American scholar to lead the way, had seen the signs in "the very features of the soil we inhabit." These, he said, should "be our pledge for the fulfillment of all that the imagination has ever pictured of the destination of man." [25] For the *West* was but another name in the transcendental vocabulary for *nature*, the nature which civilization had eradicated.

In England, Emerson said, he was "quite too sensible of this." For a moment he recalled the America in which nature lies "sleeping, overgrowing, almost conscious." "There," he wrote, "in that great sloven continent, in high Alleghany pastures, in the sea-wide, sky-skirted prairie, still sleeps and murmurs and hides the great mother, long since driven away from the trim hedge-rows and over-cultivated garden of England" (*C*, V, 288). There was the scope the spiritual faculties needed and that he assumed the material struggles of frontier life would awaken. If the English became spiritually bankrupt, then, he concluded his "Manchester Speech," "the elasticity and hope of mankind must henceforth remain on the Alleghany ranges, or nowhere" (*C*, V, 314).

He shared this conviction with most transcendentalists who warmed to the spiritual mission of America, and especially with Thoreau, who considered the *West* another name for the wild or instinctive life, and who saw in the wild the "preservation of the World." Thoreau believed with Emerson in the magnetism of nature and discovered that its leadings were always westward. That way was the future and an unexhausted and richer world — the free world of sympathetic correspondence. He said it was hard for him "to believe that I shall find fair landscapes or sufficient wildness and freedom behind the eastern horizon." He knew, and Emerson knew, that the prospect was poor in that direction. The race, he believed, progressed from east to west, from restraints to freedom, toward Oregon, not Europe. Eastward was only history, institutions, works of art, and literature — the past; westward was the future and the prospect that the "spirit of enterprise and adventure" would realize itself. And in the westward course he thought that men would take on the spiritual and physical grandeur of the continent: "Will not man grow to greater perfection intellectually as well as physically under these influences? . . . I trust that we shall be more imaginative; that our thoughts will be clearer, fresher, and more ethereal, as our sky, — our understanding more comprehensive and broader, like our plains, — our intellect generally on a grander scale, like our thunder and lightning, our rivers and mountains and forests, — and our hearts shall even correspond in breadth and depth and grandeur to our inland seas." [26]

Here was Emerson's vision writ large for the nation: man would complete himself and justify his moral individualism by completing the nation, and the nation would be justified by the men it produced. This fusion of Western destiny with the moral destiny of man supplied part of the charm his vision of the spiritual democrat had for the multitudes who heard him. This was his most suggestive correspondence, joining practical and spiritual needs and spiritualizing the actual.[27] But the quest for spirit, which was his foremost aim and to which action was subordinated, was all too easily forgotten in the quest for action. Enterprise and wealth and invention might be interpreted, as he himself did with consistency on the spiritual level, as the reward of the spiritual quest and the power of mind to transform nature. Individualism, which he had controlled by a dependence on spirit and by the duty of social benefit, found its sanction in the boldness and ecstasy of endeavor, and however extravagant, rapacious, or unrestrained might appeal to the spirit.[28] Reading Emerson's affirmation on the level of commodity, America willingly read its own gospel into his faith in the spiritual power of individual men. What he had spoken in the interest of the whole man, using the expanding frontier to envisage the spiritual promise of America, was applied by practical men to the physical frontier, and in that conquest a new materialism, as constraining as Darwin's, extinguished the transcendental spirit.

But perhaps that was the transient in Emerson's work. There was still a deeper message to be read on the spiritual level by those for whom the frontier was the mind and the nature of man. To these he was "an opener of doors," an example of greater and greater importance in post-Darwinian America of one who in the search for truth had resisted the urge to "make the universe a blind alley" (*J*, VI, 525). For the new generation — the generation to which Emerson felt he was really speaking — had come of age with Darwin and had soon enough to engage in another revolt against formalism (*J*,

IX, 366).[29] They, too, felt the need to reassert the self-reliance of man in a world of circumstances, and they shared with William James the will to believe he found expressed in Emerson: "And we are now men . . . not minors and invalids in a protected corner, not cowards fleeing before a revolution, but guides, redeemers, and benefactors, obeying the Almighty effort, and advancing on Chaos and the Dark." [30] By believing in the inseparability of man and the universe, Emerson was the man who, Justice Holmes acknowledged, had set him on fire.[31] Nor could he have failed the praise of Dewey, who ranked him with Plato; for he had turned nature to the spiritual uses of man, had put all to the test of individual experience, and had fashioned the democratic man in whom being and character, thought and action were one.[32]

He had done this by creating what he believed to be a metaphysics "to the end of use" (*C*, XII, 13). He had built his vision on the needs of men, in answer to the spiritual wants he felt when he wrote in an early sermon: "We want such views of life and duty as shall harmonize all we do and suffer; as shall present us with motives worthy of our nature, and objects sufficient for our powers of action" (*Y*, 99). By showing that man could not be reduced to logic, that the heart was the organ of living faith in the whole man, he affirmed the possibility of sympathetic correspondence with the life of the universe. Through sympathetic correspondence he had a way of using nature for moral growth. And in the moment of perception that he enjoyed in merger with the stream of life he felt the relationship of the atoms of experience and was armed with the ideas that nullified circumstance. This was the basis of his self-reliance, of the hydrostatic paradox by which he symbolized the relation of man to nature, the nation, and the universe (*C*, VIII, 217, 221). Established at the center of the universe and partaking of the moral force of the Over-Soul, man, he wrote, "counterpoises" the dismaying immensity of nature and "bereaves it of terror" (*C*, VIII, 225). With the wings of affection, the intellect could launch itself into the void, and with its power be safely borne across it (*C*, VIII, 228). For the void was in man himself, created by the separation of intellect and affection. Once he became whole, the terrors vanished from the face of nature: nature became "sanative, refining, elevating" (*C*, VIII, 224).

The miracle of perception was the life of this vision, and he wished to domesticate it, to teach all men how to live a sympathetic existence and share the power of spirit. He was able to live by his perception, able to live serenely in the optimism generated by a cosmically guaranteed and significant conduct of life. But the basis of his will to believe was correspondence — one of those "profound convictions," he said, "which refuse to be analyzed" (*C*, VIII, 229). For him the angle of vision was a religious perspective and correspondence the prism through which his natural eye spiritualized the facts of life. Through it the fire of his piety could infuse the natural facts with the warmth of his desire. To iron-lidded men, however, men who disdained to believe in the possibility of sympathetic existence, the prism was opaque. Among them he knew that the vision he had created was good only as "a lonely faith, a lonely protest in the uproar of atheism" (*C*, VIII, 74). He recognized that in the age of Darwin the age of faith was doomed, that after his generation mysticism would "go out of fashion for a long time" (*J*, VII, 19), that the reconciler of the next generation would have to create a vision corresponding to the new revelations of science. And knowing that his vision was only a momentary balance in the silent revolutions of thought, he was willing to pass on the burden of seeing and mediation to those who could do it freshly for their time. This willingness to let the generations seek their truth and to make their experiments on life was what he affirmed, and in his own way and for his own time, as much by the effect of his character as by his words, enacted.

Notes

Notes

CHAPTER I. THE LINEAR LOGIC

1. See Harold Clarke Goddard, *Studies in New England Transcendentalism* (New York, 1908), pp. 2 ff., for a still usable distinction between the philosophic and popular meanings of transcendentalism. An article much like those today on existentialism, "What is Transcendentalism," *The Knickerbocker*, XXIII, 205–211 (March, 1844), a dialogue by a thinking man, objects to what it labels "transcendental" on these grounds: "The spiritualism which I like, looks through nature and revelation up to GOD; that which I abhor, condescends hardly to make use of nature at all, but demands direct converse with GOD, and declares that it enjoys it too; a sort of continual and *immediate* revelation; Itself is its own authority. The ultra-spiritualist contains within himself the fulness of the Godhead. He allows nothing external. . . He has abolished nature, and to the uninitiated seems to have abolished GOD himself." See also Emerson, *L*, III, 18–19.

2. In the sermon, "Find Your Calling," delivered in 1832, Emerson said: "A man is born under the shadow of ancient institutions by the side of whose strength his own strength is insignificant. Men are observed to be of their fathers' religion. Men frequently follow, especially in old countries, their fathers' profession. And so it is said, man is formed by these institutions. But observe, on the other hand, how strong is the effect of individual character in each man to change the complexion of the same pursuits in his hands. In a degree he always is affected by the nation, age, family, profession, friendship he falls upon; but he exerts influence as well as he receives it. And that, in proportion to the strength of his character. . . And as any man discovers a taste of any new kind, any new combination of powers, he tends toward such places and duties as will give occasion for their exercise. And this because great powers will not sleep in a man's breast. Everything was made for use. Great powers demand to be put in action, the greater they are with the more urgency. *Every man is uneasy until every power of his mind is in freedom and in action; whence arises a constant effort to take that attitude which will admit of this action*" (*Y*, 165 ff., italics supplied).

3. See James Elliot Cabot, *A Memoir of Ralph Waldo Emerson* (Boston, 1888), I, 217. See also *C*, VI. 159.

4. "Words Are Things," November 6, 1831, an unpublished sermon, used with the permission of the Ralph Waldo Emerson Memorial Association.

5. Orestes Brownson, reviews of "Emerson's *Phi Beta Kappa* Oration," and "The Divinity School Address," *The Boston Quarterly Review*, I, 107, 504 (January and October, 1838).

6. Stephen E. Whicher, "The Lapse of Uriel: A Study in the Evolution of Emerson's Thought, with special reference to the period between his first and second journeys to Europe (1833–1847)," Harvard dissertation, 1942, pp. 58 ff. This study is a landmark in Emersonian scholarship.

7. "Oration on Genius," *Aesthetic Papers*, edited by Elizabeth P. Peabody (Boston, 1849), p. 60.

8. William Ellery Channing had sounded the same note: "No man can be just to himself — can comprehend his own existence, can put forth all his powers with an heroic confidence, can deserve to be the guide and inspirer of other minds — till he has risen to communion with the Supreme Mind" ("Remarks on National Literature," *The Works of William E. Channing*, one-volume edition; Boston, 1899, p. 135).

9. See Dorothy Emmet, *The Nature of Metaphysical Thinking* (London, 1945), p. 13.

10. In *The Education of Henry Adams* (Modern Library edition; New York, 1931), Adams commented on Emerson: "The less aggressive protest of Ralph Waldo Emerson, was, from an old-world point of view, less serious. It was *naif*" (p. 35). Like Alcott, he got at one sympton when he wrote: "Books remained as in the eighteenth century, the source of life" (p. 39).

11. Perry Miller, review of Ralph L. Rusk's *The Life of Ralph Waldo Emerson, New York Times Book Review*, May 22, 1949. Bronson Alcott said in *Concord Days* (Boston, 1872), p. 31, "He has chosen proper times and manners for saying his good things; has spoken to almost every great interest as it rose."

12. "The Editors to the Reader," *The Dial*, I, 1–3 (July, 1840).

13. See the critical essay on Emerson's *Essays* (second series), written by Margaret Fuller for the *New York Daily Tribune*, December 7, 1844. Margaret Fuller, whose literary judgments remain remarkably solid, was not exaggerating out of her devotion to Emerson when she wrote:

"If only as a representative of the claims of individual culture in a nation which tends to lay such stress on artificial organization and external results, Mr. Emerson would be invaluable here. History will inscribe his name as a father of the country, for he is one who pleads her cause against herself.

"If New England may be regarded as a chief mental focus of the New World, and many symptoms seem to give her this place. . . if we may believe, as the writer does believe, that what is to be acted out in the country at large is most frequently first indicated there . . . we may hail as an auspicious omen the influence Mr. Emerson has there obtained, which is deep-rooted, increasing, and over the younger portion of the community far greater than that of any other person." In sketching out the area of his influence, she says, "This circle is a large one if we consider the circumstances of this country and of England also, at this time" (*The Writings of Margaret Fuller*, edited by Mason Wade, New York, 1941, pp. 389–390). Just as Carlyle's American audience was greater than his English audience, so Emerson at this time had more English than American readers.

14. See, for example, Orestes Brownson's comments on *The American Scholar* in *The Boston Quarterly Review*, I, 108–110 (January, 1838).

"He has deep faith in a heavenly Father of souls, reverence for each brother as a child of God, — respect for his own reason as a divine inspiration, — too much love for men to fear them, — a conscientious hungering and thirsting for truth, — and a serene trust in the triumph of good. He seems to us true, reverent, free, and loving. We cheerfully tolerate therefore any quaint trappings, in which a peculiar taste may lead him to deck his thoughts. . . At the same time we will freely express our regret that Mr. Emerson's style is so little a transparent one. There are no thoughts which may not be simply expressed. . . He cordially welcomes us to his summits of speculation, and to the prospect they command, in full faith that our sight is as keen as his. But he forgets that he has not pointed out the way by which he climbed. His conclusions are hinted, without the progressive reasonings through which he was led to them. Perhaps he does not come at them by any consecutive processes. . . There are no developments of thought, there is no continuous flow in his writings. We gaze as through crevices on a stream of subterranean course, which sparkles here and there in the light, and then is lost. The style is in the extreme aphoristic. But again, another cause of his obscurity is a fondness for various illustration. He has a quick eye for analogies and finds in all nature symbols of spiritual facts. His figures are occasionally so exquisitely felicitous, that we have hardly the heart to complain of this habit of mind, though, we confess, that not seldom we are attracted from the feature of his thoughts to the splendid jewelry of their attire, and yet oftener annoyed by the masquerade of rural and civic plainness, in which they see fit to march." See also Margaret Fuller's description of various responses to Emerson, in *The Writings of Margaret Fuller*, edited by Wade, pp. 391 ff.

15. Emerson remarked in his journal, "It was said of Jesus that he 'taught as one having authority,' a distinction most palpable. There are a few men in every age, I suppose, who teach thus" (*J*, II, 296).

16. "Preliminary Essay," Coleridge's *Aids to Reflection* (Burlington, 1840), p. xxxiii.

17. See Emerson's "Historic Notes of Life and Letters in New England" (*C*, X, 305 ff.); W. D. Wilson, "The Unitarian Movement in New England," *The Dial*, I, 409 ff. (April, 1841); Theodore Parker, "Transcendentalism," *The World of Matter and the Spirit of Man* (Centenary Edition; Boston, 1907), pp. 1–38. See also these secondary works: Goddard, *Studies in New England Transcendentalism*, and O. B. Frothingham, *Transcendentalism in New England: A History* (New York, 1876).

18. Orestes Brownson, "Philosophy and Common Sense," *The Boston Quarterly Review*, I, 85 (January, 1838). Brownson's remarks show the common tie between patriotism and intellectual speculation: "We young Americans, who have the future glory of our country and of Humanity at heart, who would see our country taking the lead in modern civilization, and becoming as eminent for her literature, art, science, and philosophy . . . must ever bear in mind the greatness and sanctity of our mission."

19. See Orestes Brownson, *New Views of Christianity, Society, and The Church* (Boston, 1836); Orville Dewey, *A Discourse on Miracles* (Cambridge, 1836); William Henry Furness, *Remarks on the Four Gospels* (Philadelphia, 1836); George Ripley, *Discourses on the Philosophy of Religion* (Boston, 1836).

20. A. N. Whitehead, *Science and the Modern World* (Pelican edition; New York, 1948), chap. iii.

21. See also Emerson's early lecture on "The Naturalist," reprinted in Kenneth W. Cameron, *Emerson the Essayist* (2 vols.; Raleigh, N. C., 1945), I, 342–343; *J*, VIII, 413–418; *L*, II, 377.

22. Whitehead, *Science and the Modern World*, p. 77.

23. *Ariel and Caliban with Other Poems* (Boston, 1886), p. 99.

24. Marsh, "Preliminary Essay," *Aids to Reflection*, pp. 48 ff.

25. Arthur O. Lovejoy, *The Great Chain of Being* (Cambridge, 1936), p. 211.

26. "Immanuel Kant," *The Dial*, IV, 410–411 (April, 1844).

27. See, perhaps an extreme, Orestes Brownson's account of his spiritual wanderings in *The Convert, or Leaves from My Experience*, cited in Clarence Gohdes, *The Periodicals of American Transcendentalism* (Durham, N. C., 1931), p. 38. "Like most English and Americans of my generation, I had been educated in the school of Locke. From Locke I had passed to the Scottish school of Reid and Stewart, and had adhered to it without well knowing what it was, till it was overthrown by Dr. Thomas Brown, who . . . revived the scepticism of Hume, and drove me into speculative atheism, by resolving cause and effect into invariable antecedence and consequence, thus excluding all idea of creative power or productive force."

28. "Lectures on the Times," *The Dial*, III, 13–14 (July, 1842).

29. Whitehead, *Science and the Modern World*, p. 60.

30. See Sampson Reed's attempt to reorient the *Growth of the Mind* around the affections.

31. "Poetry, Myth, and Reality," *The Language of Poetry*, edited by Allen Tate (Princeton, 1942), p. 9.

32. Emerson wrote: "How many changes men ring on these two words *in and out*. It is all our philosophy. Take them away and what were Wordsworth or Swedenborg?" (*J*, II, 440).

33. "The Senses and the Soul," *The Dial*, II, 374 (January, 1842).

34. *The Language of Poetry*, p. 10.

35. Emerson wrote: "There are people who can never understand a trope, or any second or expanded sense given to your words, or any humor; but remain literalists, after hearing the music and poetry, and rhetoric, and wit, of seventy or eighty years. They are past the help of surgeon or clergy. But even these can understand pitchforks and the cry of Fire! and I have noticed in some of this clan a marked dislike to earthquakes" (*C*, VI, 140).

36. "Works and Days," *C*, VII, 180. "Life is good only when it is magical and musical, a perfect tuning and consent, and when we do not anatomize it . . . The world is enigmatical . . . and must not be taken literally, but genially."

37. I. A. Richards, *Coleridge on Imagination* (London, 1934), pp. 157 ff., 164 ff., 177–178.

38. *The Biblical Repository and Quarterly Observer* (Andover and Boston), VI, 177–178 (July, 1835), reprinted in Cameron, *Emerson the Essayist*, II, 78. Emerson's *Nature* seems to me to be especially indebted to Hubbard's emphasis on the uses of nature. This distinction is especially clear in Whitman's poem, "When I heard the learned astronomer."

39. See Frederic H. Hedge, "Coleridge's Literary Character," *The Christian Examiner*, XIV, 119 (March, 1833). Here by distinguishing the interior active consciousness from the passive common consciousness, Hedge tries to rid "free intuition" of mystical misinterpretations.

40. One of the complaints Emerson suffered was made by Margaret Fuller, who certainly knew his transcendental temperature. "We doubt," she wrote, "this friend raised himself too early to the perpendicular and did not lie along the ground long enough to hear the secret whispers of our parent life" (*The Writings of Margaret Fuller*, edited by Wade, p. 393. See also, *The Memoirs of Margaret Fuller Ossoli*, edited by R. W. Emerson, W. H. Channing, J. F. Clarke, Boston, 1882, I, 290).

CHAPTER 2. THE STAIRCASE OF UNITY

1. Vision usually has an emotional coherence, unlike philosophical systems which rely on logical cement. Norman Foerster's impression of Emerson's coherence is accurate: "In Emerson . . . there was an impressive inner harmony, of which everything he did was a faithful expression — like rays from a shining light" (*American Criticism*, Boston, 1928, p. 52). For the difference between systems and vision, see Austin Warren, *Rage for Order: Essays in Criticism* (Chicago, 1948), pp. v–vi; and for the need of techniques of vision, see John Dewey, "The Philosophy of William James," *Problems of Men* (New York, 1946), p. 385.

2. See Kenneth W. Cameron, *Emerson the Essayist* (2 vols.; Raleigh, North Carolina, 1945).

3. This is hardly a summary of the sources of Emerson's thought. We know, for example, that he was never an accomplished reader of German, which he learned in order to get at Goethe, and that his knowledge of German philosophy was scant and second-hand (see Rene Wellek, "Emerson and German Philosophy," *New England Quarterly*, XVI, 41–62, March, 1943). Nevertheless, he appreciated the Kantians (*J*, VIII, 529–530). His distinction between imitation and originality and his belief that translation retained the concrete expression of books, made it possible for him to gather what he needed in popularizations and histories. Reading to fortify his thought, or reading for "lustres" and inspiration, Emerson, at least, did not feel that *his* thought was derivative. "He must be a superficial reader of Emerson," he said, "who fancies him [Emerson] an interpreter of Coleridge or Carlyle" (*C*, V, 387). He said as much of Schelling, whom he seriously read only as late as 1845 (*L*, III, 298). He said that he could find nothing in Cousin and Jouffroy, that Cousin had an analytical mind and had never had an inspiration, but later he praised him (*J*, IV, 400, 404; IX, 147; VII, 56). For, after all, to be dependent on outside sources was as "bad" as depending on circumstances for one's thought; he was the attractive force, the true source, and what and how he used the books of others depended on him, as the essay "Quotation and Originality" testified. Elsewhere he settled the matter of sources to his own satisfaction: " 'Then it is very easy to write as Mr. Pericles writes. Why, I have been reading the books he read before he wrote his Dialogue, and I have traced him in them all and know where he got the things you most admire.' Yes, and the turnip grows in the same soil with the strawberry; knows all the nourishment that it gets, and feeds on the very same itself; yet it is a turnip still" (*J*, VI, 23). Emerson's indebtedness, however, can be seen in his loyalty and service to Carlyle, even when Carlyle's thought — during and after the Civil War — became increasingly anti-democratic. For more than books, Emerson needed a concrete, living ideal, a representative man.

Carlyle was one; Alcott, Thoreau, Newcomb, Very, to whom he was devoted, were others. (See also James Elliot Cabot, *A Memoir of Ralph Waldo Emerson*, Boston, 1888, I, 289 ff.)

4. *The Friend* (Burlington, 1831), p. vii.

5. Cited in Cameron, *Emerson the Essayist*, I, 225.

6. *Ibid.*, p. 226.

7. See John S. Harrison, *The Teachers of Emerson* (New York, 1910), and Stuart Gerry Brown, "Emerson's Platonism," *New England Quarterly*, XVIII, 325–345 (1945). Brown says that Emerson covered his Platonism with German idealism and oriental mysticism of the day because they were the current cultural fads (p. 326). Brown, I think, misinforms when he says that Emerson wanted to emphasize Plato's conclusions and that Platonism best explains Emerson's inconsistencies. He overlooks Emerson's activism and the contribution of German idealism to the transformation of the essentially static Platonic epistemology.

8. See Frederic Hedge on German metaphysics in his reviews of Coleridge's works, "Coleridge's Literary Character," *The Christian Examiner*, XIV, 108–129 (March, 1833).

9. Emerson's distinction between masculine and feminine powers also fits the vertical and horizontal metaphor. Lamenting the lack of American geniuses, he wrote, "They are all feminine or receptive, and not masculine or creative" (*J*, IV, 87). Again, "To create, to create is the proof of a divine presence" (*J*, IV, 253).

10. See Josiah Royce, *Lectures on Modern Idealism* (New Haven, 1919), p. 120.

11. Joseph Warren Beach finds the key to Emerson's motivation as a nature-poet in "the emotional urge to put off all sense of homelessness and isolation." Beach says that "the metaphysical aspect of this is the assertion of the identity of matter and spirit, objective and subjective — of the essentially spiritual, or ideal, character of the universe" (*The Concept of Nature in Nineteenth-Century English Poetry*, New York, 1936, pp. 353–354).

12. Cabot, *Memoir*, I, 218.

13. Alice Snyder, *Coleridge on Logic and Learning* (New Haven, 1929), p. 12.

14. Cabot, *Memoirs*, I, 218.

15. Snyder, *Coleridge on Logic and Learning*, p. 15.

16. See Chapter 3.

17. Snyder, *Coleridge on Logic and Learning*, p. 35.

18. See I. A. Richards, *Coleridge on Imagination* (London, 1934), p. 59.

19. *The Friend* (Burlington, 1831), pp. 397, 404.

20. *Ibid.*, p. 409.

21. Richards, *Coleridge on Imagination*, p. 62.

22. Snyder, *Coleridge on Logic and Learning*, p. 136.
23. *Aids to Reflection* (Burlington, 1829), p. 286.
24. Snyder, *Coleridge on Logic and Learning*, p. 136.
25. *Aids to Reflection*, pp. 224–225.
26. *The Friend* (Shedd Edition; New York, 1854), II, 470–471. This paragraph, which served as a summary, was omitted in the Marsh edition.
27. *The Friend*, p. 408.
28. *Ibid.*, p. 456.
29. *Ibid.*, p. 414.
30. *Biographia Literaria*, edited by Shawcross, I, 184.
31. *Ibid.*, p. 185.
32. *Ibid.*, p. 167.
33. See Richards, *Coleridge on Imagination*, pp. 160–161.
34. *Biographia Literaria*, I, 167.
35. *Ibid.*, p. 167.
36. *S. T. Coleridge's Treatise on Method*, edited by Alice D. Snyder (London, 1934), p. 6.
37. *The Friend*, pp. 431–432.
38. Cameron, *Emerson the Essayist*, I, 18.
39. See earlier record, *J*, III, 235 ff., where he adds: "The *first* Philosophy, that of mind, is the science of what *is*, in distinction from what *appears*. . . These laws are ideas of the Reason, and so are obeyed easier than expressed."
40. See Cameron, *Emerson the Essayist*, I, 162–169.
41. *The Works of William Ellery Channing* (one-volume edition; Boston, 1899), p. 272.
42. *Ibid.*, p. 126.
43. *Ibid.*, pp. 124–125.
44. *Ibid.*, p. 129.
45. *Ibid.*, p. 132.
46. *Ibid.*, "The True End of Life," pp. 981–982.
47. "Historic Notes of Life and Letters in New England," *C, X,* 339.
48. *The Works of William Ellery Channing*, p. 498.
49. William Cullen Bryant gave his second "Lecture on Poetry" in New York in 1825. Apparently indebted to Channing (he ended the lecture with a long quotation from him), he devoted the lecture to the value and uses of poetry. Among the uses of poetry he gave one which, as we have already seen, was close to Channing's thought. "Among the most remarkable of the influences of poetry," Bryant wrote, "is the exhibition of those analogies and correspondences which it beholds between the things of the moral and of the natural world. I refer to its adorning and illuminating each by the other — infusing a moral sentiment into natural objects, and bringing up images of visible beauty

and majesty to heighten the effect of moral sentiment. Thus it binds into one all the passages of human life and connects all the varieties of human feeling with the works of creation." And he was quick to add that "any one who will make the experiment for himself will see how exceedingly difficult it is to pervert this process into an excitement of the bad passions of the soul." None of the transcendentalists who experimented failed Bryant in his expectations *(Prose Writings of William Cullen Bryant,* edited by Parke Godwin, New York, 1884, I, 19).

50. An enthusiastic reader of the *Edinburgh Review,* Emerson recorded in his journal at the age of twenty a note about the "excellent condensed view of his [Alison's] theory," that he had read. His reading list for the same year mentions Alison on *The Nature and Principles of Taste (J,* I, 293, 298).

51. William Charvat, *The Origins of American Critical Thought, 1810–1835* (Philadelphia, 1936), pp. 29, 32 ff.

52. *Ibid.,* p. 48.

53. *Ibid.,* p. 50.

54. *Ibid.,* p. 93.

55. *Ibid.,* p. 75.

56. *Ibid.,* pp. 71, 75.

57. *Ibid.,* pp. 91–92.

58. See also *J,* II, 232 ff.

59. Jeffrey's article was an adaptation of Alison's theory and was printed in the *Encyclopedia Britannica* and unfavorably reviewed in *The North American Review* in 1818 (Charvat, *Origins,* p. 51).

60. Francis Jeffrey, "Essay on Beauty," *Essays on Beauty and Taste,* edited by A. Alison (London, 1871), pp. 41 ff.

61. Snyder, *Coleridge on Logic and Learning,* p. 12.

62. S. T. Coleridge, *The Statesman's Manual* (Shedd edition; New York, 1884), I, 437–438.

63. Clarence Hotson, "Emerson and the Doctrine of Correspondence. III," *The New-Church Review,* XXXVI, 311 ff. (July, 1929).

64. *Ibid.,* pp. 311–312.

65. Compare Swedenborg's explanation in Nos. 89–90, *Heaven and Hell:* "The whole natural world corresponds to the spiritual world, and not merely the natural world in general, but also every particular of it."

66. Mark Schorer's *William Blake: The Politics of Vision* (New York, 1946) shows that even Blake, early a disciple of the New Church, did not use the doctrine of correspondence without amending it. "The system of correspondence was useful to Blake because it enabled him to write . . . an intricately symbolic poetry, dense with layers of meaning; because it allowed him to include within single images, the individual, society, and the universe, one lapsing into the other without fixed boundaries anywhere. For this reason he followed Swedenborg in

making the ancient concept of macrocosm and microcosm the central aspect of the doctrine; but it was central to Blake for a reason different from Swedenborg's. It was the metaphorical tool that enabled him to counter the prevailing mechanical view of man and the universe with his own organic view" (pp. 108–109). Blake, Schorer says, "had no interest in simply taking over a static theological system of analogies" (pp. 110–111). For Baudelaire and the relation of correspondence to the symbolists poets, see Renato Poggioli, "Correspondence of the Arts," *Dictionary of World Literature,* edited by Shipley (New York, 1943), pp. 125–127.

67. Austin Warren, *The Elder Henry James* (New York, 1934), pp. 40–41, writes: "His exploration of Genesis suggested to his mind that its early chapters were mystical rather than scientific, intended not to 'throw a direct light upon our natural or race history' but to reveal in symbolic form 'the laws of God's *spiritual* creation and providence.' Indeed his own reflexions at this period adumbrated the doctrine of correspondences he was soon to find systematically put in Swedenborg; for in 1843 he writes his friend, Professor Henry: 'Again and again I am forced by scriptural philosophy to the conviction that all the phenomena of physics are to be explained and grouped under laws *exclusively* spiritual — that they are in fact only the material expression of spiritual truth — or as Paul says the visible forms of invisible substance.' "

68. See Cameron, *Emerson the Essayist,* I and II, *passim.*

69. In his Harvard dissertation, "Emerson and Swedenborg," 1929, and in 4 articles taken from this dissertation and printed as "Emerson and the Doctrine of Correspondence," *The New-Church Review,* XXXVI, 47–59, 173–186, 304–316, 435–448 (January, April, July, October, 1929), Hotson has conveniently isolated from Emerson's printed works 173 passages expressing the idea of correspondence. This catalog shows the pervasiveness of the idea and its longevity in Emerson's thought, but it does not conclusively demonstrate Emerson's dependence on Swedenborg or the specific derivation of the idea from him. Hotson, no doubt, is right in emphasizing the importance of Swedenborg in giving this idea currency; but as important was the changing climate of opinion which made men eager to receive it. Emerson was receptive, but where an idea takes hold and does its work in his thought, he switched the Swedenborgian direction the idea took in such typical books as M. Edgeworth Lazarus's *Comparative Psychology,* vol. I: *Vegetable Portraits of Character, Animal Portraits of Character, with analogies of sound and color, Passional Hygiene;* George Field's *Universal Analogy-Chromatics-Chromatology;* Wilkinson's *The Human Body and its Connexions with Man;* or Sampson Reed's *The Correspondence of the Sun, Heat, and Light.*

70. Cited in Clarence Hotson, "Sampson Reed, a Teacher of Emerson," *New England Quarterly*, II, 258 n. (April, 1929).

71. Sampson Reed, *The Growth of the Mind* (Boston, 1829), pp. 31, 84, 22.

72. *Ibid.*, p. 82.

73. Henry James, Sr., named one of his sons after Wilkinson.

74. *Aesthetic Papers* (Boston, 1849), p. 118. The remaining quotations are from this source.

75. See Thoreau's *Walden* for the application of this idea to his hut and to his ideal house.

CHAPTER 3. THE ANGLE OF VISION

1. In his lectures on "Human Culture" (1837–1838), he devoted one lecture to the "Eye and Ear." In this lecture, Emerson calls the eye and ear "ministering senses with which all the information we owe to the other senses appears trifling." But the lecture does not develop the contribution of the eye. Emerson is more concerned with the general education of the senses as a way to increase the response to beauty. He wants to purge the senses, make the perceiver aware of the beauty in nature as well as in art-objects, and by means of a total response to nature overcome the partial relations most people have. His distinction between art and taste is based on this complete sympathetic correspondence with nature: the poet touches the circumference of nature at every point and has "art" — he is the Ideal man. The Actual man has only partial relations and has only "taste." For Emerson the eye was the ensphering organ. This lecture is in the Houghton Library and is used with the permission of the Ralph Waldo Emerson Memorial Association. See also James Elliot Cabot, *A Memoir of Ralph Waldo Emerson* (Boston, 1888), II, 734–735.

2. A manifestation of his difficulties in finding his best working attitude or calling, his loss of sight (see *J*, II, 68, 70–71) was also connected with his belief in compensation (*J*, II, 72 ff.; *Y*, 103). For a revealing biographical passage on illness and vision, see *Y*, 103. The parallel case of William James is instructive (see Ralph Barton Perry, *The Thought and Character of William James*, briefer version, Cambridge, 1948, pp. 119–126).

3. Reed, *Growth of the Mind*, pp. 71, 72.

4. Dorothy M. Emmet, *The Nature of Metaphysical Thinking* (London, 1945), pp. 41 ff.

5. *Ibid.*, pp. 41 ff. Emerson describes this "aesthetic seeing" in *Nature* (*C*, I, 49–50).

6. See Sherman Paul, The Wise Silence: Sound as the Agency of Correspondence in Thoreau," *New England Quarterly*, XXII, 511–527 (December, 1949).

7. "On Point of View in the Arts," *Partisan Review*, XVI, 823 (August, 1949).

8. *Ibid.*, p. 831.

9. See *English Traits*, chap. xiv.

10. Ortega, "Point of View in the Arts," p. 831.

11. *Ibid.*, p. 824.

12. Melville also emphasized the need for love in the rapacious commercialism of mid-nineteenth-century America (see Sherman Paul, "Melville's 'The *Town-Ho's* Story,'" *American Literature*, XXI, 212–221, May, 1949). And Hawthorne, too, condemned the unsympathetic eye of the scientist — what Emerson called "Aristotelian eyes" (*L*, II, 342).

13. Ortega, "Point of View in the Arts," p. 835.

14. *Ibid.*, p. 825.

15. *Ibid.*, p. 825. See also Thoreau's entry in his journal for August 24, 1841: "The universe is built round about us, and we are central still. By reason of this, if we look into the heavens, they are concave. . . The sky is curved downward to the earth in the horizon, because I stand in the plain. I draw down its skirts" (*The Writings of Henry David Thoreau*, 20 vols., Boston and New York, 1906, VII, 274).

16. Ortega, "Point of View in the Arts," pp. 825–826.

17. *Ibid.*, p. 833.

18. *Ibid.*, p. 831.

19. Landscape painting at this time also shows a similar desire for the distant (or perhaps the sublime). Perhaps the need to humanize the landscape by including small human figures, usually in the foreground, came about from the painter's own need to represent himself as an angle of vision in which the panorama becomes significant. And of course, the human figure in the landscape became *the measure* by which to judge the immensities of nature.

20. But he knew "that our hunting of the picturesque is inseparable from our protest against false society" (*C*, III, 178).

21. George Meredith, according to Charles Morgan, also used the stars as his "emblem of the supreme harmony" ("George Meredith's Return," *The Atlantic*, CLXXXIV, 80, August, 1949).

22. See his sermon "Astronomy," *Y*, 170–179.

23. See *The American Library of Useful Knowledge* (Boston, 1831), I, 267–320.

24. "Hegel and His New England Echo," *The Catholic World*, XLI, 59–60 (1885), reprinted in Cameron, *Emerson the Essayist*, II, 409.

25. R. M. M., "American Philosophy — Emerson's Works," *Westminster Review*, XXXIII, 360 (March, 1840), reprinted in Cameron, *Emerson the Essayist*, II, 406–407. The eyeball seems to have gained considerable currency as a jibe at the ludicrousness of transcendentalists. For example, Charles Newcomb's sister used it to chide him (see *The Jour-*

nals of Charles King Newcomb, edited by Judith K. Johnson, Providence, 1946, p. 21). Another famous picture of an eyeball, perhaps symbolic of the astronomical basis of Poe's thought in *Eureka,* is a lithograph of a huge balloonlike eyeball ascending into the heavens, beneath which is written, *"L'oeil, comme, un ballon bizarre se dirige vers L'INFINI."* The lithographs were done by Odilon Redon in 1882 to illustrate Poe's work and are now in Houghton Library. The importance of the eye to the nineteenth century was indicated, perhaps by Emerson when he wrote that one of the symbols of the age was the mirror (*J,* VIII, 98–99).

26. See *J,* VIII, 280, for man as a battery, and so forth.

27. See his comments on the "female mysticism" of Margaret Fuller (*J,* VIII, 142–143).

28. Emerson's use of primary and secondary, though inverted, derives from Locke; form, for example, he identified with intellect, and color with sentiment (*C,* VII, 300). But he was more concerned with the color of things, with what the mind actively contributed in perception, than with the given or Lockean primary qualities.

29. An important Coleridgean word used by Emerson to distinguished vision from observation.

30. City dwellers, he believed, although they never doubted the permanence of the natural order, did not refer their "subsistence . . . to the rain and the sun and the soil" (*Y,* 40).

31. Emerson needed to feel the universe as gentle and protective, and his notion of ambience, of atmospheric enfolding, supplied it. See, for many instructive glosses, Leo Spitzer's "Milieu and Ambience," *Essays in Historical Semantics* (New York, 1948), pp. 178–316.

32. See Maud Bodkin, *Archetypal Patterns in Poetry* (London, 1934), p. 74.

33. Paul, "The Wise Silence," 513.

34. See his poem, "Days." "Hodiernal" is a favorite Emersonian word.

35. History was also a way of distancing facts, of getting them in perspective, in time (see "History," *C,* II, 5).

36. See "Summer," *Y,* 42 ff.

CHAPTER 4. THE ARC OF THE CIRCLE

1. For the notion of expression as outgoing, see M. H. Abrams, "The Mirror and the Lamp: A Study of the Transition to Romantic Theories of Poetry and Criticism," Harvard dissertation, 1940, pp. 38 ff.

2. See Susanne K. Langer, *Philosophy in a New Key* (New York: New American Library, 1948), pp. 32, 49.

3. See Martin Foss's distinction between metaphor and symbol, the metaphor conveying the tension of process and the symbol hypostatizing it, and his attempt, like Emerson's, to keep experience alive by the

metaphor, in *Symbol and Metaphor in Human Experience* (Princeton, 1949).

4. See Emerson's comments on Mary Moody Emerson and her reading in *C*, X, 402. See also Ralph L. Rusk, *The Life of Ralph Waldo Emerson* (New York, 1949), pp. 24–25.

5. Johann B. Stallo, *General Principles of the Philosophy of Nature* (Boston, 1848).

6. Harry H. Clark, "Emerson and Science," *Philological Quarterly*, X, 247 (July, 1931).

7. See his awareness of employing this method, in *C*, II, 96.

8. *S. T. Coleridge's Treatise on Method*, edited by Alice Snyder (London, 1934), pp. 37–38. Almost identical passages are to be found in *The Friend* (Burlington, 1831), pp. 415–416. For an instructive study of dialectic, see Kenneth Burke, "Three Definitions," *The Kenyon Review*, XIII, 178–181 (Spring, 1951).

9. *The Writings of Margaret Fuller*, edited by Mason Wade (New York, 1941), p. 391.

10. See Emerson's stream metaphor, perhaps an anticipation of William James, in *C*, XII, 16.

11. *S. T. Coleridge's Treatise on Method*, p. 38.

12. "The Dialectic Unity in Emerson's Prose," *The Journal of Speculative Philosophy*, XVIII, 195–202 (April, 1884). Harris also pointed out the unity in Emerson's poetry in "Ralph Waldo Emerson," *Atlantic Monthly*, L, 238–252 (August, 1882).

13. "Emerson's Literary Method," *Modern Philology*, XLI–XLII, 81 (November, 1944). For a current example of the misunderstanding of Emerson's method, see Karl Shapiro, *Essay on Rime* (New York, 1945), pp. 33, 38, 39.

14. Emerson always felt incapable of consecutive expression, and the piece-method of the dialectic made the best use of his working habits. He also liked to think that within the dialectic he could create "brisk shocks of surprise" (*C*, II, 34) by showing the "legitimate series but suppressing one or more of the terms" (*J*, VII, 59). He was aware, too, almost from the beginning of his preaching career that his method was unusual (*Y*, 27–28) and that the lecture as he employed it was a new method of expression, an indirection (*J*, V, 189, 324).

15. Sampson Reed, *Growth of the Mind* (Boston, 1829), p. 21.

16. *Ibid.*, pp. 40–41.

17. *Ibid.*, p. 21. See also *J*, III, 350; and Alcott's *Concord Days* (Boston, 1872), p. 72, for his praise of "a geometry of ideas, a rhetoric of images."

18. See Emerson G. Sutcliffe, *Emerson's Theories of Literary Expression*, University of Illinois Studies in Language and Literature, VIII, 27 ff. (February, 1923).

19. Less crudely, perhaps, this later became Emerson's standing image of bias of temperament (see Chapter 5).

20. Compare this passage with Robert Frost's "Stopping by Woods on a Snowy Evening."

21. One reason Emerson left the ministry was the burden of sermons, which he found too excessive for his cycles of inspiration (see *L*, I, 267).

22. Emerson also transcribed Reed in the remainder of the paragraph (see Reed *Growth of the Mind*, p. 9).

23. *Ibid.*, p. 22.

24. There is perhaps a hint of this idea in the critical dictum, "the style is the man." Recently it has been used as a critical tool by Mark Schorer in restoring submerged metaphors ("Fiction and the 'Matrix of Analogy,'" *The Kenyon Review*, XI, 539–560, Autumn, 1949).

25. William Cullen Bryant seems always to reflect palely the ideas Emerson made so thoroughly his own. He wrote that passion was needed to intensify expression, that passion was "naturally figurative." "The great spring of poetry is emotion. It is this power that holds the key to the storehouse where the mind has laid up its images, and that alone can open it without violence" ("Lectures on Poetry," *Prose Writings of William Cullen Bryant*, edited by Parke Godwin, New York, 1884, I, 10; see *J*, IX, 311–312).

26. Alcott also found walking a stimulus to image-formation: "Admidst the scenes of nature, under the wide cope of heaven, treading erect the plane of earth, man finds all his faculties addressed. Thought at once seizes its images. . . Study is perfect only when aided by the presence of nature" (*The Journals of Bronson Alcott*, edited by Odell Shepard, Boston, 1938, p. 107; see also Alcott's *Concord Days*, p. 42).

27. Perry Miller said in *The New England Mind* (New York, 1939), p. 213: "It is truly strange that the generation of Emerson and Alcott should have had to go to Emmanuel Swedenborg for a doctrine of 'correspondence', since something remarkably like it had been imbedded in their own tradition for over two hundred years" (see also pp. 162–163). He also extended this insight in his *Jonathan Edwards* (New York, 1949), and in his study of Edwards' *Images or Shadows of Divine Things* (New Haven, 1949). Kenneth B. Murdock's study of colonial style, *Literature and Theology in Colonial New England* (Cambridge, 1949), especially the chapter, "The Puritan Legacy," shows that Emerson appreciated the plain style of his ancestors.

28. See the passage Emerson copied from Reed's *Growth of the Mind*, p. 63.

29. Edwards, following Locke, tried to create the sense of the heart by an accumulation of imagery which he amassed and heightened within

the framework of the Puritan sermon. He tried by a multitude of images *to fill* the abstraction with feeling. Emerson's method was analogical, each portion of an essay, raising the subject to a higher platform, each portion in its polarities preparing one for his own perception.

CHAPTER 5. SPHERAL MAN

1. See also Theodore Parker's *A Discourse of Matters Pertaining to Religion*, in *The Collected Works* (London, 1876), I, 126 ff., for the clearest philosophical discussion of this need. This discourse appeared in Boston in 1842.

2. For the germ of this idea, see William Ellery Channing, "Likeness to God," *Works* (one-volume edition; Boston, 1899), pp. 294–295. See also Hawthorne's "The Great Stone Face," in which this idea is artistically expressed.

3. *Movements of Thought in the Nineteenth Century* (Chicago, 1936), p. xxxiv.

4. Emerson never reveals the origin of this name. Perhaps he meant it to mean *man of mouths* (os), the man with many channels opening into the universe.

5. "Domesticate" and "adaptiveness" are favorite words for Emerson (see *J*, VI, 12).

6. Isaac Ray, in reviewing Combe's *Constitution of Man*, saw in phrenology, as many transcendentalists did, a support of the faculty theory. "The present state of our knowledge warrants us in rejecting any ethical or metaphysical system, that does not recognize and explain the adaptation of the human constitution to the circumstances in which it is placed, its reference, in every particular, to its sphere of action and the purpose of its being. . . . Phrenology, therefore, establishes the fundamental principle, that for every special end and object of our existence, nature has provided us with an original and distinct power, and its results to be necessary in maintaining the relations of the constitution, as an harmonious and consistent whole, to the world around it" ("Moral Aspects of Phrenology," *The Christian Examiner*, XVI, 225–226, May, 1834). Emerson thought highly of Combe's work in 1830: ". . . the best sermon I have read for some time" (*L*, I, 291).

7. The faculty theory was also a part of the Puritan legacy, as can be seen in Mrs. Alcott's journal entry: "These have been great years for my soul. Wise discipline, circumstances the most diversified, have conspired to bring great energies into action. I have not been always wise, or prudent; I have looked too much to consequences, not enough to principles and motives; but I feel encouraged. Defeat has given me strength" (*The Journals of Bronson Alcott*, edited by Odell Shepard, Boston, 1938, p. 143).

8. Self-culture was a frequent theme of Unitarian discourse (see, for example, William Ellery Channing's "Self-Culture," *Works*, pp. 12–36). Baron de Gérando's *Self-Education; or the means and art of Moral Progress* had a considerable reception in the 1830's, especially in Elizabeth Peabody's translation, the second and less metaphysical edition appearing in Boston in 1832.

9. This is a representative example of Emerson's early method of expression, and also shows the religious matrix from which were derived his more secular doctrines. It is interesting to note that he prefaces this sermon with the distinction between inner and outer worlds, spirit and matter, thought and body.

10. Alcott wrote in his journals for October 12, 1830: "Our education is incomplete, until all our faculties of *perceiving* and *loving* are addressed by their corresponding objects; til the whole nature has communed with itself and its author, through the aids of observation, reflection, and experience." In 1834, he added, giving the correspondential theory of education: "Education is that process by which *thought* is opened out of the soul, and, associated with outward . . . things, is reflected back upon itself, and thus made conscious of its reality and shape. It is *Self-Realization*. As a means, therefore, of educating the soul out of itself, and mirroring forth its ideas, the external world offers the materials. This is the dim glass in which the senses are first called to display the soul, until, aided by the keener state of imagination . . . it separates those outward types of itself from their sensual connection, and in its own bright mirror recognizes again itself, as a *distinctive* object *in* space and time, but *out of it* in *existence*, and painting itself upon these, as emblems of its inner and super sensual life which no outward thing can portray. Education, throughout all its stages, is but a mirroring forth of this inner life by . . . symbols. . . He who is seeking to know himself, should be ever seeking himself in external things, and by so doing will he be best able to find, and explore his inmost light."

11. This, of course, was what he felt the "times" were denying his generation (see again, "The Editors to the Reader," *The Dial*, I, 1–2, July, 1840).

12. *Growth of the Mind* (Boston, 1829), p. 36.

13. Theodore Parker in *A Discourse of Matters Pertaining to Religion* best expressed the role of the spiritual philosophy in fulfilling the wants of the higher faculties: "This theory ['Spiritualism' or Transcendentalism] teaches that there is a natural supply for spiritual as well as corporeal wants; that there is a connection between God and the soul, as between light and the eye, sound and the ear, food and the palate, truth and the intellect, beauty and the imagination; that as we follow an instinctive tendency, obey the body's law, get a natural supply

for its wants, attain health and strength, the body's welfare; as we keep the law of the mind, and get a supply for its wants, attain wisdom and skill, the mind's welfare, — so if, following another instinctive tendency, we keep the law of the moral and religious nature, we get a supply for their wants. . . As we have bodily senses to lay hold on matter and supply bodily wants . . . so we have spiritual faculties to lay hold on God, and supply spiritual wants; through them we obtain all needed spiritual things" (p. 138).

14. See Alcott's "Orphic Sayings," XXXIX in *The Dial*, I, 95 (July, 1840) "Man is a rudiment and embryon of God; eternity shall develop in him the divine image."

15. *Growth of the Mind*, p. 31. The best summary of the nature of this inner principle was given by Elizabeth Peabody in her record of Alcott's Temple School. The best way of getting education was "not by accumulation, but by growth; for there is something at the foundation of the human soul, analogous to the organization of a plant [both Reed and Emerson often spoke of the mind as a plant], which does indeed feed on the earth from which it springs, the air in which it flourishes, the light of heaven which comes upon it from afar; but which admits nothing that it cannot assimilate to itself. We may assist a plant, if we will study its nature, but there are things which might be put round one plant, which will destroy another. And so we may assist a soul, but there is only one way . . . we must offer the individual those elements alone, which it needs, and at the time it needs them, and never too much, and always enough. Then we shall find that each soul has a form, a beauty, a purpose of its own. And we shall also find, that there are a few general conditions never to be shut out: that, as the light of heaven, the warmth of earth, and space to expand, are necessary to the plants; so knowledge of God, the sympathy of human love, and liberty to act from within outward, are indispensable to the soul" (*Record of a School: Exemplifying the General Principles of Spiritual Culture*, third revised edition, Boston, 1874, p. 244; original edition, 1836).

16. *Growth of the Mind*, p. 82.

17. Joseph Warren Beach points out that in the evolutionary metaphysics of Coleridge and Schelling, sensibility, the highest stage of organic life, corresponded to magnetism on the physical level (*The Concept of Nature in Nineteenth-Century English Poetry*, New York, 1936, p. 332).

18. Alcott reveals the way science was used by transcendentalists: "Professor Faraday, I read, is about presenting some discoveries of his to the Royal Society on the relation of Electricity and Magnetism to Light. I venture the conjecture that the three are states of One Substance, and that this, by whatsoever name it shall be designated, is the

immediate Breath of Life, the nexus of Spirit and matter" (*The Journals of Bronson Alcott*, p. 171; see also Alcott's "Orphic Sayings," XLIII, in *The Dial*, I, 96, July, 1840). Emerson purchased a magnet in 1829 (Ralph L. Rusk, *The Life of Ralph Waldo Emerson*, New York, 1949, p. 144).

19. For some of Emerson's dreams, see *J*, VI, 178–180; IX, 120–121, 354; X, 174, 314.

20. Emerson often spoke of the aim of character in terms of "the erect man." In the vertical-horizontal diagram, the erect man was obviously one who had risen from the linear, brute level. Uprightness was the result of perception: "He that perceives . . . rights himself, he stands in the erect position, and therefore is strong" (*J*, IV, 277). How important perception was to character can be seen in Emerson's almost automatic use of this image: in an early sermon he said," the whole creation cannot bend him whilst he stands upright" and in his journal he recorded, " 'Stand up straight,' said the stagecoachman, 'and the rain won't wet you a mite' " (*J*, VI, 441).

21. *Growth of the Mind*, p. 81. Reed also pointed out, what many besides him praised, the advantages of free America in providing room for a choice of calling (p. 83). See also Orestes Brownson's review of Cousin in which he emphasizes America's mission, to provide for the full development of the ideal man ("Cousin's Philosophy," *The Christian Examiner*, XII, 34, September, 1836).

22. In V of his "Orphic Sayings," Alcott briefly summarized this idea of self-culture as a vocation: "Engage in nothing that cripples or degrades you. Your first duty is self-culture, self-exaltation. . . Either subordinate your vocation to your life, or quit it forever" (*The Dial*, I, 86, July, 1840). Alcott was true to this instruction.

23. Aunt Mary Moody kept his literary ambitions, stifled by his ministerial routine, alive (see Rusk, *Emerson*, p. 136).

24. The life of Jones Very is the best example, as his writing is the best expression, of the attempt to make reason and inspiration *all* of life, to transcend sense altogether. See his poem, "The Garden" for the fusion of the senses and their objects (*The Works of Jones Very*, Boston and New York, 1886, p. 76).

25. *The Journals of Bronson Alcott*, edited by Shepard, p. 225. See also Alcott, *Concord Days*, p. 40, where Emerson is called "the merchant-man of ideas"; and Ripley's comment in O. B. Frothingham's *George Ripley* (Boston, 1882), p. 268: "The practical shrewdness interwoven with his poetical nature is one of the secrets of his power." Rusk's *Emerson* confirms this with ample detail.

26. See Orestes Brownson, *New Views of Christianity, Society and the Church* (Boston, 1836).

27. In "Literary Ethics" he diluted this to "The man of genius should occupy the whole space between God or pure mind, and the multitude of uneducated men" (*C*, I, 182).

28. A favorite word of Alcott, but also common in transcendentalist language (see his "Orphic Sayings," XXIV, *The Dial*, I, 91, July, 1840).

29. Theodore Parker believed that in this Emerson had led the youth of his generation astray, with his claims for ecstasy and intuition ("The Writings of Ralph Waldo Emerson," *The Massachusetts Quarterly Review*, III, 223–233, March, 1850).

30. See *L*, I, xxxvi, 59, 63, 86, 380.

31. This resolution of social usefulness and individual choice of ideals is, I think, for all the differences, the germ of Josiah Royce's *The Philosophy of Loyalty* (New York, 1908).

32. This control was also necessary to thought: "Every existing thing is an analogon of all existing things. Thence appears to us Being ever at once sundered and connected. If we follow the analogy too far, all things confound themselves in identity. If we avoid it, then all things scatter into infinity. In both cases, observation is at a stand, in the one as too lively, in the other as dead" (*J*, IV, 28).

33. The life of Charles K. Newcomb is perhaps the best example of the decay of powers, repressed in his youth, and dissipated in the dilettantism of his old age. See Newcomb's philosophy of action, which unfortunately reflected the desire for action he never fulfilled (*The Journals of Charles King Newcomb*, edited by Judith K. Johnson, Providence, 1946). Emerson was deeply sympathetic with Newcomb's plight and regretted the great waste of his gifts.

34. Alcott noted in *Concord Days*, " 'Deeds are masculine, words feminine' " (p. 133).

35. The relation of Emerson's unfitness to the fabric of his vision should not be underestimated. Compensation, the faculty theory, and self-reliance are the expressions of the demands he had to make on the universe in order to accommodate himself and his gifts (see *C*, IV, 184).

36. *The Journals of Bronson Alcott*, p. 87.

37. See Emerson's catalog of reading in "Books" (*C*, VII, 187 ff.). He also believed that history and biography were controls, that is, objective like nature, and thus safe ways of studying the self (*J*, IV, 158, III, 355, 362–363, 440; *C*, II, 61, 66).

38. Samuel Ward and, later, John Murray Forbes were his ideals of the social man.

39. In this judgment he seems to have followed Jones Very's "Shakespeare," *The Works of Jones Very* (Boston and New York, 1886). Emerson read it in manuscript.

40. Jesus had been the central figure in the bitter exchanges of the Unitarians and Transcendentalists over the nature of man. Perhaps Emerson felt this association too deeply to include him.

41. Edward Everett Hale, *Ralph Waldo Emerson* (Boston, 1899), pp. 67, 68, 69, 73, 74.

42. Later on he presented Lincoln as an ideal (*C*, VIII, 318).

43. John S. Harrison, *The Teachers of Emerson* (New York, 1910), pp. 223 ff. See *Symposium*, 190.

44. *The Journals of Bronson Alcott*, p. 221.

CHAPTER 6. FRIENDSHIP

1. "The Art of Life – The Scholar's Calling," *The Dial*, I, 176 (October, 1840). The "scholar," of course, is the equivalent of the present day "intellectual."

2. "American Literature," *The Boston Quarterly Review*, II, 20, 26 (January, 1839). Parker, too, believed that Emerson "would lead others to isolation, not society" ("The Writings of Ralph Waldo Emerson," *The Massachusetts Quarterly Review*, III, 234, March, 1850).

3. Hubert H. Hoeltje, *Sheltering Tree: A Story of the Friendship of Ralph Waldo Emerson and Amos Bronson Alcott* (Durham, N. C., 1943).

4. Self-and-God was the meaning of nature as Emerson focused the problem of his generation in *Nature*.

5. He wrote this when he heard that Carlyle was not coming to live with him at Concord.

6. See *L*, IV, 50: "I fear," he wrote Lidian, "to have people kind to stones like me."

7. In the privacy of his journals, he preferred "mob" to "multitude" (then being used by democratic reformers).

8. This was what Thoreau meant when he wrote, "A man cannot be said to succeed in this life who does not satisfy one friend" (*The Writings of Henry David Thoreau*, Boston and New York, 1906, XV, 272).

9. *The Journals of Bronson Alcott*, edited by Odell Shepard (Boston, 1938), p. 98. Parker wrote that "persons seem of small value to him – of little value except as they represent or help develop an idea of the intellect" ("The Writings of Ralph Waldo Emerson," *The Massachusetts Quarterly Review*, III, 234, March, 1850). Margaret Fuller was less generous than Alcott (see Chapter 1, note 40).

10. Throughout the letters he frequently uses the imagery of ice, crystals, and so forth. See *L*, II, 351, "Ice has its uses," and *L*, II, 352, "But tell me I am cold . . . I become a cake of ice. I can feel the crystals shoot & the drops solidify." In this he shares with Hawthorne, who was even more self-reliant than Emerson, and whose preoccupation with solitude and society was also a central concern.

11. See also his remarks on the loss of Margaret Fuller (*J*, VIII, 117), and his personal list of representative friends. What *Representative Men* meant to Emerson might be discovered in the following comparisons:

Plato and Alcott, Swedenborg and Jones Very, Shakespeare and Charles Newcomb, Montaigne and W. E. Channing (the younger), Napoleon and Thoreau, and — of course — Goethe and Emerson (*J*, VIII, 62). Where was the contemporary Jesus, or Socrates?

12. In a way Emerson was justified in choosing Concord, because, for him, his decision to remove there in the 1830's was, although individual, an anticipation of what Ripley found necessary for the group.

13. The importance of Emerson's name in forwarding new enterprises was always recognized. He was, however, unwilling to lend his name where he did not also give active support, that is, leadership. Although he broke with Ripley gently — and Ripley nevertheless never forgave him — his wrath at being freely used and not on his terms can be seen in the correspondence with Theodore Parker over *The Massachusetts Quarterly Review* (see *L*, III, 409; IV, 106–107, 108–109, 111, 112, 114).

14. Brownson, in attacking the scholarly class as aristocratic, advised that in America the scholar could not "safely be exempted from the ordinary duties of practical life. The scholar must be a man of business, and do his own share of the drudgery" ("American Literature," *The Boston Quarterly Review*, II, 10, January, 1839).

15. He was instrumental in organizing the Town and Country and Saturday Clubs, and was a very active and faithful member (see *J*, VIII, 103–105, 324–325; *J*, IX, 469, *J*, X, 12, 18, 296). He gave his philosophy of clubs in "Clubs." "Thought is the native air of the mind, yet pure it is a poison to our mixed constitution, and soon burns up the bone-house of man, unless tempered with affection and coarse practice in the material world." In the form of clubs, society was the best tonic (*C*, VII, 225). It provided the conversation — the "vent of character as well as of thought" (*C*, VII, 236) — and a compensation for the solitude of nature (*C*, VII, 244). For the aging Emerson, who, as he said of the scholars, "does not wish to be always pumping his brains," it supplied gossip (*C*, VII, 245).

To those who had once witnessed the individualist of "Literary Ethics," this was a new Emerson. Henry James said: "His nature had always been so innocent, so unaffectedly innocent, that when in later life be began to cultivate a club-consciousness, and to sip a glass of wine or smoke a cigar, I felt very much outraged by it. I felt very much as if some renowned Boston belle had suddenly collapsed and undertaken to sell newspapers at a street corner. 'Why, Emerson, is this *you* doing such things?' I exclaimed. 'What profanation! Do throw the unclean things behind your back!' But, no; he was actually proud of his accomplishments!" ("Mr. Emerson," *The Literary Remains of the Late Henry James*, edited by William James, Boston, 1885, pp. 293–294).

16. *The Dial*, III, 86–90 (July, 1842). Also partly restated in "Historic Notes," *C*, X, 325–370.

17. New York, 1844. See especially chapter X, where Godwin explains Fourier's theory of Universal Analogy and supports it with Swedenborg's Doctrine of Correspondences.

18. Compare, in "Swedenborg," "A horse signifies carnal understanding; a tree, perception; the moon, faith; a cat means this; an ostrich, that; an artichoke, this other" (*C*, IV, 121).

19. He misunderstood this part of the system which was intended to give each man an opportunity to employ all his faculties by engaging at short intervals in all the specialties suited to his growth.

20. Elizabeth Peabody, in "Fourierism," *The Dial*, IV, 473–483 (April, 1844), came to the same conclusion: "The question is, whether the Phalanx acknowledges its own limitations of nature, in being an organization, or opens up any avenue into the source of life that shall keep it sweet, enabling it to assimilate to itself contrary elements, and consume its own waste; so that Phoenix-like, it may renew itself forever in great and finer forms" (pp. 481–482). She also reported Dr. Channing's argument "from the analogy of nature" in defense of individual property. This is especially valuable in showing the distance Emerson had traveled from Channing. Channing inverted the Emersonian emphasis that "life was forever tending to individuality of expression" by subordinating it to assert that "individual property was the expression of this universal law" (p. 474).

21. Zimmermann's treatise was, Kenneth Cameron tells us, the standard work on solitude throughout Emerson's life. It was available and widely read in several translations: *Solitude, or the Effect of Occasional Retirement* (2 vols.; London, 1779); *Solitude Considered with Respect to its Influence on the Mind and the Heart* (translated from the French by J. B. Mercier, London, 1795); *The Advantages and Disadvantages of Solitude Considered* (London, 1808); *Solitude* (2 vols.; Exeter, 1836) [*Emerson the Essayist* (Raleigh, N. C., 1945), I, 411]. He probably found Baron de Gérando's *Self-Education* (second edition; Boston, 1832) another support. See de Gérando's chapter, "Solitude and Society," pp. 301–312.

22. Ralph L. Rusk has shown the depth of Emerson's life-long attachment to his child-bride (*The Life of Ralph Waldo Emerson*, New York, 1949, pp. 131–150).

23. Zimmermann's "reflection" meant to Emerson all that "self-culture" did. "Solitude is that state in which the soul freely resigns itself to its own reflections. . . The mind surrenders itself in retirement to the unrestrained enjoyment of its own ideas" (*Solitude*, Mercier translation, pp. 2, 5).

24. *Ibid.*, p. 130.

25. The title itself, with society first, is suggestive of the change in his attitude.

26. Ripley wrote of Emerson in 1867, "I really think he grows softer and more human in his old age" (Frothingham, *George Ripley*, p. 257).

CHAPTER 7. PROSPECTS

1. In his review of Cousin, Brownson wrote: "The great mission of our age is to unite the infinite and the finite. Union, harmony, whence proceed peace and love, are the points to be aimed at. We of the nineteenth century appear in the world as mediators. In philosophy, theology, government, art, industry, we are to conciliate hostile feelings, and harmonize conflicting principles and interests. We must bind together . . . by meliorating instead of destroying." In eclecticism he saw the solution of the philosophic problem (*The Christian Examiner*, XXI, 61, September, 1836).

2. This pursuit is not alien to contemporary philosophy (see F. S. C. Northrup, *The Meeting of East and West*, New York, 1946).

3. Emerson's disapproval of Sampson Reed, his early mentor, suggests this (see Ralph L. Rusk, *The Life of Ralph Waldo Emerson*, New York, 1949, p. 118).

4. "Life of Herder," *The Christian Examiner*, XVIII, 214 (May, 1835).

5. Reed, *Growth of the Mind* (Boston, 1829), pp. 41–44.

6. Harold Clarke Goddard points out that "transcendentalism is itself a naturalistic interpretation of the world . . . founded . . . on the conception of law, and welcomed, as if it were its very own, every conquest of science in the diminishing domains of the supernatural" (*Studies in New England Transcendentalism*, New York, 1908, pp. 78–79).

Emerson believed that Jesus, although indisputably the greatest moral force in history, was not a complete man because he was deficient in the love of science (*J*, III, 578).

7. James Elliot Cabot, *A Memoir of Ralph Waldo Emerson* (Boston and New York, 1887), II, 710–712.

8. Hartford, 1849.

9. Emerson said that the finest tool, the one nearest to the mind, was language (*C*, VII, 163). As his image theory shows, he believed that language was the instrument of correspondence.

10. *God in Christ*, pp. 21–22.

11. The age was captivated by the power of analogy. For example, one of the formative books in Alcott's early years was Francis Wayland's *A Discourse on the Philosophy of Analogy* (Boston, 1831). Parke Godwin wrote an ecstatic account of analogy in his chapter on Fourier's "Univer-

sal Analogy." "Analogy," he said, "is the enchanted prism through which Nature shows herself in the most graceful forms and most pleasing colors" (*A Popular View of the Doctrines of Charles Fourier*, New York, 1844, p. 104).

12. See Richard Hildreth on the consequences of Reason (the faculty of analogy) in putting a stop to the war between science and religion in *A Letter to Andrews Norton on Miracles as the Foundation of Religious Faith* (Boston, 1840), pp. 17–18.

13. *Society the Redeemed Form of Man* (Boston, 1879), p. 31.

14. *God in Christ*, p. 98. For a more detailed exposition of Bushnell's views on language, see Sherman Paul, "Horace Bushnell Reconsidered," *ETC.*, VI, 255–259 (Summer, 1949).

15. *The Dial*, III, 40 (July, 1842).

16. *God in Christ*, p. 46.

17. *Indoor Studies* (Boston, 1899), pp. 73–77, cited by Harry H. Clark, "Emerson and Science," *Philological Quarterly*, X, 225 n. (July, 1931).

18. "Theodore Parker's Experience as a Minister," in John Weiss, *Life and Correspondence of Theodore Parker* (New York, 1864), II, 503.

19. "Emerson and Evolution," *The University of Toronto Quarterly*, III, 474 ff. (July, 1934). This essay is especially valuable in giving an analysis of how Emerson used science. See also Frothingham, *George Ripley*, p. 268.

20. A. N. Whitehead, *Science and the Modern World* (Pelican edition; New York, 1948), p. 88.

21. Acknowledged with the permission of Houghton Library, Harvard University.

22. Emerson said that the tree was his peculiar symbol and the stream Thoreau's. Thoreau used the stream as the basis of his spiritual journey in *A Week on the Concord and Merrimac Rivers*. There it joined the two levels of the actual and spiritual, the flow of inner thoughts and outer being. For Emerson on the river, see *J*, IX, 413, 430, and "Two Rivers." The tree in Swedenborg's "dictionary" of symbols represented perception (see Clarence Hotson, "Emerson and the Doctrine of Correspondence," *The New-Church Review*, XXXIV, 438–439, October, 1929). Carlyle contrasted the world-machine with a tree in *On Heroes, Hero-Worship and the Heroic in History* (Carlton Classics edition; London, 1923), II, 214–215, 218. Edwards said that trees were made to represent men (see *Images or Shadows of Divine Things*, edited by Perry Miller, New Haven, 1948, p. 98). See also Robert Frost's poem "Tree at My Window," and Thoreau's journal entry on the tree, *The Writings of Henry David Thoreau*, XIV, 140–141.

23. J. Hector St. John Crevecoeur, *Letters from an American Farmer* (London and New York, 1907), p. 55.

24. "Cousin's Philosophy," *The Christian Examiner*, XXI, 34 (September, 1836).

25. "Progress of Society," *The Christian Examiner*, XVI, 20 (March, 1834).

26. "Walking," *The Writings of Henry David Thoreau* (Boston and New York, 1906), V, 222–224. See also Margaret Fuller, "American Facts," *Life Without and Life Within*, edited by A. B. Fuller (Boston, 1860), pp. 108–109.

27. See *The Dial*, I, 4 (July, 1840).

28. See John Jay Chapman, *Emerson and Other Essays* (New York, 1898), pp. 12–13.

29. See Morton G. White, *Social Thought in America: The Revolt Against Formalism* (New York, 1949).

30. James selected this for the motto of a book (F. I. Carpenter, "William James and Emerson," *American Literature*, XI, 50, March, 1939).

31. "The Holmes-Cohen Correspondence," *Journal of the History of Ideas*, IX, 15 (January, 1948). See also *Holmes-Pollock Letters*, edited by Mark Howe (Cambridge, 1941), II, 264.

32. *Characters and Events*, edited by Joseph Ratner (New York, 1929), I, 69–77.

Index

Index